What is History For?

Beverley Southgate

Routledge
Taylor & Francis Group

LONDON AND NEW YORK

First published 2005
by Routledge
2 Park Square, Milton Park, Abingdon, Oxon OX14 4RN

Simultaneously published in the USA and Canada
by Routledge
270 Madison Ave., New York, NY 10016

Transferred to Digital Printing 2008

Routledge is an imprint of the Taylor & Francis Group, an informa business

© 2005 Beverley Southgate

Typeset in Garamond by
Taylor & Francis Books

Printed and bound in Great Britain by
TJI Digital, Padstow, Cornwall

British Library Cataloguing in Publication Data
A catalogue record for this book is available from the British Library

Library of Congress Cataloging in Publication Data
Southgate, Beverley C.
  What is history for? / Beverley Southgate.
        p. cm
Includes bibliographical references and index.
ISBN 0-415-35098-0 (alk. paper) -- ISBN 0-415-35099-9 (pbk. : alk. paper)
    1. History--Philosophy. I. Title.
D16.8.S6836 2005
901--dc22   2004024555

ISBN 978-0-415-35098-0 (hbk)
ISBN 978-0-415-35099-9 (pbk)

What is History For?

What is History For? is a timely publication that examines the purpose and point of historical studies. Recent debates on the role of the humanities and the ongoing impact of poststructuralist thought on the very nature of historical enquiry, have rendered the question 'what is history for?' of utmost importance.

Charting the development of historical studies, Beverley Southgate examines the various uses to which history has been put. While history has often supposedly been studied 'for its own sake', Southgate argues that this seemingly innocent approach masks an inherent conservatism and exposes the ways in which history has, sometimes deliberately, sometimes inadvertently, been used for socio-political purposes. With traditional notions of truth and historical representation now under question, it has become vital to rethink the function of history and renegotiate its uses for the postmodern age. History in the 21st century, Southgate proposes, should adopt a morally therapeutic role that seeks to advance human hope and happiness.

This fascinating historicisation of the study of history is unique in its focus on the *future* of the subject as well as its past. *What is History For?* provides compulsive reading for students and the general reader alike.

Beverley Southgate is Reader Emeritus in the History of Ideas at the University of Hertfordshire. His publications include *History: What & Why?* (1996), *Why Bother with History?* (2000), and *Postmodernism in History* (2003).

For Sheila again, and for those others who continue to give meaning to my narrative and teach me what life (as well as history) is for – including especially Victoria, Benjamin, Susannah, Ellen, and Lily.

Contents

Figures

Preface

My aim in this book is to consider what history has been, is, and might be *for*.

Charges of heresy follow hard on the heels of anyone so much as asking that question, 'What is history for?' After all, history, as a supposedly straightforward and truthful representation of the past, is not meant to be *for* anything: history just *is*. As soon as you start talking about what it's meant to be *for*, you're in the minefield of ideology and politics – in danger of the past being abused for your own or someone else's purposes, and in danger thereby of sullying history's virginal reputation (as well as disrupting its funding). But Claude Lévi-Strauss noted decades ago that there can be no way in which history can ever correspond to any 'reality' of the past: 'a truly total history would confront [historians] with chaos'. So history, he concluded, is inevitably partial, incomplete, selective, 'biased'; it's 'never history [pure and simple], but [always] history-*for*'.[1] The interesting question, then, is *what* it's for.

That question needs to be considered at a time when (once again) the whole point of the humanities in general is under question, and when history more particularly has been a repeated object of attack, both from outside and from inside the academy. External threats to the subject periodically recur from political modernisers, whose visions for the future purport to render obsolete any earlier traditions; and such recent advocates of a trendy brave new world have dispensed with respect for anything that savours of the 'old' or 'past'. A new diverse society is perceived as having different needs from earlier models, whose strength was supposedly rooted in some shared and homogeneous background; and any pomp and circumstance derived from that historic background (and still manifested in a few allegedly outdated institutions) is seen as an irritating irrelevance ripe for removal. Conventional visions of the past are held suspect – as anomalous intrusions from a now alien world whose time has passed. Such history is history.

And that politically motivated relegation of history to a past that's no longer needed has found support in intellectual movements within, or bordering closely on, the academic discipline of history itself. During the last few decades, theorists have undermined the conventionally accepted foundations of the subject, digging sufficiently deep to expose its scientistic pretensions and to question any disingenuous claims to be telling it (the story of the past) 'as it actually was'. Some ostriches remain, with heads burrowing ever deeper into an empirical mire, while others have pragmatically made adjustments to their earlier hubristic claims. But the overall effect of a sustained bombardment has been to render quite impossible the continuation into the future of history in the form that it has previously assumed.

So it's high time to rethink its proper function – to consider what, in our changed world, a changed history might actually be *for*. And paradoxically, as some might think, that entails (I continue to believe) some historicisation of the question: to see how history's functions might change, those functions are best seen as not essential but contingent – as having changed in the past, and as being in practice what *can* be changed in the future. Thus, in Chapter 1, I consider how, from Plato through to Wittgenstein, some thinkers have advocated a 'therapeutic' role for the humanities – have been concerned that their seemingly esoteric theories impinge on 'real life' and contribute in practice to a better future; and my overall argument in this book is that it may be time for historians to present their own subject now, not just as another self-indulgent entertainment, or as a vehicle for marketable skills, but rather as something that might and should contribute to human betterment and hope.

So after addressing, in Chapter 2, the traditional model of an elusive (and possibly self-indulgent) history supposedly pursued 'for its own sake', I look in Chapter 3 at some purposes that have been openly professed by historians: at the claimed transference of practical skills; at the hypothetical acquisition of some appropriate personal qualities; and at the injection into the public consciousness of some myth-breaking actuality. Some other purposes that history might have less obviously fulfilled are considered in Chapter 4: the roles that historians, sometimes all too unconsciously, have played –

not least as puppets for political masters, often justifying the status quo not only in politics but also in the discipline of history itself. In Chapter 5, I go on to consider some of the needs that individuals and societies might have in our condition of postmodernity (a term I'm using here simply to refer to the historical epoch in which we live), in order to ascertain an appropriate contemporary role for humanities and history; and in the light of that, I argue in Chapter 6 for a revised historical study which may serve, in Richard Rorty's phrase, the cause of 'social hope' and greater human happiness. That entails seeing history, as he sees philosophy, as potentially 'an aid to *creating* ourselves rather than to *knowing* ourselves';[2] and so it takes on huge importance as (in the words of one recent commentator) 'the ... supremely "meaning-giving" discipline'.[3] In Chapter 7, I look further at such aspirations, and in particular identify some human qualities that we might hope to derive from historical study; and, bringing theory firmly back to practice, I discuss in Chapter 8 four actual examples of what seem to me to be models of history for our time.

In the early twentieth century, John Dewey proposed a 'reconstruction' in philosophy, and suggested that his revised subject, having surrendered 'its somewhat barren monopoly of dealings with Ultimate and Absolute Reality, will find compensation in enlightening the *moral* forces which move mankind and in contributing to the aspirations of men to attain to a more ordered and intelligent *happiness*'.[4] If for philosophy we now substitute 'history', we have some indication of what I believe that it too might now be *for*.

Acknowledgements

My thanks are due again to my editor Victoria Peters for her continued encouragement and guidance, and to her team at Routledge, including importantly Ruth Jeavons, whose sympathetic handling of my manuscripts (and my pedantic self) is greatly appreciated. Jayne Bloye at the University of Hertfordshire has again helped me enormously with her readiness to find time to print my various drafts; and I have received encouragement along the way from Dennis Brown and Robert Rosenstone. I am also indebted to Alun Munslow and Barbara Tischler, as Routledge readers, for their sometimes critical but always positive and helpful comments; and for their friendship and intellectual stimulation, I remain particularly grateful to John Ibbett and Keith Jenkins. Finally, and most importantly, Sheila has continued to provide for me the physical, intellectual, and emotional environment in which writing is not only possible but pleasurable.

Chapter 1

Humanities and therapeutic education

> I want to demote the quest for knowledge from the status of end-in-itself to that of one more means towards greater human happiness.
>
> (Richard Rorty)[1]

Teachers of the humanities – by which I mean here in particular history, philosophy, and literature – have often prided themselves on learning for its own sake: the idea that their subjects may be of some mundane practical use has even been seen as somehow demeaning – as potentially detracting from the value of what they do. And, periodically faced with the philistinism of politicians (seemingly of all political persuasions) obsessed with undefined 'clear usefulness',[2] I have personally shared that view: assaulted by demands for 'relevance' and the transmission of 'transferable skills', I too have insisted on the inherent value of the humanities themselves, and on their value as enhancing the more 'spiritual' (and in practical terms maybe even 'useless') side of human life, on their contribution to the Socratic ideal of cultivating the soul.

But I wonder now, in the twenty-first century, whether it isn't time to reconsider, and in view of the state of the world – with its wars, environmental crises, 'global terrorism', human-rights abuses, and ever louder totalitarian style assertions of Manichaean black/white, right/wrong distinctions – more directly and explicitly to apply our humanitarian resources (importantly including our historical study) to answering such perennial questions as that posed by Arthur Lovejoy nearly a century ago – 'What's the matter with man?'[3] – and to join forces with Richard Rorty in his rejection of knowledge 'for its own sake', in favour of a quest for greater human happiness.

There's nothing new about suggesting that history, and the humanities more generally, can – and even should – do more than provide a platform for seeking knowledge as an 'end in itself', but should, rather, perform a practical and essentially 'therapeutic' role in an education that might actually constitute another route to 'greater human happiness', and give us cause for hope. In history more specifically, emphasis has admittedly often been placed either on the supposed virtues of 'own-sakism' or on vocational banalities. But the humanities have also, after all, always been concerned (by definition, or supposedly) with 'humanity' itself – with what it might actually mean to be a human being, with how human beings can be developed and enabled to realise (make real) their full potentials (their latent powers); and by implication they've been concerned too, as Lovejoy implied, with what at any time is wrong with us, and with what might be done about it. 'I study history,' as R. G. Collingwood explained, 'to learn what it is to be a man [or person].'[4]

For it has always been clear that people are not as they should or could be – that something needs to be done to improve or redeem them, that they've slipped and fallen from their ideal state in the Garden of Eden or some more secular Golden Age, and that they're capable again of something better. So the task of the humanities sometimes has been, and now, following Richard Rorty's lead, decidedly *is* (surely *must* be) to facilitate that improvement – that restoration and return to health and human happiness. That implies for Rorty that philosophy and, I'm now proposing, history too, should be seen 'as an aid to *creating* ourselves rather than to *knowing* ourselves'.[5] One of the main points of 'knowledge' – including here especially what we'll provisionally call 'historical knowledge' – becomes the act of self-creation.

As a philosopher, Rorty himself stands in a long tradition. His philosophical aim, of happiness and hope, may well sound strange to many who have been brought up in the mainstream western version of the subject as it has evolved in the Anglo-American tradition (but not the continental European or the eastern) over the last four centuries. An emphasis on rationality and the intellect has all but overridden – indeed, made academically suspect if not disreputable – an earlier approach concerned with such mundane and practical matters as how best (or at least better) to live. But that was the primary concern of many, if not most, philosophers in antiquity, and culminated in the explicitly therapy-orientated philosophies of the Hellenistic period – a period of great monarchies and emperors, when it seemed to ordinary people that little could be done to affect life at a political level; so that what became important was to consider how, within existing constraints, individuals might best live as private individuals.

That then became the underlying concern of such philosophies as Epicureanism, Stoicism, Cynicism, and Scepticism. In the first century BC, the Roman poet (and enthusiastic Epicurean) Lucretius wrote of people's mental sickness – of how they don't really know what they want, and 'everyone [is] for ever trying to get away from where he is'. They rush from one place to another, driving from the town to the country, and then back again as they immediately get bored. Such behaviour may not be unfamiliar to us. But what it means, explains Lucretius in words that a psycho-therapist today might well approve, is that all the time, in self-hatred, 'the individual is really running away from himself'.[6]

Stoics and Cynics share with Epicureans the belief that philosophy can bring relief from such self-hatred and frenzied frustration, and can show the way to happiness through the attainment of freedom – freedom from any desire for such distractions as wealth, power, and bodily pleasures. For them all, the point of knowledge and wisdom is very practical: that it should lead to real happiness, with philosophy 'keep[ing] one on the correct course as one is tossed about in perilous seas'.[7] But of all these ancient philosophies, it's Scepticism that is perhaps most relevant and interesting here, as most closely resembling contemporary (postmodern) thought.

Now, to link Scepticism of all things with the provision of any form of therapy may seem particularly perverse, since that philosophy is notorious for having itself often, and on the contrary, provoked serious mental distress. On its revival in the seventeenth century, Scepticism was described by one thinker as nothing short of a 'destructive contagion'[8] that was liable to result in personal and professional demoralisation. An acceptance that truth can never be known, it was argued, simply led to a universal indifference that undermined the basis of morality. But the original objective of early sceptical philosophers is clear: namely (in Greek), *ataraxia* – a word that can best be understood by looking briefly at its derivation. The verb *tarassein* meant to stir up, to trouble, to disturb; so the *tarassomenoi* are those whose minds are agitated, distracted, troubled, confounded, frightened; and it's freedom from such *dis*-ease that is denoted by 'a-taraxia'. In short the sceptical philosopher's goal is untroubled calmness, even in the face of adversity – just the sort of quality that we associate with being 'philosophical'. Thus, the founder Pyrrho recommended as a role-model the pig he saw on a ship: the pig calmly went on doing what pigs do, despite the great storm by which all on board were threatened, and it thereby exemplified 'the unperturbed state in which the wise man should keep himself.[9]

That state of unperturbedness is reiterated as a goal by arguably the greatest philosopher of the twentieth century, Ludwig Wittgenstein. 'The real discovery,' he writes, 'is the one that makes me capable of stopping doing philosophy when I want to. – The one that gives philosophy *peace*, so that it is *no longer tormented* by questions.' The link with therapy is made explicit: 'The philosopher's treatment of a question is like the treatment of an illness.' For 'What is your aim in philosophy?' he asks of himself, and replies: 'To shew the fly the way out of the fly-bottle.' Humans, he observes in Lucretian mode, are caught, trapped like flies in a bottle – a bottle from which there's an easy way out if they'd only stop buzzing around so frenetically and unconstructively, and take proper stock of their situation. Just like buzzing flies, humans need to calm down and come to realise what their problem is. And as often as not the solution lies ready to hand: it's just that we haven't seen it, because it's so obvious and has always been there. 'The aspects of things that are most important for us are hidden because of their simplicity and familiarity.' It's a commonplace that we can't see what's always before our eyes, so that 'we fail to be struck by what, once seen, is most striking and powerful'. The philosopher's task, then, is to open eyes to what's already there – to reveal what's gone wrong and (reverting to Lovejoy) what's the matter with us; which is to diagnose the illness and so enable therapy.[10]

It's not only philosophers who have claimed such therapeutic concerns. Literary theorists too, from the time of Aristotle's acknowledgement of the cathartic (cleansing) effects of tragedies that 'purge' the mind of pity and terror, have often seen an explicitly therapeutic function for their subject. The nineteenth-century poet Matthew Arnold, for example, has been seen as applying his main effort to being 'a physician of the human spirit', at what he himself describes as 'an iron time of doubts, disputes, distractions, fears'.[11] Sounding like a social commentator in the twenty-first century, he writes of the time when one discovers that for many 'the whole certainty of religion seems discredited, and the basis of conduct gone';[12] and similarly in his poem 'The Scholar-Gipsy' (1853), he refers to 'this *strange disease* of modern life,/ With its *sick* hurry, its divided aims'. He compares the scholar, described by the seventeenth-century writer Joseph Glanvill as having acquired traditional knowledge and skills from the gipsies, with people of his own time, 'Who fluctuate idly without term or scope,/ Of whom each strives, nor knows for what he strives,/ And each half lives a hundred different lives'. Having tried many things without success, they are reduced to 'sick fatigue' and 'languid doubt', and succumb to the strong '*infection* of our mental strife'.[13] No wonder, then, that in a letter of 1870, Arnold writes of his hope to provide, in such 'troubled times', 'a *healing* and reconciling influence'.[14]

In the following century, that therapeutic emphasis was followed by two very disparate literary critics and theorists – I. A. Richards and F. R. Leavis. The former, paradoxically, had such serious doubts about the value of English literature as a discrete academic discipline that he actually thought about retraining as a mountain guide, and in fact went off for a time to teach in China. Indeed, it was his study of the Chinese language that left him more receptive to what he came to see as the *inevitability* of linguistic ambiguity – and hence of ultimate failure in communication. He concluded that, however precisely authors try to express their thoughts and feelings, a residue of ambiguity must always remain. Individual words are never 'univocal', or susceptible to one conclusive definition; and meanings are therefore never conveyed with that ideal clarity to which we might aspire. Meanings indeed (as we all know, having so often been misunderstood) remain elusive: different readers offer alternative interpretations; and, as in cases of any historical evidence, we lack any sure criterion for determining their relative merits. How, for example, could we ever penetrate to Milton's intended meaning in *Paradise Lost*, without entering somehow into the poet's own head in the context of his times? Which is obviously an impossible task: we may edge our way towards some such 'empathetic' gesture – but we can never actually achieve it, or even know when we've got near. So just as for us in postmodernity, it's necessary to accept the 'aporia' – that impasse in meaning, beyond which we can never hope to go.

But that, Richards believed, is not to be seen as negative – any more than postmodernists believe it is for us. Indeed, it's just there – in the 'aporia' – that the moral and therapeutic dimension of literary study comes in. For an appreciation of ambiguity can be seen as equivalent to (or as resulting in) an openness to alternatives – a recognition that one *must* be limited and may be wrong, that there's a whole range of possible meanings, available to different minds from different contexts. And that very recognition can hardly fail to necessitate a more tolerant disposition towards the views of others.

That's one way, then, in which a careful study of literature might have a moral point. But tolerance of multiple meanings in literature (and hence in society more generally) does not, for Richards, imply that some order, however provisional, has not been attained: poetry, for all its ambiguities, remains a means of overcoming the disorder by which we're otherwise threatened; like an historical narrative, its cohesive power enables the construction of a unitary route (however provisional) through surrounding chaos. And apprehension of that imposed poetic order provides a form of psychic therapy for the individual – as well as a stabilising function for society. 'Man,' as Graham Swift puts it in his novel *Waterland*, 'is the story-telling animal. Wherever he goes, he wants to leave behind not a chaotic wake ... but the comforting marker-buoys and trail-signs of stories ... As long as there's a story, it's all right.'[15] 'All sorrows,' as the story-teller Isak Dinesen has more recently indicated, 'can be borne if you put them into a story, or tell a story about them.'[16] And poetry (and literature more generally) is one way of enclosing individual sorrows within a universal human story. The desirability of such ordering of human experience remains, for Richards, as a psychological and political presupposition; and, given that goal, poetry (properly studied) provides one means of attaining it. Literature thus proclaims its own essentially therapeutic function, and may well in that respect have some lessons for history.[17]

As a second example of a literary theorist, F. R. Leavis is imbued with a moral earnestness that has served to make him sound hopelessly dated – even an object of ridicule. Fashions come and go, and Leavisites are now far from *à la mode*. But Leavis again well illustrates my contention that there has been a therapeutic function assigned to literary studies – therapeutic not in the physical sense, of course, but in the moral. So Leavis identifies what he describes as 'the great tradition' of English novelists, and in it places Jane Austen, George Eliot, Henry James, and Joseph Conrad; and what these authors have in common, he asserts, is their significance 'in terms of the human *awareness* they promote; awareness of the possibilities of life'.[18]

For Leavis, then, literature is closely linked to life: it has a moral point, and in the promulgation of that moral point lies its essentially therapeutic function. Writers who seem to him to lack a suitably moral approach to life itself cannot be admitted to the literary pantheon. So Arnold Bennett is refused admission, since, as Leavis claims, he 'seems to me never to have been disturbed enough by life to come anywhere near greatness'; and he similarly quotes with approval D. H. Lawrence's repudiation of Flaubert, as having 'stood away from life as from a leprosy'. The great are to be distinguished, rather, by their 'reverent *openness* before life, and a marked moral intensity' – characteristics amply embodied in George Eliot, who incorporates into her writings the moral problems and tensions that she perceives in her own life. It is her consciousness of such aspects of life itself, and her incorporation of them in her work, that make her a great writer: 'Without her intense moral preoccupation,' as Leavis concludes, 'she wouldn't have been a great novelist.' Likewise it's his noble celebration of 'certain human potentialities' that sets Henry James apart: 'He creates an ideal civilised sensibility; a humanity capable of communicating by the finest shades of inflexion and implication.' And Joseph Conrad similarly 'is the servant of a profoundly serious interest in life', and is 'peculiarly alive' not only *in* his time but *to* it. That is to say, he is 'sensitive to the stresses of the changing spiritual climate as they begin to be registered by the most conscious'. 'Amid all this mass of destruction and disintegration,' as D. H. Lawrence puts it and as Leavis might, 'one must speak for life and growth.'[19]

Similar concerns have been expressed by literary critics in the United States. Lionel Trilling in particular, writing after the Second World War, emphasises the moral or, as I would put it here, the therapeutic importance of the novel. By being forced to consider the moral dilemmas and choices faced by fictional characters, readers are provoked to reconsider their own positions. They are also presented with a diversity of possible viewpoints, some of which may challenge their own; and so they are encouraged to extend the range of their understanding and tolerance. The novel, then, acts as a moral agent by teaching 'the extent of human variety and the value of this variety', and by suggesting to the reader 'that reality is not as his conventional education has led him to see it'.[20]

Within the humanities, then, both philosophers and literary theorists have claimed not only a didactic but, in moral terms, a therapeutic role for their subjects. But what of history? Far from being any form of therapy, it has been suggested, historical study itself constitutes and/or induces sickness, sometimes even unto death: in their unhealthy search for origins, historians may originate their own demise. Following Jacques Derrida's reference to 'Archive Fever', Carolyn Steedman, for instance, has recorded how the dust of the archive may indeed, not only metaphorically but even literally, set up a fever in the historical researcher – a fever, whether psychological as a result of professional pressures, or physical in the case of those (like the nineteenth-century French historian Jules Michelet, it seems) exposed to too much toxic dust.[21]

But despite these little publicised disciplinary hazards, there's nothing new either about the idea of history itself being therapeutic – as being medically beneficial, that is, both for practitioners (the writers of history) and for their readers. For history, as the study of the past, can take one's mind off the troubles of the present; it can serve to put one's own problems into longer chronological perspective; and it can provide models for how to lead a better life. The Renaissance scholar Petrarch is just one example of a man who admitted to being so repelled by his own time that he chose to take refuge in the past: in order to forget the present, he wrote letters to long-dead ancient Romans, feeling more at home with them than he did with his own contemporaries. For whatever reason, but in seemingly similar mode, the nineteenth-century historian W. E. H. Lecky suggested that, caught up in 'childish recollections' of more dramatic times, we might identify first with the political divisions of the seventeenth century rather than those of our own time; so that 'we are Cavaliers or Roundheads before we are Conservatives or Liberals'. The renowned twentieth-century historian Geoffrey Elton thought it 'no wonder ... that men concern themselves with history', as being an escape from a 'burdensome' present and from the prospect of a 'dark' future: 'only the past', he believed, as 'dead and finished, bears contemplation.' And today temporal tourists are invited to sample 'sixteenth-century living' at Hampton Court (near London) as '*the antidote*' to 'twenty-first century living'.[22] The foreign country of the past has many advantages, with more congenial companionship and exemplary life-styles; and altogether it provides a therapeutic distancing from our native life and times.

Since its professionalisation in the nineteenth century, such theoretical justifications for historical study have been superseded by a supposedly more 'grown-up' perception of history as a discipline – as a mode of rigorous intellectual training, an autonomous study in its own right, that needs no external rationale or justification. As we shall see in Chapter 2, history has simply been presented as an unquestionably good thing in itself. But it has degenerated until it has come to be, in the words of one contemporary historian, 'disparaged as nothing more than a bunch of names and dates about long-ago events and dead people'.[23] So it's time now, I want to argue, with our own needs in the condition of postmodernity (as will be diagnosed in Chapter 5), to envisage a therapeutic function for the subject, and to enlarge on the claim made by Elizabeth Fox-Genovese in relation to Lionel Trilling, that 'history also engages its readers in moral reflection upon the extent and value of human variety'.[24] For therapy has been described as 'an experience which involves the individual in systematic reflection about the course of her or his life's development'; and in that process the individual is required 'to harmonise *present* concerns and *future* projects with a psychological inheritance from *the past*'. It's only by self-consciously developing a coherent narrative in which to locate oneself, that one can succeed in 'escaping the thrall of the past ... [thereby] opening oneself out to the future'.[25]

It's not only the individual but humanity itself that stands open to the future. For, as Richard Rorty reminds us, it too has no closed definition, but is 'an open ended notion', with 'the word "human" nam[ing] a fuzzy but promising *project* rather than an essence'.[26] In joining in and contributing to that project, a refigured history might even help to give us hope? And the suggestion anyway provokes a more general consideration of what history has been, is and might be *for*.

Chapter 2

History for its own sake

I Introduction

> I do not know what history is about, nor what social function it serves. I have never given the matter a thought.
>
> (Richard Cobb)[1]

People rarely do things for no reason at all – whether it's chewing gum, gazing at a landscape, or writing history. They may, like Richard Cobb, sometimes claim to be acting (in his case, writing history) without any awareness of what they're doing or why; but usually, if pressed, they can give some account of what they're acting for. Cobb himself soon comes clean about his own motivation in doing history: 'I am happy in it,' he admits, 'and that is the main thing.' And for some – perhaps many, or even most – historians, such self-indulgence is no doubt sufficient justification for what can be seen as a labour of love. Happiness, after all, is no bad goal.

But by others that love for which they labour is claimed to be not just self-indulgent self-love, but love of humanity more generally. In other words, historians have often claimed to be acting altruistically – to be doing some good to other people through their history, benefiting them in some way, and helping future generations to live better. That can be done, so they have claimed, first, by providing examples – examples of the morally good, or the politically or militarily or artistically successful: these can then be emulated, while corresponding models of failures can henceforth be avoided. And second, helpful conclusions can be drawn from the past: general laws can be deduced, and at least some tentative hypotheses drawn up concerning the impact that our various present actions might have upon the future. (As the United States and Britain prepared for war with Iraq in February 2003, arguments were presented that were based on alleged historical parallels with appeasement in the 1930s, and there was an assumption that such arguments drawn, however spuriously, from history would prove cogent.)

Learning from history, though, or drawing lessons from the past, depends on certain things remaining constant. In particular, there's a presupposition that human nature and the laws governing human behaviour stay more or less the same: the past may be a foreign country, but despite some admitted variations in language, culture, and values, the inhabitants of that country are nevertheless essentially similar to ourselves. As the mid-nineteenth-century Anglican H. H. Milman puts it:

> Man is the same, to a great extent, in every part of the world, and in every period. Society is part of his nature, and social forms, being circumscribed in their variations, will take the same character, enact the same provisions, establish the same ranks and gradations, aim at the same objects, and attain the same ends.[2]

That, of course, had been the starting-point for the ancient Greek historian Thucydides. He specifically tells us that he wants his history of the Peloponnesian War to remain as 'a possession for all time', and it makes sense to aspire to such immortality only because, human nature being what it is, the future is bound to resemble the past. What's needed, then, 'as an aid to the interpretation of the future', is 'an exact knowledge' of that past – which is what Thucydides, as an historian, aims to provide.[3]

It's also what subsequent historians have aimed to provide, and often for the same reason: the purpose of their histories has determined its nature; and their essentially helpful, educational, progressive purpose has continued to require 'an exact knowledge of the past'. Unsurprisingly, then, the assumption that such 'exact knowledge' can be attained has characterised history through the centuries: it has come to be what has justified any study of the subject and any claims it might have to be an academic 'discipline' in its own right – a discipline distinct in particular from 'literature', which in many respects it often so closely resembles. For as Thucydides claimed, as he contrasted his own historical work with the poetic accounts of Homer, literature is altogether more transitory – its own aim being merely to provide some instant gratification or, in the historian's derogatory words, to 'charm for the moment'.

In the long and ongoing disciplinary wars of academia, supporters of literature have, of course (as we saw in Chapter 1) made their own claims for their subject – and not least (certainly no less than historians) for their subject's power as a teacher. The moral high ground has always been contested territory, and for good reason. But that's not our concern here – or not except inasmuch as it relates to our own central theme of history; and I want to revert briefly to the sort of subject that history has more recently become. For having, as we have just seen, long been based on the assumption that 'exact knowledge' of the past could be acquired, it has, during the last few decades, been assailed by so-called 'theorists' who have challenged the very possibility of any such knowledge. And while I don't want to get involved here in the arguments, I do want to suggest that they have fundamentally changed the way that it's appropriate to think about history – and that that must obviously have profound implications also for our beliefs and aspirations concerning what history might be *for*.

First, though, let's consider those who, like Richard Cobb, have repudiated any form of instrumentalism – or any suggestion that history might be *for* anything outside itself; those who have insisted that their subject is of *intrinsic* value – that it can and should be studied purely 'for its own sake'.

2   The Holy Grail of truth

> Yes, yes ... but what does one do with the Grail once one has found it?
>
> (Benjamin Jowett)[4]

For the Pre-Raphaelite painter Edward Burne-Jones in the nineteenth century, the Holy Grail represented the end-point of life's most serious quest. In mediaeval romances, the Grail (sometimes identified with the cup used by Christ at the Last Supper) was a vessel with extraordinary spiritual powers, and was most famously sought by the pious Perceval – one of the knights associated with King Arthur and his Round Table (Figure 1). So with his self-conscious reversion to an earlier Age of Faith, Burne-Jones used it as

Figure 1 The Holy Grail: symbol of historical truth for its own sake. Fifteenth century french manuscript illumination, Round Table with the Holy Grail from *L'Estoire de Saint Graal* by Robert de Boron.

a symbol for the goal of spiritual aspiration when painting his murals of the Arthurian stories in the Oxford Union. As at the University of Princeton in the USA, where Walter H. Camm (1881–1967) used the same legend in a stained-glass commission in 1919, the Arthurian quest was seen as an appropriate theme to inspire students in their own search for perfection; and Burne-Jones must have been horrified by the response attributed to Jowett (the renowned Master of Balliol College) to his idealistic message. The quest for the Grail was surely an end in itself: its attainment would be its own justification; one doesn't have to *do* anything *with* it.

And in that respect, the Holy Grail is, in what I shall call 'modernist' terms, just like historical truth, which too has been seen as the object of a life-long dedicated quest, without need of any utilitarian justification. Modernist history – by which I mean the model of history that evolved from antiquity and culminated in the nineteenth-century professionalisation of the subject – presupposed a past reality that could, with proper diligence, be ultimately retrieved by historians. Admittedly aware of problems deriving from human prejudice and partiality, from deficiencies of evidence and pluralities of interpretation, historians have nonetheless aspired to such 'objectivity', and such 'detachment' from the object of their study, as enabled them to aim at, and ultimately in principle to reach, the 'truth' about the past. That is what, for some (from the time of Thucydides, as we've just seen) has distinguished historians from that lesser breed of literary folk, who deal in the products of imagination. Attempting clearly to distinguish his own subject from literature, the great Dutch historian Johan Huizinga concluded that 'If the deeply sincere desire to find out how a certain thing "really happened" is lacking as such, he [the writer] is not pursuing history.'[5]

Like mediaeval knights, then, historians have pursued their subject (and their objective) – the discovery of what 'really happened' in the past – with religious fervour and intensity, one of the last relics of an earlier age of faith. For the historian, the great Leopold von Ranke confirmed, 'The first demand is pure love of truth'. 'History,' in the words of one of his disciples, 'is not the truth and light; but a striving for it, a sermon on it, a *consecration* to it.' 'History,' in the words of another, 'is *divine service* in the broadest sense.'[6] And with such sentiments, historians associated themselves with a broader intellectual-cum-spiritual approach to truth that emanated from the time of Socrates in ancient Greece, that flourished through the nineteenth century, and that has persisted in some quarters even up to our own time.

In his representation of Socrates' last days, Plato clarifies the philosopher's key belief, that it is the (immortal) soul that's all-important: the body is nothing more than a prison – a prison from which the soul needs to be freed in order to reach enlightenment and truth. So, as Socrates reassures his friends shortly before he drinks the hemlock, death, as merely constituting that long-desired separation of soul from body, is by no means to be feared: rather it is something to be welcomed, as a liberation of the soul from its bondage. Freed from all physical constraints, the soul will finally be in a position to enjoy that true knowledge to which it has always aspired. It is that ultimate release to which philosophers devote their lives – 'ever pursuing death and dying'.[7] They may have to wait until actual physical death for their final goal to be realised, but they can in the meantime strive to release, so far as possible, their soul from its physical restraints; they can attempt to transcend their bodies – and so facilitate the acquisition of true knowledge even here on earth.

That ascetic denial of the flesh, in the interests of a purer, higher form of knowledge, passes into the Christian tradition and re-emerges strongly in the nineteenth century.[8] That great Victorian moralist Samuel Smiles recommended self-denial as one of the crowning virtues, needful for the man who 'would get through life honourably and peaceably'. Smiles cites the example of Michael Faraday as one exceptional man whose self-denial had enabled him nobly to resist any temptation towards material affluence and instead to 'follow the path of pure science'; he may have died a poor man, but for forty years Faraday enjoyed the honour of being a veritable beacon of English science. And some historians too, as Smiles reveals, had been similarly blessed with virtue and reward: the French historian Anquetil had shown such self-denial in the face of pressure from 'the Napoleonic yoke' that, determined to retain his financial independence, he was reduced to living on bread-and-milk; but in spite of bodily hardships, he lived on happily until the age of ninety-four. As Smiles concludes elsewhere, both 'the man of science … [and] the man of letters, *forgets himself* in his pursuit'.[9]

Self-denial, then, was a Victorian virtue with important consequences for life, including intellectual life. In whatever field – whether science, or history, or literature, or aesthetics – the idea became a commonplace, that, in order to reach that Holy Grail of truth, the body – the very self – had to be denied: the truth, whether of nature or the past, was there waiting to reveal itself; but revelation was reserved for those who merited it – for those disinterested, disembodied seekers, whose very purity enabled receptivity. Knowledge becomes a function not so much of empirical investigation as of moral worth – and that moral worth was characterised above all by self-denial.

So, as the Irish physicist John Tyndall clarifies in relation to science, 'if a man be not capable of this self-renunciation – this loyal surrender of himself to Nature and to fact, he lacks … the first mark of a true philosopher'; and he goes on to emphasise the need for 'sacrifice of self' as a prerequisite for acceptance of 'the truth, no matter how it may present itself'. It's only in that way, with the renunciation of personal vanities, that prejudice and bias can be removed, and the scientist can actually 'become Nature's organ'.[10] It was that sort of moral discipline, according to another physicist, William Whewell, that made Newton's achievements possible: Newton had subordinated himself to the mysteries of nature – his *intellectual* success deriving from *moral* superiority.

That blending of the intellectual with the moral is reiterated by statistician and eugenicist Karl Pearson, who similarly insists on the need to remove the fallible self so far as possible from the activity of knowing: 'The scientific man,' he makes clear, 'has above all things to strive at *self-elimination* in his judgments.' His assessments must be 'unbiased by personal feeling': it's the *detachment* of its practitioners – effectively the death of any personal input – that justifies any authority that science has. For that science ideally consists of 'judgments *independent of the individual mind*'; the 'scientific frame of mind' implies the 'habit of *dispassionate* investigation'. And, importantly for us here in relation to history, that is not, as Pearson insists, something to be confined to physical problems alone: it may, on the contrary, 'be acquired by all', and is 'applicable to social as well as physical problems'. It is, indeed, a potentially universalisable moral position, even 'an essential of good citizenship'; and it will naturally be adopted, so far as possible, by all those who aspire to the condition of scientists – and that, of course, includes not least historians.[11]

The link between science and history in this respect is illustrated by the most renowned of nineteenth-century scientists, Charles Darwin, when he applied himself to history in the form of his own autobiography. The claimed avoidance of any intrusion of 'self' into this most obviously self-centred of activities can hardly be clearer: 'I have attempted,' Darwin explains, 'to write the following account of myself *as if I were a dead man* in another world looking back at my own life.'[12] Rather like Socrates, it's by killing off his self – by effectively dying – that he will become able to know, that he'll gain that uninvolved detachment from his subject (even when that subject is himself) which enables him to reach the truth.

And that, of course, has remained the ideal of the scientifically orientated historian up to our own time: any intrusion of a living self – a self encumbered by all those human failings we all share – is to be deplored, and indeed is sufficient to disqualify the contaminated product that results from what counts as history. So it's hardly surprising that, like Perceval and Burne-Jones, historians are often shocked by any questioning as to what that truth to which they're consecrated might all be *for*. Let's look further now, then, at their own 'own-sakist' tradition.

3 'For its own sake'?

> Such is the constitution of the human mind that any kind of knowledge, if it be really such, is its own reward.
>
> (John Henry Newman)[13]

With his devout Christian belief, the nineteenth-century theologian and educational theorist John Henry Newman believed that all kinds of knowledge had a common goal of 'Truth'. For practical reasons, he conceded, universities have to map out 'the territory of the intellect, and [see] that the boundaries of each province are religiously respected', with no 'encroachment nor surrender on any side'; but such institutional empire-building (with which we have subsequently become all too familiar) does not pre-empt the essentially unitary nature of knowledge. Different academic subjects deal with different aspects of experience, giving only 'partial views' of the whole; but they are all ultimately interrelated, and 'all taken together form one integral subject'. And the goal of that subject, again, is 'Truth'. It is to knowledge of truth that humans aspire: such knowledge needs no further justification; it is, like virtue, 'its own reward'.

With such claims, Newman joined a debate that had been going on from the time of classical antiquity – a debate, that is, concerning the relative merits of what we might call, on the one hand, 'pure' or (as I have described it in Chapter 1) 'therapeutic' education, and, on the other hand, the sort of 'vocational' or 'instrumentalist' education that is so fashionable today. In the fifth century BC, Socrates expressed contempt for the market-orientated emphasis of his contemporaries, the Sophists, who unashamedly sold practical skills to their students. His own concern, as he frequently re-emphasised, was with the soul – with how to live a good life, and so live happily with oneself. And that idealistic stance has been adopted, against more pragmatic and materialistic challengers, through the centuries. 'Here's to pure mathematics!' as one professor (however ironically) toasted only a few decades ago – 'and may it never be of use to anyone!' An ideal form of mathematics, it's implied, has its own inbuilt justification: it somehow justifies itself, without the need for any reference to things external to it; it does its practitioners good, purely in its own terms. Just as Archimedes supposedly long resisted demands to put his mathematical knowledge to the pressing practical demands of military technology, and finally died through being more interested in a geometrical problem than in the challenge of a Roman soldier, so – in the continuing Platonic tradition to which Archimedes was assigned in conventional historiography – any contact of abstract 'pure' mathematics with material physical 'reality' is seen as nothing less than contamination and defilement.

An analogy may, perhaps, be drawn here with the courtly (and Arthurian again) ideal of romantic love – the idea, that is, that there is some essence of another person that has value in and of itself. A man ideally loves a woman purely 'for herself' – not for any physical or social or economic or any other tangible advantage she may bring, but for her very essence. And in such a relationship, any idea of taking into account the possibility of some utilitarian benefit would be absolute anathema – the very denial of what that relationship is meant to be about.

And, however unworldly and romantic it may sound, a similar tradition has often prevailed in the field of historical study, where again any attempted practical application has constituted a form of disciplinary betrayal – and more particularly, with more sinister implications, a surrender to such notorious abusers of the past as politicians and ideologues. An historian, wrote Houston Stewart Chamberlain in one of his more idealistic moments, 'should give shape, but only to that which is already there ... He is but a servant, the servant of truth'.[14] 'I suppose,' proclaimed another eminent historian, William Stubbs, in 1867, 'that it is truth we are all seeking'; and, echoing J. H. Newman with his belief in an ultimate multi-disciplinary unitary truth, Stubbs went on to insist 'that though the sorts of truth [of theologians, scientists, historians and philosophers] are distinct and the ways that we work in are very different, when we have found what we seek for, we shall find all our discoveries combine in harmony'.[15] Such harmonious unitary truth needs no external justification: it is, again, its own reward.

That emphasis on truth in a history studied for its own sake was perpetuated by influential voices through the twentieth century, and for good reason. For after the Great War of 1914–18, it became clear that historians had forfeited their intellectual independence.

Whether from free choice, a sense of patriotic duty, or political manipulation, they had played a key role on both sides, in justifying the conflict and in stoking up nationalist fire in the bellies of the opposing peoples. German history had been made to reveal the superiority of a race providentially destined to rule the world; and both French and English historians had been able just as easily to justify their own nations' opposing position. Not only the Christian God but history too had fought on both sides, and their perceived political involvement invited fundamental reassessment of the proper roles of their respective representatives. If religious leaders had proved amenable to nationalistic manipulation, so too had historians. Abandoning that academic detachment which would have enabled them, as intellectuals, to maintain some distance from contemporary events, they had fervently committed themselves to the service of their state and their political paymasters. Patriotism was defined by subscription to the credo of 'my country, right or wrong', so that 'A true German historian,' insisted one, 'should especially tell those facts which conduce to the grandeur of Germany'. 'Even if the country is wrong,' confirmed another, 'we must think it in the right.'[16]

Such political commitment was subsequently perceived as representing a betrayal of history – and, worse, a betrayal of everything for which intellectuals more generally had always stood. In his famous essay, *La Trahison des Clercs* (published in 1928), Julien Benda identified a class of thinkers (in his terminology 'clerks') who had traditionally upheld certain humane values, even in the face of more popular 'lay' opposition. Their values were absolute, transcending the specificities of time and place, and as such they provided a touchstone by which, rationally and calmly, to assess ideas and events. Passions could thus be restrained: even at the height of a storm, the 'clerk' (like Pyrrho's pig and ideal sceptic) is enabled to keep calm, to maintain a balanced, philosophical approach – and thus ensure continuing survival. That restraining influence, Benda insists, had been hugely important – widely recognised as being there, even if not always effective; so that, even while doing evil, men had been compelled to remain ever conscious of their own shortfall from good. They had been prevented from 'setting up their actions as a religion' (representing them as actions of a god), and prevented 'from thinking themselves great men as they carried out these activities'. There were still some absolute values and standards, of which they were conscious of having fallen short.

But now (in the 1920s) that 'clerkly' role had been renounced, and it was the loss of any transcendental values – and indeed the derision heaped upon anything claiming to be above or beyond the particular and sensible – that Benda found so lamentable. A longstanding tradition of idealistic cosmopolitanism had been superseded by pragmatic and parochial nationalism; and historians in particular had become nothing other than 'men of politics who make use of history to support a cause whose triumph they desire'. They had taken it upon themselves to assume the role of God: there was no higher court to which appeal could be made. There was no longer any consciousness of human limitations; and while men may have always had a tendency to forget their own mortality, the new danger derived from the lack of anyone now able or willing to remind them of it. The world was, in Renouvier's words quoted in an epigraph, 'suffering from lack of faith in a transcendental truth'.

Intellectuals (including historians, of course) had not just withdrawn to the sidelines: they had actually changed sides; as a final act of 'treason', they had gone over to the enemy. Far from retaining their own 'clerkly' beliefs and values, they had actually been converted to those of the laymen, so that, in imitation of their erstwhile opponents, they too now preached the virtues of material advantage, of political and military power, and of worldly 'success'. Strong government, discipline, submission to authority – these were now openly approved, as were such characteristics as courage, harshness, and cruelty, which were required in time of war. Indeed, Benda concludes, 'Today the "clerk" has made himself Minister of War ... The "clerk" is not only conquered, he is assimilated'.

That moral abnegation of the intellectuals was exemplified by Germany in 1914, when men 'set themselves up as the sole judges of the morality of their actions', and in a strangely prescient conclusion, Benda claims that 'the logical end of the "integral realism" professed by humanity today [i.e. in the mid-1920s] is the organised slaughter of nations or classes'. The fulfilment, within two decades, of that terrible prophecy added considerable weight to Benda's argument, and must have confirmed the need for 'clerks' – and especially perhaps for historians – to retain their own ideals as independent of any external contamination. The moral surely was that they should continue in their own quest for the Holy Grail of truth, irrespective of any outside pressures: if religious faith had proved inadequate, then faith in history must be confirmed, and must not be betrayed.

So 'Omnia veritas,' wrote Geoffrey Elton, with his own e:
ence of another war only adding weight to Benda's argument. '
is what matters: 'truth is everything', and it's the function of historians to reveal that aspect of the truth with which their own
discipline is concerned – namely 'the rational reconstruction of the
past' – without regard to anything outside itself. It's 'the search for
truth', the reconstruction of the past as it really was, that is the one
thing on which historians must concentrate. They must never
deviate from the central disciplinary tenet that 'the past must be
studied for its own sake'; or as J. H. Plumb reiterates a few years
later, 'the past must be studied in its own right, for its own sake'.[17]

It has continued to suit historians to present themselves as
unconcerned with anything other than serving truth. For it's their
assumed 'objectivity' in that service, and their much vaunted
'impartiality', that gives them their authority: any perceived concession to some personally adopted 'position' in relation to their
material must render them suspect; their work, it is assumed, will
then inevitably be tainted by politics or ideology – or by having
some ulterior motive – and it's then invalidated. And as a closely
related second point, such explicitly 'tainted' history is bound, in
liberal democracies, to lose the support of politicians and paymasters. In more totalitarian régimes, there is little compunction about
using (or abusing) history for ideological purposes, but in democracies that use is less overt.

It has, then, remained both personally and politically expedient
to persist with the mythical ideal of history 'for its own sake' –
expedient, that is, for the maintenance of historians' own feelings of
self-worth, and for the maintenance of public support for history as
an important ingredient of education. But the problematic nature of
that ideal has often been revealed, even in the numerous protestations uttered on its behalf. The Roman orator, politician, and
philosopher Cicero is sometimes invoked as someone properly
concerned with the pursuit of 'pure' truth; but he himself is
adamant that any such 'search of truth' should not be at the expense
of 'the more necessary duties of active life': 'the knowledge of
things,' he insists, 'unless it is accompanied with that sort of virtue
which consists in ... the maintenance of human society, is but a
barren and fruitless accomplishment.'[18] Much more recently, proponents of the 'own-sakist' tradition appear to have been similarly
torn in their allegiances – on the one hand persisting in their politically correct position, but on the other hand revealing their own

deeply (semi-consciously?) held beliefs about what history is actually for.

The respected military historian Michael Howard, for example,
in his significantly entitled Inaugural Lecture at Oxford, 'The
Lessons of History' (1981), strongly repudiated any idea that history
might be 'socially useful' or 'relevant': any history designed 'to meet
contemporary social or political needs, has no place in a university
or anywhere else'. That sounds like a renewed plea for a useless and
irrelevant history in the 'own sake' tradition; yet he goes on, in the
very next paragraph, to assert how important it is – and not just a
matter 'of purely scholarly interest' – to be aware of such historical
issues as Hitler's responsibility for the Second World War, of the
extent of Germany's losses in the bombing of Dresden, and of
American motivations in the dropping of atomic bombs on Japan.
He later goes on to oppose ethnocentrism in historical study, as
feeding a parochialism which, as in the 1940s, 'can have pretty
disastrous results'; so that he's finally forced to confront his own
confusion. Can he, he asks, marvelling at his own inconsistency, be
conceding that history should, after all, be 'guided by some criterion of civic usefulness? In a sense I must admit that I am'! For
historians, he comes to realise, can perform a vital function, by
encouraging students 'to step outside their own cultural skins', and
by teaching 'the importance of comprehending cultural diversity
and equipping oneself to cope with it'. In the end, the historian
must, however great his own 'intellectual and moral detachment',
be *committed* – and must be committed not least 'to the values, and
to the society, that enables him to remain so detached'.[19]

Michael Howard's confusion in relation to the 'own-sakist' tradition is replicated by others. The philosopher Raimond Gaita, for
example, has recently written of how 'A love of the past is always
more than a prudential concern for how knowledge and preservation
of it may serve our present and future interests'. That suggests again
that 'love of the past' is as pure, and untainted by practicalities, as
(in the Arthurian tradition) some mediaeval knight's. But only a
few lines later, Gaita comes clean, revealing his belief that 'love ...
of the past of one's people nourishes the deepest forms of communal
identity'.[20] In other words, it's 'communal identity' that constitutes
his Holy Grail – and it's that that he hopes will be nourished by
history. Gerda Lerner similarly, in her own consideration of why
history matters, swings in consecutive paragraphs from talk of
'dedication to understanding the past *for its own sake* and in its own

light', to the suggestion that 'It is history ... that enables us to delineate goals and visions for a communal future'.[21] And as a penultimate example, Alan Kors, in an invocation of 'historians' common capacity for fascination with knowledge *for its own sake*', has written with amazing equanimity (or is it complacency?) of his approval of how 'Historians in general ... have *not* chosen to nurture the sort of knowledge that the world so desperately needs now', and has repudiated any claim to the propriety of their 'intellectual leadership'.[22]

Now admittedly, it may be presumptuous for historians to lay some special claim to 'intellectual leadership'; but for whom would that not be the case? And Kors himself goes on to propose what constitutes a leading intellectual role – and not least for historians, presumably – when he describes how 'The best educators always have preferred open, critical minds to spell-bound disciples'; and when he writes of how history, through its presentation of diverse 'others', can provide a 'great antidote to parochialism'. That finally discloses once again what is the actual point – what history should be *for*: Kors is not after all concerned with history for its own sake, but rather with history for the sake of encouraging 'open, critical minds', and providing an 'antidote to parochialism'.

Gaita's nourishment of 'communal identity' may not be to everyone's taste, but I personally can't fault Kors's educational objectives, which interestingly parallel those of Michael Howard. And the point is, surely, that the obsessive pursuit of a perfect but useless Holy Grail can lead (and has sometimes led) to a form of history that is of not the slightest consequence or interest to anyone except its own producer. 'Perfect knowledge,' as Hugh Trevor-Roper long since said of history (and literature), 'may be so fine and so uninteresting that nobody, except its discoverers, will wish to possess it.'[23] That sort of study becomes, in other words, a form of self-indulgence.

And none the worse for that, we might think, if we can, like Richard Cobb, get away with it; and happiness with their self-imposed task is probably sufficient justification for most historians. M. C. Lemon has recently reaffirmed the pleasure that derives from the actual doing of history. Historians, he claims, have and require no external motivations for continuing with their subject: the very doing – the writing and reading – is, as it were, its own reward; it is done purely 'for its own sake'. In that context, Lemon himself distinguishes between what he calls 'practical' and 'theoretical' studies – with the former concerned with some practical outcome, while the latter (including history, of course) are ends in themselves, requiring (and permitting) no extraneous motivation. Practically orientated texts, then, are essentially ideologically based, rhetorical, propagandist: their writers have an agenda in mind. But as engaging in an essentially 'theoretical' study, historians, on the other hand, are free from any external pressures or commitments: they are to be seen as disinterested observers, having no aims extrinsic to their own subject, deriving their justification and their satisfaction from simply seeking 'the truth'.

Many of the perennial problems associated with history seemingly evaporate for Lemon, as he unfashionably reverts to an essentially representational brand of truth. 'Facts', he believes, can be readily distinguished from fiction, for 'any "fact" is either true or false depending upon whether what it states to be the case is, or was, the case'; and it's seemingly by 'common sense' (rooting out anomalies, or what doesn't fit our expectations) that we ascertain the case. The writer of fiction is 'always *practically* motivated' and 'constantly "angling" his narrative to achieve his end'; but historians have no such 'axe to grind', so are left free to look impartially at everything. 'They will explore *all* avenues of their topic ... and will consider *all* angles from which it might be understood.' These are extraordinary claims, and are hardly borne out by Lemon's own (inevitably) selective use of material, evidence, and examples in his own historical narrative. But his confidence knows few bounds as he goes on to claim that historians of all people are well equipped to detect 'ideological bias', whether in themselves or in others. With the heightened self-awareness associated with their discipline, they are able 'to bring what might have been in "the unconscious" into consciousness'; so that they can recognise and remove any 'bias, distortion, or partiality' (in themselves or others), and persist in their own determination 'to give a "true" account' – an account again that is necessarily presented simply 'for its own sake'.[24]

Lemon's late reversion to an own-sakist tradition is premised on a representational theory of truth, which has (as we shall re-emphasise in Chapter 6) been seriously challenged – and, I would argue, totally undermined. Still writing in the Eltonian tradition, Lemon reasserts the independent reality of a past which it's the function of the historian to reveal. That past has to be allowed, as it were, to speak for itself – to be approached without any extraneous agenda: that's what Lemon's 'theoretical' (as opposed to 'practical') approach involves; and it implies that there are not only 'facts', but a whole story (a narrative of past events) out there awaiting rediscovery. Against that position, postmodernists would argue that, though the past admittedly existed, it can't be simply accessed (let alone known) as an entity, but only through others' representations – through others' inevitably partial and selective descriptions – and that it can never be approached with the naivety and theoretical purity that seems to be implied by such commendatory words as 'objectivity'; one can't help but be in some way 'positioned' in relation to any object of study.

And indeed it's quite clear that Lemon's own account of the philosophy of history is far from being innocently or impartially presented. Embracing as it does the whole span of human history, how could it possibly be? How could he ever 'explore *all* avenues' and 'consider *all* angles'; and how, in the face of a virtually infinite amount of material, could he ever hope to be other than 'partial'? It's just not possible to do it all: there's no single thread to be found and followed through the labyrinth of past thoughts and actions; one necessarily chooses one's own – for one's own (whether stated or unstated) purposes. And Lemon, of course, in fact explicitly reveals his own agenda – by the very act of advocating a history written (or read) 'for its own sake'. For him, the pursuit of such knowledge, uncontaminated by practical concerns, is the very 'telos' or end for human life, and it's that that he therefore recommends; that's what his history is *for*.

In that classically inspired advocacy, Lemon shows himself well aware of how it has long been politic for historians to make additional claims, and to claim in particular that study of their subject results in highly desirable *practical* outcomes; and to some of these we'll turn in Chapter 3. First, though, to conclude this chapter, it's worth confirming how, despite all the theoretical debates of the last decades, many other traditional modernist assumptions about history's nature – and so potential purpose – still prevail.

4 Straw men?

Postmodernists are often accused of attacking 'straw men', those caricature figures whose exaggerated characteristics make all-too-easy targets, but who don't of course in reality exist at all. Traditional historians, it's claimed, are simply misrepresented in various ways – as extreme empiricists, for example, who refuse to take any theoretical considerations whatever into account; or as Arthurian-style pursuers of the Holy Grail, who fanatically retain their belief in absolute objectivity and truth, and their power to re-present the past 'as it was'. Such descriptions, it's alleged, are gross distortions: they fit no one in practice, but are presented simply in order to make the opposition look ridiculous. The historical profession itself, regardless of any external pressures, has moved on, away from any such arrogance and theoretical naivety.

So it's important to realise just how tenacious some modernist beliefs remain. By representing the present as the culmination of a long progressive development, historians have often confirmed and ratified the *status quo*, making it appear as nothing less than 'natural'. That has been their purpose and their role: that's what history has been for. And that has given to historians a very central and defining position, with enormous influence and power, and the sort of prestige that's unlikely to be given up without a struggle.

That means in turn that historians have a vested interest in retaining modernist assumptions and beliefs: they have good self-interested reasons to reject any theoretical questioning of their current practice; and they no less have good reasons to persist in their quest for historical truth and understanding – to retain their own faith, and that of others, in the whole project of modernist history. So words such as 'fact' and 'objectivity', 'knowledge' and 'understanding', still fall from lips unsullied by doubts about their meaning and proper application. 'I never asked the question – how do historians know?' confessed A. J. P. Taylor of himself as a history undergraduate at Oxford; 'I increased my knowledge of history, my *understanding* of it not at all'; Geoffrey Barraclough confirmed that, before the Second World War, 'few of us [historians] ... questioned the credentials of what we were doing, or the premises of our work'; and Charles C. Gillispie has recently confessed that, when writing his classic work in the history of science, *Genesis and Geology* (1951), 'Nothing was farther from my thoughts than methodology'.[25] And for many, such 'theoretical' questions as understanding what it is that history *is*, still, a half-century on, remain irrelevant – or perhaps too frightening to contemplate. Despite some allowance for periodic heretic-revisionists, largely conformist versions of past events continue to be transmitted as generally accepted dogma – and as our heritage – through the generations; for that's the implication of accepting a professional peer-group with a shared 'paradigm', or model that by definition excludes 'anomalies' – or those recalcitrant ideas that fail to fit professional expectations.

It's hardly surprising, then, that people at large have failed to keep up with contemporary thought, so that the old model of reportage of events prevails – as is evidenced almost daily in our newspapers. Reporters themselves assume the possibility of an unproblematised 'objectivity' and 'balance' (and are roundly condemned by politicians when they're thought to lack it). 'Last week,' proclaims John Simpson with reference to a newly opened memorial in 2002, 'the past *as it really was*, not as we choose to remember it, received its proper due at last.'[26] Well-paid revelations, such as those by Paul Burrell, former butler to Diana, Princess of Wales, are unhesitatingly claimed (and no doubt often accepted) as 'the true story as it is'.[27] And in February 2003, the British Prime Minister Tony Blair complacently awaited 'the judgement of history' for his stand on Iraq: his contemporaries may disagree with him, but he is confident that, as at the last judgement, his stance will ultimately be vindicated by some 'objective', all-seeing, all-comprehending tribunal known as 'History', when everything will presumably appear 'as it really was' (rather than as we currently might think it is).

Reporters, butlers, and Prime Ministers only follow historians themselves. So 'we certainly shouldn't be confusing pupils by giving them different interpretations of history', as Professor Niall Ferguson is reported as insisting, following a meeting of educationalists set up by Prince Charles in October 2002. What's needed is a good story, like that of Henry VIII, the English Civil War or the Second World War, in all of which, he claims, 'there are goodies and baddies and a clear result'! And Professor David Starkey, another influential voice, apparently agrees. 'Historical "process" [by which I take him to mean theory, or philosophy of history] is desiccated, tedious, pointless. What matters is the product' – that 'product' consisting presumably of his own true version of the past. For there has, he complains, been a tendency to tell students 'that interpretation is what matters ... [But] all this is absolutely wrong. Teachers poison the minds of the young by suggesting that everything is open to interpretation'. Altogether too much attention is paid to 'so-called documentary evidence, which encourages a patchwork approach'. What is needed, rather, is to teach children *facts*.[28] In the context of such historiographical confidence, then, it's small wonder that in announcing a re-run of its 1964 documentary, the BBC in February 2003 feels justified in claiming to present 'the definitive history' of the Great War – where 'definitive' surely implies that it's the last possible word on the matter.

Biographers, too, having immersed themselves in their research for years, can sometimes feel confident that they've penetrated to the essence of their subject – that they've actually got to *know* the person with whom they have been so intimately concerned for so long; and others certainly attribute such attainments to them. So, for instance, we read that, in his study of historians' various treatments of Hitler, John Lukacs 'reveals the contradictions that take us back to *the true Hitler* of history'.[29] There's an unquestioned assumption that there's a single 'true Hitler' back there in 'history'; so that, first, any earlier 'contradictions' and then, finally, the truth can be revealed. It's possible, again, as claimed for a recently (2002) published biography of Jack the Ripper, to produce, in the words of its sub-title, '*The Definitive History*'.[30]

Even as a theoretically aware and philosophically concerned historian, Mary Fulbrook seems similarly to retain her belief in historical 'truth', and has no compunction about writing about '*the realities* of the past'. She can then attribute the aim of 'not getting the story wrong' (which surely must mean getting it 'right') to those working in the subject. Indeed, she remains confident that 'The historian [who happily has 'some notion of ... what, precisely, the past is made up of'] knows what clues to look for, which suspects to interrogate, which of the diversity of contemporaneous elements can be safely ignored'; so that this omniscient researcher can present findings with some confidence in their adequacy, as having 'a degree of plausibility, *even certainty*', and there can be progressive development in 'what we *actually know*'.[31] And that progress, according to another historian and journalist, seems likely somehow to be aided by modern technology; for, despite all the admitted difficulties of selection and editing, the television camera can contrive to bring us 'closer than any other medium to *how things really were*'.[32]

It's hard to believe that this sort of attitude still prevails among historians, but, as so often, they in turn are following in the footsteps of scientists who, however eminent, can still themselves remain theoretically naive. Steven Weinberg, for example, a Nobel laureate in physics, remained confident as late as 1996 that his scientific findings had absolute validity: 'if we ever discover intelligent creatures on some distant planet and translate their scientific works, we will find that we and they have discovered the same laws ... Science is cumulative, and permits definite judgements of success or failure.'[33] Weinberg's sanguine assessment of his subject is clearly justifiable in a context in which science is still seen – as it is by Stephen Hawking – as likely soon to reveal nothing less than 'the mind of God', to be shown in a unified theory of the whole world.[34] And some philosophers too remain similarly convinced of their ability to reach the Holy Grail of truth. Raimond Gaita, for example, concedes that 'it requires disciplines of mind and character to "see things as they are" as opposed to how they appear to be', but that is to imply it's not impossible. Some ascetic detachment may (as in the case of history, as we've seen) be necessary; but given that, it seems possible to ensure 'that our fears, fantasies and affections do not interfere with our sense of what is objectively the case', and (whether in physics or poetry or, presumably, in history) our aim remains to '"see things as they are" rather than ... how they appear from distorting perspectives'.[35]

The didactic, priestly role continues to be claimed, then, by some scientists, philosophers, and of course historians. For all their professed disinterestedness, they all have their own quasi-theological, psycho-therapeutic, as well as ideological, aspirations. From the time of Descartes, thinkers have prided themselves on their role – their role as intermediaries between God (and the 'reality' of his nature, or the past) and human beings. Like the priestesses at the Delphic Oracle, they have been the interpreters of messages whose meanings might be less than transparent to mere mortals, but to them are unambiguous. And however hollow their promises may now appear, such 'straw men' still exist.

5 Conclusion

> Hitherto perhaps you have learned names and dates, lists of kings, lists of battles and wars. The time comes now when you are to ask yourself, To what end?
>
> (J. R. Seeley)[36]

Well over a hundred years ago, J. R. Seeley, as Regius Professor, was encouraging Cambridge history undergraduates to take some thought about what they were studying *for*, and it may be time to reiterate and re-emphasise his question, 'To what end?' The thoughtless learning of names and dates, and lists of kings and battles, has admittedly become unfashionable, but there's still a core of accepted 'historical knowledge' that students are expected to ingest, and there are still voiced aspirations to attain the Holy Grail of historical truth; and it's as well periodically to consider why. What's it actually all for?

'When I meet a person,' Seeley wrote elsewhere, 'who does not find history interesting, it does not occur to me to alter history – I try to alter him.'[37] It's still inconceivable to many that history could or should be altered: history, it's assumed, like Moses' God, just is, and any attempt to alter it must constitute transgression of some natural or even spiritual order. But history, when it's historicised, or shown itself to be a part of history, is seen to be not a naturally existing entity at all, but rather something that's been constructed by human beings for their own purposes – something that's been developed over time, and with particular agendas in mind. Those agendas, as we'll see, often have much to do with power. History (or those 'professionals' who guard its gates) enjoys enormous power, not least by controlling the very categories in which history is written – its chronologies (or the way the past is split up, to make it manageable, or enable it to manage), its language (its naming and definitions), its choices (of whom and what to consider 'relevant' and memorable), and its evaluations (or unavoidable moral judgements on the past). Recognition of such power to define the nature and direction of the past exposes any pretension to selfless own-sakism as at best disingenuous; and it indicates that one important role for history is to investigate the history of history itself. For such study shows that history – as well as everything else – could have been, and so could be, quite different; and that contingency, both in and of history, opens up the possibility of choice and of change in a hopeful direction for the future.

By looking at what we think history should be for, then, we may indicate some ways in which the subject might be changed: as our purposes are modified, and our agendas re-negotiated, so we may need to change the sort of history that we do – and that may even lead in turn to our meeting fewer people who don't find history interesting.

First, though, in the next chapter we'll consider some of the purposes that historians themselves have claimed for their subject in the past.

Chapter 3

Professed purposes

I Introduction

> It would be useless to speak about its [history's] utility since
> nobody doubts it.
>
> (Leopold von Ranke, *c.* 1830)[1]

There may never have been unanimous support for Thomas Carlyle's
claim that history – as 'the letter of Instructions, which the old
generations write and posthumously transmit to the new' – 'recommends itself as *the most profitable of all studies*';[2] but as his
contemporary Ranke suggests in the quotation above, nobody has
seriously doubted that history can, in one way or another, prove
useful. As we noted in relation to Richard Cobb, it's hard to do
anything for no reason at all; and even Geoffrey Elton, for all his
belief in doing history 'for its own sake', concluded that 'any
thoughtful historian must at times ask himself whether he has a
purpose beyond his own satisfaction'.[3] And while, as we'll see in
Chapter 4, historians have sometimes been manipulated, have
sometimes had their own hidden agendas, and have sometimes
inadvertently achieved more (and other) than they themselves
intended, many have tried to answer Elton's question and have been
quite open in acknowledging what their history is *for*. It's some of
these openly professed purposes that we'll consider in this chapter.

To introduce this topic, we can return to William Stubbs.
Writing of the purposes of history in 1877, he indicated that, in the
tradition that we've just been considering, history 'may be read for
its own sake'; but it may also, he went on, 'be learned as a mental
discipline, and it may be acquired as a piece of the furniture or
apparatus of cultivated life'.[4] The last of those aims, referring to a
'cultivated life', may initially sound remote from our experience,

but I'll return to that in Section 3. First, though, let's consider the second function, of providing 'a mental discipline'; for this has been much promoted during the last half-century in association with the educational fashion for so-called 'transferable skills'.

2   Transferable skills

During the latter half of the twentieth century, there was increasing pressure on teachers of the humanities to justify their subjects on instrumental, vocational grounds: learning 'for its own sake' was seen as a luxury that could no longer be afforded, an indulgence of a previously privileged class whose time had passed, a frivolous diversion from the real business of making money. Students, subsidised as they were by a capitalist society, should be taught the essentials of getting on in the 'real' world of 'the market economy', where Perceval's quest for the Holy Grail had long since been superseded by international companies' unholy quest for world domination. Education, as one British university (not untypically) claims in its publicity for 2003, is 'for the skills you need in the real [sic] world'[5] (and not, by implication, for anything needed in an unreal world of effete layabouts in ivory towers).

Thrown on to the defensive, teachers of humanities often attempted to take refuge in a list of so-called 'transferable skills' – those skills of analysis, synthesis, personal expression, writing, oral presentation (anything to do with that much-prized ideal of 'communication') – which were supposedly acquired by any student and which could then be duly applied in other contexts to the 'world of work'. The ability to read and analyse a selection of literary texts, to formulate a synthesis, arrive at a conclusion, write an essay or report, and give a seminar presentation, is not, it was claimed, so different from the ability to do likewise in a commercial or business situation; the subject-matter may be different, but the skills required to deal with it remain the same.

Quite apart, though, from the essential skills that supposedly derive from a study of the humanities in general, history in particular has set itself apart with some self-justificatory mission-statements. Towards the end of the nineteenth century, W. E. H. Lecky was already asserting the *practical* value that he believed could be ascribed to history, as being 'one of the best schools for that kind of reasoning which is most useful in practical life. It teaches men to weigh conflicting probabilities, to estimate degrees of evidence, to form a sound judgment of the value of authorities'[6]; and such protestations became increasingly common through the twentieth century. So more recent historians have re-emphasised the old claim that we need, in E. H. Carr's words now, 'to master and understand ... [the past] as the key to the understanding of the present'. The point of history, Carr believes, is indeed very practical – namely, to increase our control over the present; and that control is gained through learning relevant lessons from the achievements and failures that have been made in the past – from the very subject-matter of history. It's the possibility of the 'transmission of acquired assets' that Carr insists on – the belief that 'man is capable of profiting (not that he necessarily profits) by the experience of his predecessors'.[7]

That optimistic belief in the possibility of learning from the past, and so of making actual progress, has been shared by many others. J. H. Plumb, for instance, implies that the study of history may increase 'man's awareness of himself', and that enhanced self-awareness in turn 'strengthens his chance of controlling himself and his environment'. The historian's purpose, then, is 'to deepen understanding about men and society, not merely for its own sake, but in the hope that a profounder knowledge, a profounder awareness will help to mould human attitudes and human actions'.[8] Peter Laslett, too, while still maintaining history's intrinsic interest ('in itself'), submits that 'all historical knowledge is knowledge with a view to ourselves as we are here and now'; for it provides, he believes, the ability better to understand ourselves by revealing contrasts with other (past) peoples and societies.[9] That implied ability to detach ourselves from our own immediate environment – from our own time as well as place – has often been seen as a by-product of a history that can be considered, in Lord Acton's words, as a potential 'deliverer not only from the undue influence of other times, but from the undue influence of our own'.[10]

Others have been more prescriptive about the improvements that history can provide, aligning them with commonly accepted ideals of liberal democracy. In the United States, for instance, it has recently been stressed that history 'is vital to our prospects for a robust and democratic society'.[11] And that position was reaffirmed in Britain by the so-called History Subject Benchmarking Group in the same year, 1999. That body was naturally concerned to re-emphasise the central importance of historical study, albeit an historical study still understood in essentially modernist terms, where 'knowledge and understanding of the human past' remained as an unquestioned and practical possibility. Understood in those terms, history, it was claimed, not only inculcated 'important abilities and qualities of mind' that were 'readily transferable to many occupations and careers', but it also conveyed 'respect for historical context and evidence, a greater awareness of the historical processes unfolding in our own time, and a deeper understanding of the varied traditions current today'. Historical education, then, should provide 'a sense of the past, an awareness of the development of differing values, systems and societies, and the inculcation of critical yet tolerant personal attitudes'.[12] Own-sakism, in a publicly accountable and closely scrutinised educational system, was no longer an option: it has, again, become desirable (even essential) to profess, however platitudinously, an acceptable social purpose. A certain sort of (democratically orientated) history is simply presupposed – a history from which appropriate lessons may beneficially be learnt.

Indeed, the political and ethical dimensions and outcomes of the subject have been recognised from the time of classical antiquity, and periodically reasserted ever since. In his witnessing of the Peloponnesian War, Thucydides was not just filling in time after his enforced retirement from personal military involvement: he had very practical moral and political messages to convey to future generations. With his belief in a universe whose morality was maintained by the gods, he determined to show that the decline and fall of Athens exemplified the working of a moral law – a law in terms of which the hubris (pride) shown by the imperialist state of Athens was inevitably followed by nemesis (retribution), in the shape of military defeat by Sparta. His own history of the Peloponnesian War thus deliberately revealed the working out of a purposeful morality, and taught a practical lesson for the future.

Practical purposes were likewise seen for history by later educators. 'The soundest education and training for a life of active politics is the study of History,' claimed the Greek historian Polybius in the second century BC. It's by knowledge of what happened in the past that politicians can act appropriately in the present: from examining past practices, they can deduce how other people are likely to proceed in the future; they can determine in what position any country or empire is, in relation to established cycles of development and decline; and they can take heart from recognising the necessity of inevitable 'vicissitudes of fortune'. By looking at history in the round – looking, that is, at particulars not just in isolation but with all their interconnections – they can 'derive both benefit and pleasure'.[13]

In that same tradition, writers specifically prescribed the subject as a most suitable training for Renaissance princes. It was essential, thought Francesco Guicciardini (1483–1540), that political leaders learn history's most useful lesson – the essential instability of human affairs. 'No one,' reiterated the Italian nobleman Maiolino Bisaccioni (1582–1663), 'should cultivate the study of it [history] more than the Prince.' That was partly because history was concerned with 'the actions of princes and great men', so that princes and great men could learn from those who resembled themselves. But most importantly of all, history 'tells of the revolutions and commotions of [ordinary] peoples' – of those 'Political Earthquakes' – which usually derive from bad government, and which obviously need to be avoided.[14]

It was, then, for such practical reasons that humanist scholars regularly placed history at the top of their intellectual and disciplinary hierarchy: 'I accord the first place to History,' wrote one teacher of humanities, 'on grounds both of its attractiveness and of its utility.' Appealing not only to the scholar but also to the statesman, history provides 'a cumulative wisdom' and 'practical lessons ... for the present day'.[15] For Leonardo Bruni (1370–1444), similarly, history served 'both public and private ends'; and, as historical scholar as well as Chancellor in Florence, he believed on both counts that it was important for citizens to be aware of their long republican tradition – that the 'struggle against tyranny began a long time ago ... [and that] Florence has always been united in one and the same cause'. History, he insisted, affords important 'lessons ... in the ordering of public policy', providing appropriate examples and enlarging 'our foresight in contemporary affairs'.[16]

It's not surprising, then, that the great Venetian painter Titian, in his symbolic *Allegory of Prudence* (Figure 2), should have made the same didactic moral point. His picture includes three faces – those of a man in youth, maturity, and old age; and the caption (in translation) reads: 'The Present does well to profit from the Past, lest Future conduct go astray.' By the mid-sixteenth century, when Titian was painting, this idea of what history was for was a commonplace: it was a part of that 'mental discipline' to which Stubbs later referred – a part of that transferable 'disciplinary force', which enabled it 'to make people honest and intelligent politicians'.[17]

That supposed moral force of history can seem particularly needful at times when moral guidance from other sources (whether

Figure 2 History as teacher: Titian, *Allegory of Prudence*, c. 1550–60.

religious or secular) is challenged, disputed, or in short supply: it's then, perhaps, when the present seems particularly in crisis and deficient in potential remedies, that lessons are most desperately sought from the past. Our own position in postmodernity (as we'll go on to consider in Chapters 5 to 7) is one such time, but a not dissimilar situation is described by writers in the middle of the nineteenth century, when too the social, economic, religious, and technological bases of life were perceived to be in flux. For Matthew Arnold in 1857, for example, the present appeared as 'copious and complex' – as 'an immense, moving, confused spectacle, which ... perpetually baffles our comprehension'. And bafflement, he believed, could be eased, if not overcome, by a study of the past:

some understanding of the others of the past may serve to clarify our own position. Or, as he puts it, we need 'to know how others stand, that we may know how we ourselves stand'.[18]

That enhanced self-understanding that supposedly derives from study of the past becomes, then, another commonplace – another assumption that historians profess when pondering what their subject might be for. Arnold's contemporary, Carlyle, goes on to recommend that people 'search more and more into the Past'; for it's there in the past, he believes, that is to be found 'the true fountain of knowledge; by whose light alone ... can the Present and Future be interpreted or guessed at'. In words that have, in one form or another, re-echoed through the centuries from the mouths of historians determined to assert the practical benefits of their studies: 'Only he who understands what has been, can know what should be and will be.'[19] Essential life-skills, in short, can be derived only from history.

One other such life-skill was identified by Geoffrey Elton, when he emphasised 'the magnificent unpredictability' that history revealed in the thoughts and actions of human beings.[20] That 'unpredictability' may, as has been noted by one critic,[21] have been imposed upon the past by Elton himself, rather than being an essential aspect of it; but (to be equally prescriptive here) any study of human beings (whether in the past or present) is bound to reveal that quality, and some recognition of its operation is bound to be salutary in the formulation of both private and public policies. Indeed, in the face of widespread political (and sometimes personal) aspirations, and even expectations, to take *control* of others, some awareness of humans' 'magnificent unpredictability' might well constitute another fitting 'skill' for historians to engender?

It's closely related to another skill that's rare but that may, perhaps, be encouraged by the sort of 'open-ended' history being developed now in postmodernity. Forced to concede the ultimately ambiguous nature of their data, and the impossibility of any final 'closure', historians are compelled endlessly to juggle alternatives – to keep as many balls as possible in the air at the same time, any or all of which may prove useful in the future. Just as physicists need to retain two models of light – as waves and particles (models which may well seem mutually exclusive) – so historians may find it counter-productive sometimes to settle for some single final ('definitive') explanation at the price of forever excluding all others. And with practice, they may come to pass what Scott Fitzgerald called 'the test of a first rate intelligence' – namely, 'to hold two opposed ideas in mind at the same time and still retain the ability to function'.[22]

To continue functioning as a self-consciously 'divided self' may, again, be a skill particularly suited to life in postmodernity, when (as we shall go on to see) concepts of identity are being questioned, and Diderot's representation of D'Alembert is becoming increasingly comprehensible as a position that might even be intellectually respectable: that 'in the morning I see probability on my right, and by afternoon it is on my left ... And by evening, recalling the rapid changeableness of my judgements, I don't believe anything'.[23] The study or presentation of open-ended histories that embrace and illustrate that sort of changeableness – where positions are at once sincerely held and seemingly incompatible – may yet foster skills (or *qualities*, as I shall go on to suggest) that are transferable (and much needed) elsewhere.

For those skills (and qualities) include, as Carlyle saw, not only practical but moral skills – having to do with what *should* be in the future. Thus, Bernard Williams has recently written of history's potential function in relation to seeing the needs of other people – a seeing that might serve to modify our vision of our own needs. It is, he suggests, partly 'by being told their historical story' that we can reach such sympathetic understanding of the needs of others – and that 'is why it may be worth one group's telling their story to others' (just as, we might add, in the case of individuals); for living together (personally, again, or globally) involves 'the question whether one lot can make sense of the fact that something different makes sense to the other'.[24]

Here, then, is another potential function for history – another answer to the question of what it might be for, another set of skills which it might engender and be appropriate for historians to profess. Such skills (or qualities) closely link – or even quite properly overlap – with the 'cultivation' that's the subject of our following section.

3 'Cultivation'

William Stubbs' third aim of history as a means to acquire 'the furniture or apparatus of cultivated life' may now sound as lifeless and outdated as a fossil – an ancient relic embedded in our texts, providing evidence of earlier and very different times. 'Cultivation' is a term we seldom use now, but as another outcome of historical study it too has a long history; and, as implying approbation of a type of civilised human being who may still win our respect, it may continue to have relevance in our consideration of what history might be for. Some characteristics may not, after all, be subject to the vagaries of fashion?

At all events, Stubbs is foreshadowed by the Renaissance scholar Leonardo Bruni, with his insistence that history (as well as serving the public interest, as we've just seen) 'must not on any account be neglected by one who aspires to true cultivation'.[25] Princes of the time, as he was well aware, needed to be not only politically shrewd, but also fitting representatives of a cultivated society – able to stand their ground with cultural competitors – and that most obviously included an appreciation of the historical roots of the culture then being re-born and deliberately brought back to life in the present. In the mid-eighteenth century, similarly, Henry St John, Lord Bolingbroke, advocates historical study as a means of achieving what might now be called multi-cultural awareness, or an enlightened cosmopolitanism, such as we might still approve. Repudiating the sort of parochial nationalism that has since his time proved all too intrusive, Bolingbroke praises the Stoic ideal of seeing oneself 'as a citizen of the world'.[26] He writes scathingly of the

> ridiculous and hurtful vanity, by which the people of each country are apt to prefer themselves to those of every other; and to make their own customs, and manners, and opinions, the standards of right and wrong, of true and false.

Such vanity can be dispelled, he believes, by a study of history, which makes one aware of – and sympathetic to – alternative values. History, that is, like foreign travel, broadens the mind and 'serves to purge the mind of those national partialities and prejudices that we are apt to contract'.[27] That is surely a part of what 'cultivation' entails.

In the following century, W. E. H. Lecky likewise proclaimed his belief that history 'expands the range of our vision':

> [it] greatly expands our horizon and enlarges our experience by bringing us in direct contact with men of many times and countries. It gives young men something of the experience of old men, and untravelled men something of the experience of travelled ones.[28]

And another century later but in similar vein, Geoffrey Elton prescribed history for its ability to equip the living 'with a much wider and deeper acquaintance with the possibilities open to human thought and action than people can ever gather from their own limited experience'.[29]

'Cultivation' of that kind might still be seen as an appropriate educational ideal, to which history might contribute? Certainly in the not distant past, it underpinned attempts to teach students of science and engineering something of the history of their own subjects, when history served as a bridge between two cultures. And if that now sounds unacceptably patronising, it does further highlight the problematic nature of 'cultivation'; and rather than simply rejecting Stubbs' term as an anachronism, historians might consider how best to update it – how to define, that is, the sort of 'cultivation' that they'd like their own histories to teach?

That question becomes increasingly insistent in the face of the utilitarian emphasis placed on the subject in government policy statements – an emphasis which, since I wrote this chapter, has provoked the President of the British Royal Historical Society, Jinty Nelson, to reassert a belief in history's 'distinctive and indispensable part in a *civilised* society'.[30]

4 Myth-breaking

History is traditionally differentiated sharply from myth. Indeed, for historians, history is the very antithesis of myth; it's precisely what myth isn't – namely, true. Myth is a story about the past that, by definition, isn't true, whereas history is a story about the past that is true – that can be empirically checked, and that has sound evidence to support it. That clear traditional antithesis between the supposedly factual and the merely fictitious has, of course, been superseded recently by a more 'nuanced' or ambivalent approach (or more bluntly by doubts that the two can be distinguished at all); but through the centuries we can detect a significant role for historians in purporting to separate the disposable chaff of myth from the wheat required for their own substantial sustenance. Indeed, we might see the supposedly progressive development of historical study as the relegation of previous 'histories' to the status of mere 'myths', and their replacement by something more historically persuasive; for historical 'revisionism' implies the replacement of one 'vision' of the past by another that is claimed to be superior and better founded.

Myths tend to be located in the past and attributed to those more naive than our sophisticated selves: they are stories that may have been believed as 'true' in the past, but that are now recognised as failing to satisfy the criteria demanded by historians to qualify as 'history'. The distinction was clearly drawn in the fifth century BC by Thucydides, who identified 'myths' as unsatisfactory bases for his own work: he recognised them, as we might say, for what they were – explanatory tales that people in the past may well have accepted, and often found attractive, but that failed his own more exacting standards for what constituted reliable evidence. He saw, in short, that the same rules that operated for him in his present had to be applied to his predecessors in the past; and he thus, as Bernard Williams has recently claimed, 'invented historical time', inasmuch as he

> imposed a new conception of the past, by insisting that people should extend to the remoter past a practice they already had in relation to the immediate past, of treating what was said about it as, seriously, true or false.[31]

So myths might have consisted of good coherent stories and offered what were, in their own terms, attractive and persuasive accounts of past events; and they might well therefore have been believed in at some level. But in the context of Thucydides' own beliefs and procedures – which had now to be applied also to the remoter past – they had to be distinguished from 'real history'.

Just as Thucydides was keen to distance himself as a 'scientific' historian from his less rigorous predecessors, so Renaissance historians assumed the role of revealing earlier myths, to which citizens innocently and erroneously subscribed, for what they were – which was something less than real 'history'. Some such myths had been perpetrated by earlier aspiring historians themselves, whose methods were defective, others by painters such as Piero della Francesca, who anachronistically depicted battles between Roman emperors and what appeared to be fifteenth-century knights – misleadingly giving 'modern dress to the ancients'.[32] It became the job of more critical historians to expose such lack of historical sense – a job in which they continue to be employed as they lambast modern film-makers for similarly confusing the 'factual' with the 'fictional' or mythical.

Sometimes, though, such myth-making is actually deliberate. 'There is,' wrote Gabriel Naudé in 1630 (and as we might still confirm), 'scarcely a nation which does not flatter itself about its origins, and take its beginning back to some hero or demigod.'[33] For there are, of course, advantages (as well as disadvantages) in postulating such origins. First concerns the matter of status: the lofty rank of our heroic or quasi-divine founding fathers reflects well on us as their presumptive heirs. As any race-horse will testify, it's good to be seen to have come from good stock: it justifies not only self-confidence within, but also appropriate deference from without; and it bodes well for the future of the race.

Importantly, too, in the second place, such myths endow both the past and the present with a surety, a fixity, a stability, that appeals to an evident need for security in relation to the future. If our nation traces its past back to some semi-divine founder, then there's no need (or room) for further speculation on the matter; any related issues can be resolved, unambiguously and finally. For our position can be seen to be, not so much the result of any historical process, as of a specific divine intervention; it becomes a matter, not of chance, but of super-human intention; not optional or *contingent*, but actually *natural* and eternal. It's no wonder, then, that such myths, as Roland Barthes has argued, have the effect of de-politicising: they remove the possibility of any *change*.[34]

That is what makes challenging such foundation-myths so important, and that's what reveals another vital role for historians – as non-conformist irritants. It was (and is) just those flattering origins, heroes, and demigods, constituting as they did the contrived foundations for various nations and power groups, that were (and are) to be challenged with the help of what were, in Naudé's time, newly developing historical methods.

An early and important victim of the new expertise in textual analysis, linked with a generally sceptical approach to both authority and evidence, was the so-called 'Donation of Constantine'. That document (dating probably from the mid-eighth century) purported to record the Roman emperor Constantine's generous 'donation' of temporal authority, throughout the western empire, to Pope Sylvester I and his successors – a particularly convenient gesture for the Roman church. By using new techniques of textual analysis, the great humanist critic Lorenzo Valla (1407–57), together with other scholars of the time, was able conclusively to expose the document as a forgery. In his *Declamation on the Donation of Constantine* published in 1439, he showed himself well aware of the very practical political privileges conferred by the pretended gift, and was scathing in his denunciation of those who had taken advantage of people's credulity. Under the terms of Constantine's mythical donation, he noted, the church laid claim to temporal authority throughout the whole of Italy, France, Spain, Germany, Britain – 'indeed the whole West' – and yet they must have known for centuries that the document on which they relied for those claims was 'spurious and forged'. It was quite obviously written not by Constantine himself, but by 'some fool of a priest who, stuffed and pudgy, knew neither what to say or how to say it, and ... belched out these wordy sentences which convey nothing'. So the pontiffs were guilty, either of 'supine ignorance', or of 'gross avarice'; from sheer self-interest they persisted in defending 'as true what they knew to be false'.[35]

Similarly mythical underpinning had been inserted into histories of Britain, at a time when antiquity still bestowed respectability. The twelfth-century historian Geoffrey of Monmouth, for example, recounted the traditional story of how Britain had been founded by the Trojan Brutus, great-grandson of Aeneas, who was himself born of a goddess and the mythical founder of Rome. Britain, he explained, had been 'uninhabited except for a few giants', before Brutus landed in Cornwall: it was Brutus who had driven the giants into mountain caves, and 'called the island Britain from his own name'.[36] The mythical (as opposed to 'historical') nature of that enduring story was exposed by the Italian historian Polydore Vergil in 1534: it could hardly be accepted as true by one who was convinced that 'the first office of an Historiographer, is to write no lye', though it has been observed by a later exposer that his own account of the 'dark' mediaeval period had its own political agenda, being designed to highlight, by way of contrast, the benefits of rule under the Tudors.[37]

'Lie', though (as in Polydore Vergil's terminology), is to put it rather strongly. Geoffrey of Monmouth is unlikely to have conceded that he was guilty of actually lying: in the case of Brutus, he was simply relaying the conventional wisdom of his time and place – naively, no doubt, but not unique in that. He and other historians of his time perpetuated myths about the Normans too – myths that have more recently been revealed as such by R. H. C. Davis, in his significantly entitled *The Normans and their Myth* (1976). Davis shows how a people originating in Scandinavia and settling widely, as 'Northmen', through Europe, were sustained through various myths that conferred much needed identity – or rather identities that were required to change over the years. The early eleventh-century historian Dudo, for instance, was concerned to convey the message that, by his time, the Normans were no longer Viking pirates but, rather, respectable citizens: in their conquest of Normandy, their early leaders were only fulfilling God's providential plan; and they had gone on to confirm their Christian credentials by being baptised and founding monasteries. Indeed, they had effectively become French, and their Norman identity was now to be seen as deriving from their being well and truly rooted in the promised land of Normandy.

As their conquests spread, needs changed; and subsequent historians, such as Orderic Vitalis in the twelfth century, fulfilled the important function of promoting a revised sense of identity – one that was now needed to unify a people whose representatives ranged far afield, from Normandy itself in northern France to Apulia in southern Italy, and subsequently to the Middle East and Britain. The new history (or mythology) placed emphasis, then, on the Normans' common ancestry, their continuing shared allegiances, and their God-given destiny as invincible conquerors. Then, when that destiny was once more confirmed by the successful invasion and conquest of England, expediency dictated further adaptations to the narrative, promoting now the Normans' reconciliation – virtually assimilation – with the English. So, in his *History of the English* (*c.* 1135–40), Geffrei Gaimar included an account of the Battle of Hastings that hardly mentioned the defeated King Harold or even any fighting; and by the 1180s, assimilation was further confirmed by intermarriage, so that another contemporary source could claim (and promulgate the message) that 'the nations are so mixed that it can scarcely be decided ... who is of English birth and who of Norman'. Indeed, as Davis himself puts it, 'the Normans projected themselves into the past and identified themselves with the pre-Norman history of England'; so that by the end of the twelfth century their own adopted and adapted 'mythology' had effectively led to their own elimination.[38] It awaited another (twentieth-century) historian to analyse and explain his predecessors' works and identify them as, not histories, but myths.

Such myths, though, continue to sustain us, and it remains the historian's self-imposed task to expose them. Jonathan Clark has recently challenged what he calls 'the American myth'.[39] Like all good myths of national identity, the American version gains persuasiveness and power (and thence longevity) by telling people what they want to hear – providing stable roots, confirming national unity and a natural sense of superiority, and establishing a progressive trajectory through time. Such myths, of course, themselves represent a deliberate re-writing of the past, and the imposition of a coherence otherwise lacking. So that, in America's case, the 1776 Revolution is re-presented as a Manichaean conflict which was, in the context of a Christian society, bound to be won by the forces of good in a triumph over evil.

That historic conflict is presented further as a struggle in which all Americans participated, to which all contributed (on the right side), and from which all were naturally destined to benefit. It marked the birth of a new nation, a new society, and a new kind of liberated individual; and the birth was successfully achieved by sloughing off the old – the old constraints, the old chains of an alien and repressive government. And once liberated, the emancipated citizens of a democratic polity provided a model for universal emulation: there was no good reason why the rest of the world could not come to enjoy the American experience. Indeed, it was the 'manifest destiny' of Americans to lead and show the way.

There was, then, again a sense of *inevitability*, not only about the past but also about the future. No alternative account seemed possible in relation to what had happened in the past: any questioning of the established version of history was (perhaps is) tantamount to a deficiency of patriotism, and any consideration of 'counterfactuals' – of what might have been – is disallowed. For the claimed inevitability of history underpins a certainty about the form and role of the American nation, and that in turn inspires its citizens with confidence – confidence in their own identities at home, and confidence in the rightness of their proselytising policies abroad. It's obviously good, after all, for the rest of the world to subscribe to those American values which form the apex of human development. The American revolution becomes 'an ongoing process, offering emancipation to all men everywhere' – the starting point for a whole 'new world order'.[40]

Professor Clark, then, advocates renewed historical enquiry in order to challenge a foundation myth which, in this case, left people 'free to shape ... [the future], but *in only one way*'.[41] He questions, for example, the *unanimity* of opposition to British rule and the demand for independence; he highlights the role of *contingency* and *chance* in military outcomes; and he denies the universal *benefit* of the successful revolution – instancing the worsened condition of Indians and slaves. And his re-opening of this history not only affects the status of a myth about the past, but (if ever heeded) might have profound implications for how Americans, in the present and the future, comport themselves both at home and in the wider world. It's not hard to see what Jonathan Clark's historical challenge to a myth might actually be *for*.

Nor is it only with the analysis of *national* myths that historians concern themselves for good reason: *personal* ones too have similarly engaged their attention. For the idolisation of public figures long pre-dates our own 'celebrity culture', and it has been one function of historians to cut such figures down to size, exposing the feet of clay often concealed by their brazen exteriors. In the 1940s, for example, Pieter Geyl charted the fluctuating historiographical fortunes of Napoleon, noting the existence of a legend, or 'Napoleonic cult', initiated by Napoleon himself, who had helpfully provided for posterity 'a [self-] portrait in which there was nought but unblemished beauty, endearing humanity, greatness, and virtue'. That myth had been adopted by a retinue of subsequent glorifiers, who had extolled the virtues of an intelligent, independent military commander who had supposedly represented the whole French people in his triumphs. But, as Geyl showed, an alternative perspective was adopted by detractors: the myth of an idealised Napoleon was challenged in another tradition of more sceptical historians; and 'the argument' – effectively the argument between 'myth' and historical 'reality' – 'goes on'.[42]

That argument by now has reached a number of controversial twentieth-century figures, where historians have continued to expose and demolish what they've seen as 'myths'. One important example is Ian Kershaw's treatment of the 'Hitler myth' – a myth which he defines as 'a "heroic" image and popular conception of Hitler imputing to him characteristics and motives for the most part at crass variance with reality'.[43] The myth was, again, deliberately cultivated from the start: Hitler himself was keen to avoid giving the appearance of having any human failings; so that, for instance, he refused to wear spectacles or to participate publicly in any sport where he might be exposed and humiliated. And the myth of some perfect super-human being was assiduously cultivated through the 1930s by a new race of propagandists (empowered by new mass media) of a sort with which we have become increasingly familiar. Hitler, then, was represented, in idealised form, as being the quintessential German, or even as essentially *being* Germany – as himself representing a unified nation, and upholding the 'true sense of propriety of the German people'. So by 1935 the Press Chief Otto Dietrich could eulogise him on his birthday as the very 'symbol of the indestructible life-force of the German nation'; and in conformity with that role, the great propagandist Josef Goebbels stressed Hitler's personal simplicity and modesty, his plain food and unadorned uniform, and his endless and altruistic toil, all on Germany's behalf. Such ideal characteristics were to be admired and emulated by all good patriotic Germans; for by 1939, as the Nazi slogan had it, 'Germany is Hitler, and Hitler is Germany'.[44]

Well-known film of the Nuremberg rallies, showing exultant crowds hailing their Fuehrer as saviour, testify to the success of the Nazi propagandists, and Goebbels himself in 1941 claimed as his own greatest propaganda achievement the creation of what he called the 'Fuehrer myth'. During the Second World War, a reputation as military genius was added to Hitler's mythical accomplishments, and early successes of his armed forces served to confirm his virtually divine status. Indeed, it was only after the defeat at Stalingrad that that myth began to be challenged and decline.

What we have in the case of Hitler, then, as Ian Kershaw reveals in his history, is a leadership myth of 'remarkable potency and resilience'; but what the historian uncovers is the great gulf between the 'fictive figure' and the 'genuine Hitler'. Despite potential problems attendant on such claims concerning the 'genuine Hitler', the revelation of that gulf is far from unimportant, as indicating again a role for history in relation to the future. For as Ian Kershaw concludes, 'Old myths are ... replaced by new'; and historical exposures such as his might go some way towards enhancing our own political awareness, and enabling us to protect ourselves against the myth-spinners of our own time – 'the marketed images of present-day and future claimants to political "leadership"'.[45]

The last and most enduring myth to which most of us wish to subscribe is that of our own immortality, and in this life-and-death matter the professed purposes of historians have varied. Some have seen their task as the bestowal of immortality upon their subjects, whereas others have seen it as their duty to serve as reminders of death's imminence. For the former, biographers are at the forefront: their essential function is to make myths and to break them (and thereby, far from incidentally, to acquire their own fame or notoriety). Looking back to antiquity, the Florentine Vespasiano da Bisticci (1421–98) came to realise that the famous men of those times would never have been remembered had they lacked historians: 'great men may well lament that, in their lifetime, there should be no writers to record their deeds'. And many have, of course, for that very reason been forgotten: 'the fame of many worthies has come to naught because there was no one to preserve in writing the memory of their deeds.'[46] Thomas Carlyle was later to remind us of the 'regiments and hosts and generations' that 'Oblivion [has] already swallowed': 'Many brave men', he notes, 'lived before Agamemnon' – before, that is, the earliest poet was available to leave any account of their dramatic exploits. The 'crumbled dust' of such forgotten people underpins our own existence – 'makes up the soil our life-fruit grows on'.[47]

In that context, a niche market had earlier been detected by the Greek historian Arrian, who noted that the Macedonian leader Alexander lacked a biographer. He describes Alexander as having called the Greek hero Achilles 'a lucky man, in that he had Homer to proclaim his deeds and preserve his memory'. Alexander himself lacked anyone equivalent: indeed, 'his one failure ... was that he had no worthy chronicler to tell the world of his exploits'; so that, Arrian explains, 'the wonderful story of his life is less familiar today [in the second century AD] than that of the merest nonentities of the ancient world'. Arrian duly sets out to rectify matters, drawing on sources already (as we need to remind ourselves) over four hundred years old. His purposes, as he himself professes, are twofold: first to record the life and retain the memory of one who 'succeeded in so many brilliant enterprises'; and second to have himself included in 'the company of the great masters of Greek literature'.[48] And in both respects he can lay claim to some success: his own reputation as an historian is assured, if only because he is one of our main surviving sources for his subject; and Alexander can account himself a lucky man as having belatedly acquired a worthy chronicler to justify his epithet as 'the Great'.

But while some historians aim to bestow immortality, others conversely see it as their function to provide contrasting reminders. An Aztec terracotta model from c. 250–700 represents a figure with three faces – a man at three different stages of development: young, old (toothless and wrinkled), and actually dead (as a death-mask);[49]

and historians, like other artists, have not infrequently seen it as a part of their job to remind us that even in the midst of life we inevitably and all the time confront death. If one of history's functions is to set us in a chronological context, one effect is to reveal the minimal nature of our own span within the whole. And if the examples from the past displayed by history teach us anything, it is that nothing and no one lasts for long: the greatest heroes and the greatest empires have their day, but their night is never far behind.

This whole matter of myth-making and myth-breaking has taken on added importance since some blatant denials of recent historical events have affronted not only historians but also the wider public. Most prominent has been the case of Holocaust denial, which has provoked responses from historians determined to set the record straight on moral grounds – seeing it as their duty to respond on behalf of historical truth against those who would 'distort reality and our view of the past', and dedicating their work to 'the six million who cannot respond themselves'.[50] More recently, too, there have been those who deny that the attack on the Pentagon on 11 September 2001 ever happened: no airliner crashed into it, but it was all 'a hoax perpetrated by the American defence establishment to advance its own interests'.[51] Like the Holocaust, it's claimed, 9/11 is just a 'myth'.

It seems, then, that 'myth-breaking', the identification of what *is* 'myth', and its replacement by something more substantial or historically acceptable, is likely to remain an important part of what history is perceived to be for – and an important purpose to be professed by historians themselves.

5 Theological confirmations and questionings

Such thoughts of death and destruction remind us that it's not only politicians who have sought stability in the past: theologians and religious leaders too have wished to see their various faiths confirmed through the determination of direct roots in the past – or of a direct route leading back to supposedly authoritative sources for their own beliefs. Political fluctuations are paralleled by the ebb and flow of theological debate; and in both contexts the need for historical support is felt particularly strongly when the *status quo* comes under threat, and advocates of both old and new are concerned to consolidate their own positions.

The Christian tradition in particular sought historically based respectability and confirmation from the outset. A virgin birth may have been attributed to Jesus, but he did not, of course, arrive unheralded. Far from it: his whole story had been foretold, and reference back to that historical underpinning served to confirm and validate his claims to moral and religious authority. As Jesus himself explains to his disciples: 'all things must be fulfilled, which were written in the law of Moses, and in the prophets, and in the psalms, concerning me.'[52] Rather than suddenly springing from the blue, he was fulfilling a longstanding and long-awaited prophecy; and while 'historians' as such may not have been directly implicated, a version of 'the past' was utilised in ways that set a pattern for the future.

That pattern became for centuries a focal point for history, its revelation and justification in Christian terms constituting an important part of what history was for. History, as Charles Rollin explained in a hugely popular early eighteenth-century treatise, 'proclaims universally the greatness of the Almighty, his power, his justice, and above all the admirable wisdom with which his providence governs the universe';[53] and with those words he exemplifies a Christian tradition in which historians have often been concerned to cultivate what has been very much their own garden – conveniently confirming their own beliefs. So they have constructed their narratives in a form that duly illustrated the guidance of events by divine providence – by the God in whom they themselves believe; and that is not to say that they necessarily set out with a didactic theological purpose, but rather that that was simply the way they saw things, interpreting them in the context of their own beliefs.

Thus, for some it was only Jesus Christ who could give any form or meaning to what had happened in the past. Even at the very end of the nineteenth century, one eminent historian proclaimed his belief that 'the birth of Jesus Christ is the most important date in the whole history of mankind'. And he went on to conclude that, 'In a certain sense we might truly say that "history" in the real sense of the term only begins with the birth of Christ'; which naturally implied the denial that any non-Christian people could actually have any 'true history' at all. So happily spared any anxieties about making arbitrary incisions into seamless webs, he duly started his own account of historical developments where he believed they actually began: in 1 AD precisely.[54] After that date, human history simply unfolded as a drama directed by a specifically Christian God: it was the historian's job to review it.

Such belief in the course of providential purpose has, of course, been perpetuated into our own time, and still indicates the sort of mono-cultural perspective from which historical study might free us. At the end of the Second World War, the British Field-Marshall Alanbrooke confided to his diary that for the previous six years he had seen God's 'guiding hand controlling and guiding the destiny of this world toward that final and definite destiny which He has ordained';[55] and although such theological parochialism may, to some, now sound curiously dated, it's worth noting that for Chamberlain and Alanbrooke, as for Thucydides and many others, there was an important corollary: history did at least have a direction and a practical point. Just as the ancient Greek historian hoped that his work would live for ever as a moral teacher, so Alanbrooke saw Allied victory as divinely vindicated; and Chamberlain too, rejecting any own-sakist approach, readily confessed to practical concerns with the present. A past understood as providentially ordered could, he surmised, surely give guidance to the present:

> to summarise the past in such a way that we no longer take pride in an empty, borrowed learning concerning things long dead and buried, but make of the knowledge of the past a living, determining power for the present! ... Surely a sublime and worthy aim![56]

That 'sublime and worthy aim' may have attracted more attention had not Chamberlain himself come to be claimed as a veritable patron saint by the Nazis. Enamoured of all things German, he went to live in Germany in the 1930s, married Richard Wagner's daughter, and managed to impress the rising Adolf Hitler with his writings – presumably not least with his declared aim to use the past as 'a living, determining power for the present'.[57] With all its idealistic rhetoric, the political use of history in the service of a religion-based crusade is something of which, in the twenty-first century, we have good reason to beware.

There have, though, been other uses to which history has been put in the service of theology. In post-Reformation England, 'revolutionary' Protestants vied with 'traditionalist' Catholics in *theoretical* religious debates that had enormous implications for *practical* politics – implications indeed for daily life and even death; and both sides enlisted the support of history. For each was determined to secure foundations for its own position – to anchor its

claims for authority in the depths of a past that required history for
its illumination. Once again the requirement was to furnish a
narrative thread – a story that began and ended satisfactorily for
present needs – and the spinning of that thread was work for the
historian.

As it developed, the theological debate between Catholics and
Protestants foreshadowed historiographical debates concerning the
respective merits of oral and literary traditions. Not without some
justification, Catholics claimed to represent an unbroken and
continuing tradition that linked them with the earliest church: they
could resort to an oral tradition – a tradition passed on by word of
mouth, from father to son, through the generations, and often
consolidated and confirmed by practical rituals. It was, after all, the
Protestants who were responsible for any schism: it was they who
had done the breaking away, and they could hardly expect to be able
to trace their own origins further back than Luther.

Luther himself, however, knew that his own position had to be
historically vindicated – justified, that is, in terms of the greater
genuineness, the greater authenticity, of his own doctrines; they had
to be shown to correspond more closely with the original teachings
of Christianity's own founder. And the only way he could do that
was by denying the validity of the tradition that had culminated in
the Catholicism of his time – by showing that, whether through
innocent misunderstanding or wilful misrepresentations and distortions, wrong directions had been taken, wrong paths followed, so
that the present condition and situation of the church was far from
anyone's original intentions.

The only problem, then, was to find the relevant evidence – and
that was what historians were for. If the validity of oral tradition
was to be denied, then resort would have to be made to literary
documents. And the most obvious and most important historical
documents relating to the early Christian church were, of course,
those inscribed in the Bible. Unsurprisingly, then, Luther determined to rely for his arguments and justification on 'scriptura sola' –
the scriptures alone.

Historians, however, may wield a two-edged sword: having
recruited the scriptural texts as historical evidence, they went on to
do what was fast becoming their professional duty, and submitted
that evidence to critical scrutiny; and that is where the required
'confirmations' were transformed into the sometimes less than
welcome outcome of sceptical 'questionings'. For if the first five

books of the Bible had been dictated to Moses by the supreme authority of God himself, then it was surprising how many glaring errors and inconsistencies could nevertheless be revealed by critics determined to treat them like any other written document – such documents being notoriously susceptible to reinterpretation, faulty transcription, and dubious amendment, as their message is transmitted through the generations.

So although not technically 'historians', such scholars as Isaac La Peyrère, Benedict Spinoza, and Richard Simon successfully applied historical techniques, to undermine the long-lived authority of the Bible as an accurate historical record: they revealed that record (or at least important parts of it) as being, as we might say in the context of the preceding section, 'mythical'. So they were acting again as myth-breakers – using history now, not so much to confirm as to question theological programmes. And that questioning of ancient authorities had ramifications far beyond the merely theological, demonstrating the more general point of what history can be for.

6   Obligations to the dead

> No one has a duty to the dead except in relation to the living. The dead can look after themselves; the living cannot.
>
> (C. V. Wedgwood, 1942)[58]

The study of *the past* 'for its own sake' (as considered in Chapter 2) may sound at best a curious enterprise and at worst a meaningless affectation; but when that past is translated into *the people* of the past – that is, the dead – we may feel differently? For some, the past is past, the dead are dead, and that is that; and that, to judge from the quotation above, seems to be how C. V. Wedgwood saw the matter. The only use or point the dead can have is in relation to our living selves: alive, we need all the help we can get, and not least from the past; whereas the dead don't warrant any more attention – they're history (which seems to be the meaning of the assertion that they can somehow 'look after themselves').

But for others, the dead (however dead) seem still to have some claim on us; or, to put it the other way round, we continue to have some responsibility towards them, and that's another thing that history is *for*. Just as, in many cultures, there's felt to be an obligation to bury the dead – to memorialise them somehow, and put them 'to rest' (if only in relation to ourselves), so too it has been widely believed that there remains some duty to *remember* them. Herodotus set out, as he makes quite explicit, to preserve the memory of the great deeds of the Greeks and, interestingly, their opponents too in the Persian Wars; and remarkably similar sentiments were expressed by the great Chinese historian Sima Qian in the second century BC:

> No offence is greater than failing the sagely monarchs by neglecting to put their virtues and accomplishments in record, erasing the names of great heroes, illustrious families, and good officials by passing over their achievements in the narration, and letting the words of our ancestors fall into oblivion.[59]

Later, as we've seen, Vespasiano da Bisticci similarly expresses his concern that some great people's reputations may be lost 'because there was no one to preserve in writing the memory of their deeds'; so he writes his own commentaries on illustrious men that he has personally known, 'that their fame may not perish'.[60] And the nineteenth-century French historian Jules Michelet more democratically concludes that: 'Yes, everyone who dies leaves behind a little something, his memory, and,' he significantly goes on, *'demands that we care for it.'*[61]

Such demands, it has been suggested, have been increasingly insistent as a result of twentieth-century horrors. We're horrified by the mass graves that follow indiscriminate slaughter – by the realisation that individuals (that we) can simply vanish from the face of the earth without any trace, without so much as a mark to indicate where and who we once were. That the Great War of 1914–18 directly affected more 'ordinary' people than any preceding conflict is attested by numberless war memorials, erected 'lest we forget'; and the Second World War provided further examples of atrocities which, in Peter Mandler's words, 'have made remembering the past a moral imperative ... Remembering is something the dead demand of us.'[62]

What that means is that the living cannot face the thought that all the suffering was for nothing: despite its apparently arbitrary nature, with the 'innocent' dying in far greater numbers than others who might have seemed to be more deserving, it must be seen to have some *point* – and that point is usually presented as a moral injunction, that 'it must never happen again'. So history is revealed once more as having some sort of therapeutic function, and not only for historians themselves: it responds to people's demands to have their memories taken care of.

However, the moral imperative of 'remembering the past' cannot, of course, be literally followed: we can't just remember 'the past'. Any moral content of our remembering derives from our own choice of *what*, from the totality of the past, to remember. .And similarly with 'demands' of the dead: it's not the dead who demand, but *we* who feel the need (or 'moral imperative') to remember certain of them. And the moral content again consists in our choice of *which* particular dead to remember: we can't after all commemorate them all – or, if we did, it would surely devalue that act of commemoration, including, as it would, those whom we might morally condemn. So the nature of any 'obligation' has to do with us and our own moral values: it's we who must decide what and whom to remember; it's we who have to decide what our histories are *for*.

That point has been illustrated in France, where the choice of memories relating to the Second World War has long been problematic.[63] For some two decades following the end of the war, the most prominent historical model of that period was what has been called 'the Gaullist Myth of Resistance' – a version of events that underpinned the claimed entitlement of France (however militarily disempowered through the occupation) to share in the Allies' triumph against Nazi Germany. That emphasis permitted self-respect, both individual and national. But the collaboration of the Vichy government and its numerous supporters proved to be a 'past that will not pass' – a past that, through the 1970s, increasingly intruded on public consciousness, with films and histories revealing the extent of French complicity with, in particular, the Nazis' treatment of the Jews. That treatment included the deportations of Jews from France – a recognition of which entailed a 'duty to memory' hitherto avoided.

Those who insisted on the restoration of that memory into consciousness were sometimes ironically labelled · 'memory militants', but it's worth noting in the context of this section that their militancy arose not just from some theoretical obligation to the past, but from a very practical programme to punish those responsible for wartime misdemeanours. They were 'militant', not in the interests of 'memory' *per se*, but of memories which, they believed, had moral significance for their present and future. Their revisionist histories, concerned as they were in part with the dead, were *for* a quite specific moral purpose that had to do with the living.

The same is true of the idealistic American historian Eric Foner, who has described how he attempted 'to put ... on the map of history' some 1,500 black individuals who had previously been ignored, or whose memories had been deliberately erased. Following the end of the American Civil War, a federal decree granted equality before the law of all citizens, black and white; and only a few years after the demise of slavery, large numbers of blacks attained public office at local, state, and federal levels. However, after the abandonment of 'Reconstruction', their numbers were greatly reduced; and it was only in the 1960s that blacks began to re-acquire their political influence. It is that short 'window' of 'inter-racial democracy' in the nineteenth century that Foner re-opened: his *Directory of Black Officeholders during Reconstruction*, albeit incomplete, 'aims to rescue from historical obscurity men who have remained virtually unknown even to specialists in the field' – unknown partly through their deliberate omission from official records, by those who considered it absurd to record 'the lives of men who were but yesterday our slaves'.[64]

And for Foner that is not a purely 'academic' matter. Indeed, he is refreshingly explicit about the practical implications of his historical researches generally. In books 'born in the archives ... [but] written from the heart', he has, as he describes, 'always begun with a concern with some present reality'. It is as one still distressed by continuing injustices and inequalities in American society that he has disinterred forgotten figures, questioned prevailing (often triumphalist) orthodoxies, and proposed revisionist accounts. For 'freedom', as he insists elsewhere, is a term that itself needs to be understood historically: often claimed as uniquely American, it has been subject to constant re-definition, constituting 'a terrain of struggle' claimed by various (and often opposing) parties, and with its story remaining 'forever unfinished'. Foner's agenda thus has little time or place for any history 'for its own sake': repudiating any solipsistic and 'complacent monologue with ourselves', he aspires rather to pay his obligations to the dead in order to provoke nothing short of 'a conversation with the entire world' – another indication of what history might properly be for, in relation to our future.[65]

Eric Foner's resuscitation of some of those dead whose memory had previously been allowed to die, or had been deliberately erased, is to be distinguished from those ritual commemorations to which we are not infrequently invited – invited, that is, to confirm the historical judgement that some selected individual or group is appropriately defined, whether as hero, victim, oppressor, or whatever; for such commemorations can themselves come to constitute something of an evasion, and (however inadvertently) prove little more than 'an easy way of giving us all a good conscience while averting our eyes from present emergencies'. It is in this context that Paul Ricoeur has warned against 'falling into the trap of "the duty of memory"', where the trap consists of our ability complacently to believe that, through the observation of some public ritual, we've fulfilled our obligations to 'the dead'.[66] All we've done, or might have done, is – however paradoxically – to have actually in some sense killed them off again, by laying them to rest in some place they (and we) can stay in comfort. For one is only finally dead, as Lyotard has suggested, 'when one is narrated' – put tidily into some accommodating story; 'the dead are not dead so long as the living have not recorded their death in narratives'.[67] So historians are left again with the challenge of resisting accepted categorisations as, continuing their work on an infinite store of memory, they try to pay their obligations to the dead by somehow keeping them alive 'in relation to the living'.

7 Conclusion

Historians, then, have themselves professed a number of important purposes – purposes important enough amply to justify the study of their subject. If the disinterested pursuit of historical truth 'for its own sake' seems less than compelling, more practical ends, in the form of 'transferable skills', can be claimed – not the least important being the ability to make some (however tentative) decision on the basis of evidence, the inevitable inadequacy of which is actually realised. That sort of decision has to be made in contexts, not only theoretical, but also highly practical – made, that is to say, not only as a literary exercise (in the form, perhaps, of compiling a report), but also as an exercise in practical politics (in the form, perhaps, of waging war). The purpose that historians profess in both cases is to heighten awareness of the complications involved, the ambiguities and subtleties and nuances of which account needs to be taken.

And that is where their role as political and moral advisers comes in. However presumptuous it may sound (and the adoption of any moral stance is sometimes held suspect), historians, by virtue of their subject, must necessarily become aware of the impenetrable complexities of human beings and of human existence; and it's their job to convey awareness of that awareness. That is surely what lay behind the thinking of those Renaissance writers who advocated history as an important part of any ruler's education: lessons could be learnt from the past – and the most important lessons had to do with the psychological complexities of human beings, their cultural variations and their unpredictability. And transmission of that message is what's intended too by those contemporary historians who still lay claim (quite properly) to the resultant tolerance that such recognition ideally should bring.

'Ideally' in that last sentence is a necessary qualification, since tolerance is not a quality that springs to mind in relation to the reality of historians' own attitudes towards their colleagues' differing approaches. All too often debates degenerate into verbal assaults that scarcely exemplify that 'cultivation' to which we've seen some historians (again quite properly) aspire. So (to risk sounding intolerably patronising) perhaps it's time for historians to lead from the front, presenting in their own persons and behaviour (and histories) the models of excellence that they believe appropriate for humanity in the twenty-first century? In some instances, as I shall indicate, this is already being done.

At all events, the purposes that historians themselves have professed, and continue to profess, indicate the enormous potential importance of their subject and the enormous power that historians in practice wield. That importance and that power do not end there, however; for, in assessing what history is for, it's not only the professed, or openly admitted, purposes that need to be taken into account, but also those agendas and those messages that are no less effective for being often hidden and implicit. It's to these that we'll now turn.

Hidden agendas

I Introduction

Historians are not the only people to have recognised history's importance: we've already seen how theologians have put it to use, but it's politicians and political theorists who have always particularly appreciated history's enormous power. That's why they have often sought to control it for their own purposes – to use it (or abuse it, as we say when we disagree with them) as underpinning for their own position, or (yet more dramatically) actually to *remove* it, when traditions and old versions of the past inhibit their own revolutionary ambitions. So when outlining the principles of his ideal state, Plato took care to propose the insertion of a new (and admittedly false) history that would convince his utopia's citizens that their present situation had indeed been determined by the past; Aristotle presented an historical account of political development that culminated in the ideal 'end' of Athenian-style democracy; seventeenth-century political theorists such as Hobbes inserted an earlier, unappetising historical period, when life was 'nasty, brutish, and short', into their advocacy of a strong government which would prevent reversion to those primitive beginnings; eighteenth-century French and twentieth-century Chinese revolutionaries did their best to eliminate a past that no longer seemed to have relevance to their visions for the future; and politicians generally are prone to emphasise (and de-emphasise) the importance of those aspects of the past that confirm (or deny) the validity of their own agendas.

Sometimes, indeed, they recruit (or press-gang) 'History' to their cause as if it were some superior being, like God or Providence or Destiny, who will ultimately authorise their own position and validate their acts – serve as some final arbiter or judge, and vindicate whatever has been done. We have already noted British Prime Minister Blair's confident expectation, in February 2003, of a favourable judgement from 'History' on his own plans for Iraq, and events over the following few months did nothing to dent his confidence, either in his own 'historic' role, or in its future vindication by some personalised (even deified) 'History'. Reassured, perhaps, by having previously (in the context of Northern Ireland in 1998) felt 'the hand of History upon our shoulders', Blair could be confident, by the time of his triumphal appearance before the American Congress in July 2003, that if any mistakes had been made in relation to the Iraq War, then 'History will forgive'. It was, as he explained to his audience, 'destiny' that had 'put you in this place in history'; and the implication clearly was that, as latter-day manifest destiny's agents, they could rest assured in the rightness of their actions. Blair and his allies were on the side of history – and history, just as importantly (if not, in the longer term, more so) was on theirs.[1] That made whatever they did seem not only natural and right, but somehow divinely ordained and so *inevitable*.

Others, of course, through the centuries, have been similarly confident in the rightness of their own cause and have similarly claimed the support of 'history' to authorise their actions. 'Pronounce us guilty a thousand times over,' proclaimed Adolf Hitler at his trial in 1924: 'the goddess of the eternal court of history will smile ... She will acquit us.'[2] Mere ordinary mortals may assess as they will the actions of those believing themselves marked out for greater things; but time, as we say, will tell, and will enable 'history' to see aright – to see the truth of the matter, just as those with 'vision' see it now.

In enormously important – and very practical – ways, then, politicians can (and do) enlist some hypothetical entity named 'History' to validate and vindicate their present policies and activities. Appeals to 'Providence' in a secular world may sound outdated, but with a similarly meaningless rhetoric, self-justificatory appeals to 'History' still endure. Such appeals may initially seem to fit ill with the contemporaneous relegation, by other politicians, of historians to the status of mere 'ornaments'; but both of those incompatible positions can in any case be maintained only in a context in which no serious thought has been given to what history is and is for. As has long been recognised, historical and philosophical ignorance plays into the hand of political manipulators.

Politically inspired manipulation of the past might seem to have received some theoretical justification in the later nineteenth century at the hands of the great French historian Ernest Renan. Discussing the then (and now) topical question of what it is that constitutes 'a nation', Renan referred to 'the possession in common of a rich legacy of memories', and 'the will to perpetuate the value of the heritage that one has received'. What is important is not what happened in the past *per se*, but the memories that we have of that past – those aspects of the past that we choose to remember together. And of course what we agree to forget, for forgetting too 'is a crucial factor': especially after national traumas, 'it is good for everyone to know how to forget'; and 'forgetting,' Renan insists, '... is a crucial factor in the creation of a nation' – even when that implies what might seem to entail 'historical error'. For it's not race or language or geography or religion, but the shared legacy of their rich cultural heritage that binds people together to constitute a nation. And although that may now, in the richer cultural diversity of postmodernity, sound dated, Renan's definition does not necessarily imply a *single* line of transmission, or one privileged and exclusive story of the past: the richness of a nation's legacy potentially embraces memories from many sources – memories that not all will have personally had (any more than that is ever possible), but that all consider worth retaining (as still worth caring about). And they will, as Renan concludes, also have for 'the future, [a shared] programme to put into effect'.[3]

That sort of political appropriation of history, though, inevitably results in the application of pressure – political pressure, that is, on the historian to convey his master's voice, and correspondingly respect his silences. Tension between historians and politicians is virtually inevitable in the light of the incompatibility – or perhaps (in their mutual quest for power) the similarity – of their respective interests; for while politicians are concerned to maintain their own and their party's and their nation's reputation, and above all to retain their control of the past (and the memory and identity that that past enshrines), historians may have a greater interest in subversion – by revealing scandals, misdemeanours, personal and public intrigues – and in making some impact of their own upon the public. While, in other words, historians claim (however disingenuously) to seek nothing more or less than 'the truth', politicians are notoriously (even brazenly) 'economical' with that commodity, as they pursue their own agendas. And the latter have the keys to the archives: politicians can (and often do) censor material (cutting, omitting, 'losing') and withhold access on alleged grounds of its 'sensitivity', or of national interest or security. They have a patriotic narrative which they are determined to retain: revisionist challenges are seen as immediately threatening and potentially even treasonable; so that maintenance of control of the past becomes a form of national duty and higher altruism. In 1629, King Charles I closed Robert Cotton's library as a potential danger to the state. He recognised that historians could use its important collection of historical documents to justify a political programme that would threaten his own monarchical position, and he believed, no doubt, as an Italian prime minister said, centuries later, of some documents in 1912, that 'It would not be right to have beautiful legends discredited by historical criticism'.[4]

'For governments,' Keith Wilson has claimed, 'patriotic history is the only legitimate kind of history', so anyone threatening to produce a history that fails to fit the line defined as patriotic by the politicians concerned, is bound to experience resistance. To take but one recent example from Britain, Noble Frankland, who was Director of the Imperial War Museum and with Sir Charles Webster wrote the history of Bomber Command in the Second World War, has revealed how 'my activity as an historian has been accompanied by almost unending struggle' – a struggle against officialdom and against 'a concerted attempt to emasculate our history so that it would fit the convenience of the mandarins in the 1950s and early 1960s'. In his autobiography, Frankland, in the words of his publisher's blurb, 'describes the battles he had to fight against the mandarins and media merchants who sought to impose a spin on history to suit their own ends, and were ruthless and unscrupulous in their methods'.[5]

Despite numerous protestations to the contrary, the imposition of some element of self-interested 'spin' on the historicised past is inevitable: any narrative thread has to be spun from something, after all – and after the event; some sense of the evidential traces has to be made from one standpoint or another. So what is interesting here is to know whether our own spin corresponds with that of others, in which case we need not be made aware or conscious of it – or whether, as with Frankland, our own conclusions fail to fit with accepted orthodoxies; in which case confrontation occurs, and self-conscious and deliberate decisions have to be made by historians about whether or not to be political puppets. We'll look at the former scenario in the fourth and fifth sections of this chapter, but first let's examine political puppetry.

2 Political puppetry: the case of Germany

> Above all, [history] should benefit the nation to which we
> belong and without which our studies would not even exist.
> (Leopold von Ranke)[6]

At a time when 'large swathes of the twentieth century' – including all reference to their war with Iran and the 1991 Gulf War, to America and Israel, and of course to their erstwhile leader Saddam Hussain – are being deliberately cut out of Iraqi school history books, a time when a spokesman for the education ministry proclaims the need for 'a consensus across the whole of Iraqi society about how to talk about our past', historians can hardly remain unaware of the obvious political (and practical) implications of their subject.[7] But there are, as is seemingly indicated in the quotation from the great nineteenth-century historian above, many examples of politically correct historians – of historians themselves being all too willing to fall into line behind politicians and act as their propagandists. In such cases, historians are aware of having an agenda that is hidden – or that is intended to be hidden – from their readers, though of course it isn't from themselves. Thus, for example, in his epic poem *The Aeneid*, the Roman poet Virgil presented an account of the past – an historical narrative – that clearly and conveniently culminated in the divinely ordained reign of the new emperor Augustus, whose cultural patronage (through the vehicle of his affluent friend and supporter Gaius Maecenas) Virgil openly acknowledged. The course of history is presented by Virgil as a progressive path, from the earliest foundation of Rome in remote antiquity, through republican strife, to the peace and prosperity guaranteed by the new dynasty. And some moral prerequisites for such progress are identified: the dutiful Aeneas is exemplary; and in an early incorporation of 'masculine' virtues at the expense of the 'feminine', his sacrifice of love – to say nothing of his lover, Dido – in the name of patriotic duty is to be applauded. Unhappy Dido, after her suicide, may have later spurned him in the underworld, but Aeneas knew that fulfilment of his destiny – the foundation of Rome – was more important; and who was a Roman emperor to disagree?

In modern times, such self-justificatory and moralising exercises have proliferated: during decades of world-wide political upheaval, historians, albeit more prosaically, have been persuaded to provide no less fanciful epic backgrounds as underpinning for political power, and imperial manipulations have continued. As we've seen in relation to myth-making, the modern emperor Napoleon was no less insistent than Augustus that the historical record support his own position. A dictated note to his chief of police in 1808 makes it clear that his own orderly and unified régime is to be favourably contrasted with the anarchic and divided hotch-potch that it had replaced:

> They [historians] are to point out the perpetual disorganisation of the national finances, the chaos of the provincial assemblies, the claims of the Parlements, the lack of regulation and resort in the administration. This checkered France, without unity of laws and administration, was rather a union of twenty Kingdoms than a single State, so that one breathes freely on coming to the period when the benefits of unity of laws, administration and territory are enjoyed.[8]

As with Augustus, 'history' is to be utilised to reveal Napoleon, not just as conquering hero, but as social saviour. But the case of Germany is yet more obvious and more dramatic, with historians playing significant roles in revolutionary politics, both before and after Adolf Hitler. The cultural historian Johan Huizinga, as long ago as 1915, pointed to 'the strongly historical inclination of the German people', suggesting that nationalism owed more to history in Germany than in other European countries;[9] and his analysis seems vindicated by developments during the short-lived Third Reich, which bequeathed long-term lessons for those concerned, as we are here, with political puppetry – or with the manipulation of historians in the service of political ends, and with the presentation therefore of history with a hidden agenda.

Indeed, the pattern was set even earlier. In 1907, Baron de Courcel had likened the German historical archives to gunpowder: it can, he explained, 'in certain cases, explode and cause damage, when it ought to be used only to defend ourselves against our enemies'.[10] And his words were taken to heart when, following the Great War, that archival gunpowder was ignited by historians mobilised to confront the victors' charge of German guilt. Assertions of guilt were based largely on the claim that Germany had started the war, and assumptions of that guilt then underpinned Allied claims made under the Treaty of Versailles. Considerable historical effort – a veritable 'historiographical propaganda campaign' – was therefore expended in Germany on re-examining the war's origins, and on demonstrating the Allies' own transgressions against international law. Holger H. Herwig has described how 'researchers were instructed to amass materials' that would put emphasis on France's expenditure on armaments before 1914, on Britain's intensive training of an army for deployment in Europe, on Italy's provocations of Austria–Hungary, and on Russia's long-term financial preparations for a war against Germany; while German leaders themselves were to be shown as having tried to avoid war rather than as having provoked it.[11]

That exercise in historical revisionism culminated in a report for presentation at the peace negotiations of 1919; and although German claims unsurprisingly failed to convince the victors to soften their position, work proceeded through the 1920s and into the 1930s on establishing an historical archive that would prove supportive of the German position. Indeed, continuing efforts were made by historians, not only in Germany itself, but also in the United States[12] (where the propaganda campaign was said to have influenced American reluctance to enter the Second World War) to rewrite the story of the war's origins in such a way as to exonerate the Germans from blame.

As we have already seen in relation to the 'Hitler myth', the political power and propaganda value of history was well recognised by the time Hitler assumed power in 1933, and he himself was naturally determined to ensure that his Nazi party retained effective control of the past. The point, he wrote in *Mein Kampf*, was not to 'know the past', in the manner of historians who stressed the importance of 'facts, dates, birthdays, names, etc.', but rather in history to 'find an instructor for the future'.[13] As far as he was concerned, that future was already determined, inasmuch as the Third Reich was destined to last for the next one thousand years. So the function of historians was clear: they were required, in short, to find a past that justified not only Hitler's own accession to power, but also the imperial role that Nazi Germany was to play in the future. As in George Orwell's dystopian *Nineteen Eighty-Four*, history was to be crucial in the educational task of refashioning the national psyche in politically appropriate ways.

The necessary materials, of course, lay readily to hand: they always do – or always can be made to. The whole of Germany's past could be summoned up in such a way as to show an inexorable progress – a march through the centuries, from the early Germanic period, through the Middle Ages, to the Prussian Empire, and on to a present that marked another climactic turning-point. That decisive historical trajectory not only established the long-lived traditions with which the German nation was identified, but also, as Hitler required, indicated future directions; for it revealed the development of a superior race of white Aryans, that would finally fulfil its due destiny of world-wide domination.

Such political supremacy cannot, of course, be expected to come easily. As in the case of Rome, the construction of whose empire, as Virgil reminded his readers, cost 'huge effort',[14] Germany's predominance resulted from a prolonged struggle: that's what history showed – and that's one lesson it taught in relation to the future. Just as Darwin had scientifically proved that in nature the struggle to survive results in the triumph of the fittest, so a scientific history was to clarify that social (and military) struggle demonstrates a similar law. There were good reasons why Germans had risen to the top: they were racially pure, physically and morally tough, prepared to sacrifice themselves to the greater good of their communities and their nation. By maintaining those qualities, and overcoming any potential threats – such as those deriving from any mixing with inferior races, or from any demoralising habits – they were enabled still to exemplify human progress in the present and for the future. The positive direction of their future was revealed as an inevitable continuation of a triumphant historical trajectory.

That triumphant march through history was clearly purposeful: it constituted the unfolding of a divine plan; it revealed the working of a higher power. There was in short a theological dimension to Germany's national story; and a religion needs prophets and high-priests. No wonder, then, that, in the words of a 1941 school textbook, 'Our history is the history of great men'.[15] One such was Frederick the Great, long-time model of an enlightened despot who, with his love of French culture conveniently forgotten, could be presented as the great Prussian imperialist, exemplifying duty, self-sacrifice, and military courage. Another was obviously Bismarck, the great unifier of the nation. And then conveniently in this roll of honour came Hitler, at one of those historical low points that appear as minor blips in the overall progressive story, a moment requiring leadership – requiring a saviour, even, and a redeemer. That quasi-theological need was early recognised by Hitler himself, who claimed that his political movement provided 'a new belief upon which they [the masses] can have absolute confidence and build, that they not be forsaken in this world of confusion, that they find again at least in some place a position where their hearts can rest easy'. And his messianic role was of course confirmed by his lieutenants: 'In you,' wrote Goering, 'this people not only found a Fuehrer, but in you the people also found a redeemer.' That redemptive role is further re-emphasised in another school history textbook of 1943. The table of contents shows progression from 'The Chaos of 1848' (a chaos calling out for, and receiving, decisive leadership), through an exposition of Hitler's own expansionist agenda – how 'The Fuehrer Builds Greater Germany' – to a concluding section displaying appropriate gratitude: 'Fuehrer, We Thank You!' Bismarck's unification of the nation had paved the way, and the stage was now set for the fulfilment of Germany's imperial destiny – after having navigated the minor (and temporary) downturn of the early twentieth century.[16]

That minor intervening blip, of Germany's defeat in the 1914–18 war, could itself be put to good use, not only at the national level, but also in the personal case of Hitler himself. For the former, it was argued (and had long been thought by some), that the armistice in 1918 should never have been agreed: given just a little more time, it was asserted, Germany would no doubt have prevailed. For such patriotic stalwarts, then, the peace that followed the armistice effectively never occurred: the struggle for which preparations were being made in the 1930s simply consti- tuted a continuation of that earlier war. But the later act was given further impetus by additional injustices that had been suffered in the meantime. The terms of the Versailles Treaty in 1919 were a continuing cause of shame and national humiliation; and the perse- cution of German minorities in neighbouring areas was another affront to patriotic sentiment. It's from such national distress that Hitler could be presented as finally providing salvation.

And Hitler too could make use of the war, in which he could be shown to have fought bravely. Indeed, he had even been wounded, so knew personally about courage and self-sacrifice; and so he could be represented as ideally qualified for his role as saviour – a verit- able reincarnation of Germany's earlier heroes. Then, as leader in the later struggles, he was to be applauded and thanked for having reunited the elements of Greater Germany and for then avenging the nation's earlier humiliations. As a school textbook was later to claim:

> The entire German folk, uniformly inspired, stands in thankfulness and devotion to their Fuehrer, who obliterated the shame of Compiègne [where peace terms were dictated to the Germans in November 1918], who burst the shackles of Versailles [where the peace treaty was signed in June 1919], and made the way free for Greater Germany's Future.

As they headed east, the German army was following in the footsteps of the Teutonic Knights (with whom Hitler himself was to be identified: Figure 3) and of Frederick the Great; so the Austrians and the Czechs could be portrayed as uniformly welcoming their

Figure 3 Appropriating the past: Hitler as Teutonic Knight. *Der Bannerträger* (The Standard Bearer). Hitler as Knight (idealised portrait). Painting by Hubert Lanzinger, 1934.

reintegration into the fatherland: 'Never,' in the words of another textbook, 'had the German people been so united ... We knew whom to thank.'[17]

Such lessons are most easily taught to the young, as being naturally most impressionable – with minds most open, and receptive to historical (or any other) impressions; which is of course why revolutionaries regularly target the youthful in their appeals. Josef Goebbels, in charge of Nazi propaganda, was well aware that 'Youth is always right, because it sees things in an unspoilt manner without inner check. For it, every "yea" is not fraught with a "but" or "however"'.[18] Black and white are not forced to merge in varying shades of grey: such words as 'good' and 'bad', 'right' and 'wrong', come more readily to lips when minds remain nearer to the blank sheets they are often claimed to be at birth; though it can hardly fail to be observed that such unqualified clear distinctions continue to be made by those (and not least politicians) whose second childhood seems to last through life.

It's especially when they wish (or need) to mobilise people behind them in some nationalistic or imperialistic enterprise, that political leaders resort to Manichaean terminology: they need clearly to distinguish their own people from any others, their friends from their enemies, the right from the wrong. And that's where some of the most obviously sinister implications of historical puppetry can be seen; or to generalise we might claim that whenever the past is portrayed in terms of black and white, historians reveal themselves as ideologically motivated.

Thus, Hitler's historians took care to emphasise the distinctive nature of the German race: Germanic superiority could be traced right back to the earliest times; and the retention of that superiority depended on the maintenance of racial purity. The implication was, of course, that any threats to that purity had to be resisted: anything defined as 'other' – or in this case, 'un-German' – had to be removed. By 1943, German xenophobia was firmly directed against the English, who, from their 'little misty, northern island on the outskirts of the world', had somehow (and enviably) contrived to gain a great empire.[19] But it was the Jews above all who had to be (and were) portrayed as the archetypal enemy – as members of a world-wide conspiracy that threatened civilisation. Back in the Middle Ages, they were held responsible for spreading bubonic plague; throughout history, in their capacity as usurers, they had oppressed the poor; they could easily be shown as dominating cultural life; and in the immediate present they could be identified with the other great ideological threat – of Marxism. The Jews, therefore, had in short to be removed: that is what history could be made to show, and that, in the hands of political puppeteers, is what it showed.

Nor did the death of Hitler and the destruction of the Third Reich in 1945 put an end to such historiographical machinations. Those events certainly marked the end of a certain sort of history, but at such ends the need for historians can actually grow; and in the following half-century Germany provides another fascinating case-study in political puppetry. The division, by the victorious Allies, of Germany into East and West created, from one root, two nation-states. Each, clearly, at that time shared the same past, but, with their quite different agendas for the future, they were destined to make totally different uses of that past. That is to say, the pre-1945 history of Germany was to be perceived and presented in two distinct ways, in furtherance of the respective political policies of the German Democratic Republic (GDR) on the one hand, and the Federal Republic of Germany (FRG) on the other; and we're thus (like psychologists with identical twins) presented with the possibility of a unique comparison between two models of political puppetry – a comparison interestingly made by Mary Fulbrook, to whom I am obviously indebted for this section.[20]

Historians in the Communist East are the more easily accused of kowtowing to their political masters – of being the more obviously aligned with a political agenda. They appear as lying within a long Marxist historiographical tradition, from which dissent was not encouraged. In the immediate post-war years, non-conforming academics did well to withdraw to the West, with its greater tolerance of intellectual diversity; but in later years, after the building of the Berlin Wall and sealing of the frontiers in 1961, emigration was no longer possible – and other (and sometimes sinister) means were used to ensure conformity. As Mary Fulbrook concludes: 'By the late 1980s, the historical profession had become a secure part of the GDR establishment.'[21] Historians in the East, then, were required at the end of the war to perform a rapid change of direction: it was necessary, after some twelve years of bolstering the cause of Nazism, to switch allegiance to a Communist régime that had previously been anathema. Past lessons had to be unlearnt and replaced by something more appropriate for the underpinning of a projected new identity. With old models discarded, a new consciousness was to be deliberately forged, for the sake of a new utopian future – the utopia this time round being Communism, and aligned with the former enemy, Russia.

Such U-turns may seem hard to effect at high speed, but history once more proved to be a versatile vehicle. The immediate problem was obviously what to do about what had just happened – how to account, that is, for the downfall of Hitler and the Third Reich. Such previous historicisations as we've just been considering above clearly had to be abandoned: far from being a providentially ordered fulfilment of German destiny, Nazism now had to be presented as an extraordinary aberration. But as an aberration, it was nonetheless explicable: it was, in Marxist mode, to be viewed as just another form of fascism, such as might be expected to breed in a capitalist environment. Explanations could then be duly offered in terms of class-conflict: Hitler himself became an unwitting puppet of capitalism, and the mass of people had been led astray by him. The people were thus conveniently enabled to perceive themselves as innocent victims – absolved from any need of guilt about their past, and ready positively to progress towards a socialist future.

That therapeutic function of history in East Germany was paralleled in the West, though the diagnosis of the relevant malaise, and the consequent remedy proposed, were of course quite different. And although there may have been greater freedom to debate the issues, and although conventional claims may have been made to such historiographical virtues as detachment and objectivity, Mary Fulbrook concedes that here too history became 'a highly politicised affair'.[22] The politics were more conservative, and the manipulations therefore less obvious; but they were nonetheless there: maintenance of the *status quo*, or restoration of the *status quo* ante, may sound unexcitingly neutral, but they still constitute an ideological positioning. Historians in the West, then, no less than in the East, found themselves clearly and closely aligned with prevailing politics – in this case the politics of Chancellor Adenauer, whose natural concern was the restoration of national morale and, after the identification and punishment of a few scapegoats, the normalisation of the post-war German situation. His agenda thus closely paralleled that of politicians in the East, and similarly implied a need to find through history some sense of continuity of German identity.

The solution in the Federal Republic, where greater emphasis on the individual was acceptable, if not required, was to view Hitler himself as an aberration – as an anomaly within the naturally progressive sweep of German history. In line with more liberal-democratic politics, he was to be seen not so much as the helpless and hapless victim of greater socio-economic forces, but rather as an eccentric madman – admittedly a charismatic leader, but essentially a criminal who had surrounded himself with a gang of like-minded evil henchmen, including in particular the notorious SS. Nazism, as the West German historian Friedrich Meinecke described in 1946, was 'the domination of a gang of criminals'; it was a 'club of criminals [who] ruled us'.[23]

That characterisation, no less than that preferred in the GDR, had the advantage of exonerating the great majority of people from any personal responsibility for what had happened: to be caught up in a totalitarian dictatorship was not unique to Germany, but a liability throughout Europe generally. And even in Germany some heroes could be identified – especially those martyrs of the so-called July Plot of 1944, who had actually attempted to assassinate their Fuehrer. There was then, after all, justification in terms of Western historiography too, for the German people generally to hold up their heads again, and start the necessary process of rebuilding.

Historians on both sides of the Wall thus initially served to heal the trauma of their country's defeat, and to minimise any feelings of responsibility for German wartime guilt. Even the Holocaust, as we now describe the effects of Hitler's attempt to find a 'final solution' to the perceived 'problem' of the Jews, was hardly mentioned – not at least until the Israeli abduction and trial of Adolf Eichmann in 1961 stirred memories. Indeed, even as late as 1985, as Mary Fulbrook has indicated, a general history virtually ignored the Holocaust, with references in just three sentences; and that, she clarifies, exemplifies 'the persistence of the self-exonerating historical pictures of the early post-war period even forty years later'.[24]

As with individuals, though (and as we've seen with France), the past could not be indefinitely repressed, and the so-called 'Historians' Debate', initiated in Germany in 1986, illuminated once more some of the political dimensions of historiography, by focusing on the issue of just what of the past should be re-admitted to memory, and how it should be treated.[25] The division within the historical profession in Germany, and the often heated debate between the two sides, need not concern us here; but it does demonstrate once again Huizinga's assertion concerning the centrality of history in the matter of German national identity.

It's not, however, only the input from German historians them-selves, with their various objectives, that needs to be considered in this context: others, with their own (often hidden) agendas, were no less concerned to use the history of that country for political purposes. So in the earlier part of the twentieth century, it has been suggested,[26] Germany was deliberately excluded from a newly constructed concept of 'the West', designed not least in the interests of an Atlantic Alliance linking western Europe with the USA. Germany, by her aggressive actions, had shown herself ineligible for inclusion in that club; she could justifiably be black-balled as beyond the pale of western civilisa-tion – a humiliation that she'd brought upon herself. And things could only get worse after defeat in the Second World War. The dispo-sition of the post-war powers necessitated the imposition on Germany of a so-called 'Allied Scheme of History' – an (obviously politicised) scheme that served to justify the aspirations of the time. Thus, it included a belief in 'western civilisation' (still excluding Germany, of course) as the apex of progressive technological and political develop-ment. Above all, it appeared now as the victorious representative of 'good' over the 'evil' of fascism; and in that it necessarily embraced Russia as a partner, in view of her own enormous sacrifices in the recent anti-fascist struggle. In conformity with that model, it also conceded to Russia her own 'sphere of influence' – an area, which included East Germany, that lay beyond the bounds of western inter-vention. And that model of history, as Norman Davies has described, persisted through the so-called Cold War, and even at the end of the twentieth century 'was everywhere evident in academic discussions and, *perhaps unknowingly*, in the conceptual framework which informs the policy decisions of governments'.[27] Histories of the time thus incorporated a hidden political agenda – all the more powerful for being unrecognised as such, but simply accepted without question, 'perhaps unknowingly'.

As the political situation changed, though, so did the brief presented to historians. Following the dissolution of the USSR, the collapse of Communism in eastern Europe, and the existence of a newly unified Germany within a fast developing European Community, historical justifications needed to be found for an alto-gether different dispensation. Histories newly revealed as myths had to be replaced by newly revealed histories; Germany (as well as other eastern states) had to be incorporated once again into the European mainstream; and historians were employed to provide underpinning for a new internationalist vision. For as the historian

A. J. P. Taylor had earlier submitted, 'European History is whatever the historian wants it to be' (at least, he might have added, when the historian is privileged to be free from political control); and Norman Davies has affirmed that any success the European Union comes to enjoy 'will owe much to the historians who will have helped to give it a sense of community'.[28] The proper function of historians today, whether working still to a hidden agenda or (surely preferably) an agenda that's made quite explicit, is not, to revert to Ranke, to 'benefit the *nation* to which we belong', but rather that *international* community to which now we all belong.

3   Justifying the *status quo*

If some historians have deliberately put 'spin' on their narratives and danced to the tunes of political puppeteers, others have sometimes worked to agendas that were hidden even from themselves, while serving nonetheless to justify the *status quo*. Richard Evans has described how 'often the impulses driving them [historians] are hidden deep inside the subconscious mind';[29] so that, like other people, they are sometimes unaware of what their own motivations are – which is not, of course, to say that they don't have any. Inevitably entangled in their own times and places, and influenced by prevailing assumptions with which they are brought up and surrounded – by the ideas, beliefs, and presuppositions that go unquestioned in any culture – historians have sometimes produced effects quite other than they themselves consciously intended; and those effects have often been to confirm and justify prevailing dispositions. As the historian Herbert Butterfield noted long ago, with the various pressures to which they are subject – essentially parochial pressures to conform to certain intellectual, professional and institutional expectations – historians 'can scarcely help it' if what they produce is a history 'most adapted to the preservation of the existing régime'.[30]

Historians, in other words, have often, however inadvertently, contributed to the maintenance of a *status quo* – to ensure that, so far as possible, things should continue as they have before, with the future resembling the past that they describe, the one a seemingly natural (if not inevitable) continuation of the other. Thus, for example, some of the earliest historical records include lists of rulers compiled by the annalists of ancient Egypt. These trace ancestries back to the third millennium BC, just as similarly later Christian genealogies lead back to Moses or Adam and Eve; and they may sound like nothing more than boring, useless lists of names. But they were not just the simple, 'neutral' (if mythical) records that they might now appear to us to be: they actually had a purpose; and that purpose, as with Virgil's *Aeneid* again, was to give the past's authority to present incumbents of power. They were, that is, clearly compiled for a specific, though unstated, political – justificatory – purpose.[31]

Similarly with histories of the Christian church. These are often not the purely descriptive narratives they may purport to be: on the contrary, through the Christian era, specific sects (including most obviously Protestants and Catholics) have been concerned (as we've already seen in Chapter 3, §5) to confirm their own validity by claiming direct links with the church's origins – by showing again that historical developments lead directly to themselves. And more generally, that self-confirming role can be seen not least in later historians' adoption of conventional chronology – that narrative trajectory from antiquity, through so-called 'middle ages', to modernity, where modernity itself is presented as the culminating point of a generally progressive development, and our own position (whatever that might be) is conveniently confirmed by accounts of everything that went before. The present dispensation is justified by history; it's the progressive course of past events that has conveyed us to this present.

And at the end of another progressive development – albeit on a smaller scale – the individual human being can be shown to have evolved (at least in our favoured western world) from 'primitive' to 'civilised'. Just like the political institutions of which we approve, and the religious (or secular) beliefs to which we ourselves subscribe, the autonomous human being can be shown as the culmination of progressive evolution and development through history. In Darwinian terms, it's as the fittest that we have, and have deservedly, survived.

History's task, then, has often been in a sense self-justificatory and self-congratulatory – confirming us in our present. We might go on to ask with Nikolas Rose: 'Who is accorded or claims the capacity to speak truthfully about humans, their nature and their problems?'[32] for implicit in the conferring or claiming of that capacity is a huge responsibility and power-bestowing privilege. And the answer to Rose's question must surely be: 'Historians!' For it is historians who have claimed (and generally been accorded) the ability to tell the truth about human characters and their problems, about their thoughts and their actions, as revealed in their pasts. It was, after all, only by presupposing some continuing truths about human nature – truths that were supposedly revealed through a study of history – that history's function as a teacher could be justified: it was only because the truth about humans remained essentially the same through history, that history could hope to teach from others' past mistakes; and it was that truth about humans, 'their nature and their problems', that it was the historian's task to uncover.

Yet that authoritative 'truth' was, of course, necessarily selective. It was constructed on its own presuppositions about what sorts of human beings should be preferred: it was within its own 'régime of truth' that history presented its models of 'man' and 'woman', 'husband' and 'wife', 'hedonist' and 'puritan', 'manager' and 'worker'. Its preferred models may have changed over time: Carlyle's 'heroes' may no longer be our own, and such Victorian virtues as self-help and thrift, as enumerated and illustrated by Samuel Smiles, may come in and out of fashion. But some implied prescription remains: history still serves to provide models for emulation, prohibitions, and justifications. These may not be explicit, but any historian's very choice of subject – whether of event or individual person – implies some value judgement. Whatever our attitude towards them, our choice of Adolf Hitler or Nelson Mandela, of aristocrat or factory worker, does affect the 'truth' to which we're concerned to bear witness. We can't do it all, so must choose, and for some reason.

A part of history's hidden agenda, then, has been to contribute to a preferred model of human nature itself – to provide some justification for our selves, as we are. The ideal autonomous self of modernity needs to be constituted in such a way as to enable that self to cope appropriately with the freedoms implicit in modernity and (even more urgently perhaps) in postmodernity. Such assumed virtues as self-discipline, self-control, self-restraint, and even self-improvement, are not confined to an imperial role in the nineteenth century, but continue as prerequisites for democratic participation into the twenty-first. Liberal democracies can't justify overt repression, but history can contribute to the constitution of an autonomous selfhood that, in its new-found freedom, can regulate itself.

In that task, it partners psychology, where too (as Nikolas Rose has shown) the study of people can be seen to affect the very nature of what it might mean to be a human being. For people are 'ephemeral, shifting, they can change before one's eyes and are hard to perceive in any stable manner'[33] – just like the past. So they have both (people and past) to be, as it were, immobilised, solidified – made graspable as an object of study, by the psychologist or by the historian. And that involves the pre-preparation of a template against which people, whether in the present or past, can be assessed; it involves having a preordained model of propriety and normality, in relation to which people can be measured. It involves, again, however unconsciously adopted, a judgement of value with its own, however implicit and hidden, agenda.

In relation specifically to history, two examples or case-studies may help to clarify this point, and we'll look at these in Sections 4 and 5.

4 Discipline and power[34]

In her detailed study of English universities in the later nineteenth and early twentieth centuries, Reba Soffer has shown how historians – some no doubt deliberately and consciously, others perhaps less so – performed a vital social, political, and moral (even surrogate-religious) function; for they served to consolidate – to underpin and justify – the dominant values of their time and place. At a point when there was little disagreement or discussion about what history was for, university academics believed their own function to lie in the production of an élite – a graduate class fully prepared to play a leading role in the drama of an empire, on whose world-wide stage the curtain never fell. The members of that class, while answering diverse needs in government, education, religion, industry, and commerce, shared common convictions, beliefs, and values – shared certain assumptions concerning individual human character and the direction of socio-political progress. And it was in the cultivation, development, and consolidation of those assumptions that historians, like other educators, saw their function. That agenda, though, remained 'hidden', in that there was no call (perhaps no ability) to make explicit what was generally and unthinkingly accepted.

History teachers at the universities of Oxford and Cambridge, then, as Professor Soffer concludes, 'treated history as a succession of lessons on the origins of private and public obligations'.[35] They could perform their traditional role of teaching by examples – by selecting those past models of human excellence to which it was appropriate to aspire – and of revealing and confirming the historical trajectory to which it was fitting to contribute. We go to history, as one tutor, H. W. C. Davis, explained to members of the Balliol College History Club in 1907, 'for a confirmation of our faith in the value of human effort; we go to it for examples'.[36] History's purpose, as Davis later clarified in his Inaugural Lecture as Regius Professor at Oxford in 1925, was to reveal the 'Sisyphean efforts' of humans to establish 'the fabric of a just, harmonious, and well-ordered state'. (Britain was not, any more than Rome or Germany, built in a day, or without a struggle.) Historians should take account of the needs of their own generation; and those past efforts, which included 'ceaseless criticism of the heritage of the past ... untiring zeal in the revision of beliefs and the reconstruction of all the organs of government', could then be properly appreciated and duly emulated. That was 'the real stuff and substance of history' – that was what it was *for*.[37]

It was clear to Professor Davis that England did enjoy a state that was indeed 'just, harmonious, and well-ordered' – a state remarkable for its stability, founded on individual liberty and opportunity, its citizens enjoying a rising standard of material living; and it was no less clear that that felicitous condition was linked with – was dependent upon – a deference to accepted moral and spiritual values. For historians, then, an important function of their subject was its revelation of the moral law of which Britain's success was an earthly manifestation. Knowledge of that law would enable the individual to play a responsible part in continuing along the proper road and so fulfilling future destiny.

The requisite education was thus not only intellectual, but just as importantly moral: properly trained in a self-sacrificing discipline, the historically educated man would be ready to devote himself altruistically to the civilising mission which was shown by history itself to be nothing less than God's own plan for his people. The link with morality, and even with religion, was made explicit by other historians themselves. At Oxford, for instance, William Stubbs had earlier described history as being second only to theology in providing 'the most thoroughly religious training that the mind can receive'. And, as we've already noted in Chapter 3, it had a practical moral point: 'the disciplinary force of the study of History is to make people honest and intelligent politicians.'[38] No doubts there, then, about what history was *for*. And the moral and religious theme was paralleled by Stubbs' counterpart at Cambridge. J. R. Seeley emphasised history's role as 'the school of statesmanship' and of 'public feeling and patriotism'.

History shows 'a man the whole of which he is a part' – provides that wider framework and 'theory of human affairs ... which serves the purpose of a chart or a compass'. With the benefit of that, we can take heart, and calmly assess our own position and the direction we now need to take: 'life, from being a wandering or a drifting, becomes a journey or a voyage to a definite port.'[39] History's agenda, then, inevitably becomes conservative again, its function to reveal the truth about the past in order to confirm the present and thence indicate appropriate directions for the future. It teaches, as Seeley himself went on, 'each man his place ... the post at which he is stationed, the function with which he is invested, the work that is required of him'; it can reaffirm, in the words of another practitioner in 1898, 'some sense, however dim, of the continuity of national life; some consciousness of the great inheritance transmitted from past generations to be handed down by us unimpaired to the generations to come'. For with certain shared presuppositions, history could be seen, as Stubbs had previously claimed, as the 'unravelling' of that 'string which forms the clue to the history of human progress'; its object of study was 'the history of those nations and institutions in which the real growth of humanity is to be traced: in which we can follow the developments, the retardations and perturbations, the ebb and flow of human progress'.[40]

History in the later Victorian age could, then, still provide justification for Britain's, and more generally for Europe's, claimed civilising role in empire: lesser countries would only benefit from subordination to materially and morally superior powers. And even as Europe later tore itself apart in the Great War, history was to retain its own moral and political agenda – its own self-justificatory use. At the outset of the war, Oxford historians, of various political persuasions and disclaiming any political agenda of their own, joined forces 'to set forth the causes of the present war, and the principles we believe to be at stake'; and they duly arrived together at the convenient conclusion that 'England stands to-day in this fortunate position, that her duty and her interest combine to impel her in the same direction'.[41] Far from raising any awkward questions, historians could actually use the war to confirm their previous practices.

If there was any doubt about the point of fighting or, later, about the price that had been paid for victory, that doubt could be conveniently allayed by reference to the larger historical picture and the continuing certainties supposedly revealed there. As Reba Soffer concludes, 'Dissent, independent or reflective thought, and critical subversive analysis were not encouraged, because greater value was given to a stable, common culture justified by a historical evolution of personal and communal goods'.[42] History, as the impartial arbiter that dispassionately revealed the rights and wrongs of what had taken place, and was of course beyond any possibility of political manipulation, was able to provide justifications, to allay fears, and to maintain personal and political calm. Its role once again, however disguised, however hidden, was to be another opiate for the people.

5 The gender of history[43]

In her fascinating work *The Gender of History*, Bonnie G. Smith has argued that the historical profession itself and *per se* has embodied another agenda, often hidden from and unrecognised by its own practitioners. That agenda has consisted essentially in a 'self-gendering' – a gendering, that is, of 'history' itself: from the professionalisation of the subject in the nineteenth century, history has been defined by 'masculine' (at the expense of 'feminine') virtues; and once established as a 'discipline', that one-sidedness has been (however unselfconsciously) self-perpetuating. That may sound initially like the paranoid raving of a latter-day feminist, but a brief summary of Bonnie Smith's argument may serve to clarify another aspect of what history, albeit unknown to its own disciples, has actually been *for*.

An essential problem, as Bonnie Smith makes clear, derives from the attempt to achieve 'scientific' status for the subject. From its reconstitution in the seventeenth century, 'science' itself has been defined in terms of what (in our own culture) has been ascribed to the 'masculine'. As one of the founding philosophical fathers of modernity, Descartes in particular was concerned to eliminate what were traditionally perceived as 'feminine' characteristics from the search for knowledge: in his reformulation of the appropriate methods for intellectual enquiry, he was largely responsible for what has been described as the 'masculinisation of thought', inasmuch as he attempted to distinguish clearly between 'subject' and 'object' – the scientist and nature, the knower and the known – and eliminate any 'subjective' input from what, by definition, had to be a purely 'rational' and 'detached' pursuit.[44] As is evidenced from writings at the time (such as those of Francis Bacon and various Fellows of the Royal Society)[45] that proposed new method was perceived as an elimination of the 'feminine' – such feminine characteristics as intuition and a sympathetic 'merging' with (as opposed to detachment from) any object of study (whether natural or human). That is not to claim any characteristics as *essentially* masculine or feminine, but to recognise that, in the period of modernity, those distinctions have conventionally been held to apply.

Feminist writers such as Susan Bordo, then, have exposed the 'gender biases' in modern science; and it's hardly surprising that similar biases can be revealed – as they have now been revealed by Bonnie Smith – in a subject that has long been deliberately modelled on such science. For in defining their own discipline, 'professional' historians have laid claim to their own 'scientific' credentials – their own essential 'detachment' and 'objectivity'. To such an extent has the intrusion of any sense of 'self' been anathema that one historian actually claimed (what many others have no doubt believed) that it is 'not I who speak, but History which speaks through me'.[46] And the language that 'History' speaks through its selfless medium or mouthpiece approaches as nearly as possible to the 'language of mathematics', claimed by Galileo as representing the very essence of (disembodied) nature. Like the natural philosophers of the seventeenth century, who strove to avoid any 'rhetorical flourishes' in their strictly 'factual' accounts, historians have eschewed any stylistic adornments or 'allurements' – anything that might seem to detract from the impersonal neutrality (and hence assumed authority) of their reports.[47]

As in any attempt to define an identity, historians, in their quest for scientific status, necessarily had resort to an 'other', with which contrasts could be made; and a model of 'amateurism' lay conveniently to hand. A long tradition of women's historical writing, long ignored as historiographically irrelevant but traced back by Smith to Germaine de Staël in the early nineteenth century, had been characterised by what we might now describe as a 'romantic' approach: starting (unscientifically) from an *emotional* engagement with the subject, early women historians resorted unapologetically to imaginative representations; unconcerned with facts and dates *per se*, they endeavoured vividly to summon up some essence of the past which remained as immanent in their own present. And that, they believed, could best be done, not through detachment and reasoned argument, but through involvement and appeal to the senses – the attempted resurrection of what eyes had seen, ears heard, and bodies felt.

Particularly interesting in the context of my claims for history's potential as in some sense 'therapeutic', the motivation for writing such histories had often been the allaying of some trauma. Authors of the time might well have witnessed political revolution and social disruption, experienced personal violence and humiliation, and resented the apparent contradiction between the public proclamations of universal equality on the one hand, and the erosion of their own personal and legal rights as women on the other. In that situation, they were then able to use their own historical writing as a form of 'therapy', seeing their work, as Bonnie Smith describes, 'as providing refuge from the sorrows, inequities, and trauma of love, a place where the self was restored, the lover forgotten, a better narrative of one's activities forged'. As against 'knowledge', such histories were 'effective for producing strong feelings of *catharsis*'.[48]

Such personal involvement was specifically repudiated by 'professionals', as the new 'discipline' of history was created; and those womanly accounts, utilising banal, everyday domestic source-material, focusing as they did on the personal and cultural rather than the public and political, were dismissively classified as 'amateur'. In that way, they were effectively consigned to the outer darkness of intellectual life, where the inner light was to be provided by men. The works of the early twentieth-century German (woman) 'amateur' historian Ricarda Huch, for instance, were catalogued and shelved in libraries as, not history at all, but 'fiction'; and the writings of (the subsequently renowned) Jane Harrison were cursorily dismissed as likely to 'appeal rather to the easy-going amateur than to the trained expert'. For, Smith argues, the new historical science was constructed 'by privileging male over female and by specifically contrasting male truth and female falsehood, male depth and female superficiality, significant male events and trivial female ones, male transcendence and female embodiment'.[49] In case this all sounds a bit over the top, we should note that tirades against the amateur still continue: Geoffrey Elton was notoriously scornful of 'the amusing amateur', who was to be contrasted with the trustworthy 'professional', on whom we must rely 'when we really want to know'; and Arthur Marwick has recently written critically of 'amateur historians [who] sometimes prefer to tempt [their] audience with books which are colourful and romantic, and unreliable ... [rather than] rigorous and analytical', as professionalism requires.[50]

If that provides some justification for Bonnie Smith's description of history as a still 'deeply gendered' profession, it's interesting to note further her suggestion that the formation of such gendering was encouraged by the education that many historians continued to receive until very recently. That education has been described as 'ascetic': starting often from an early age in boarding-schools (where boys would be largely deprived of feminine influence), it put emphasis on precise grammatical and linguistic skills, and encouraged above all the development of 'manliness' (which included unemotional personal detachment). And that of course in turn provided the ideal qualifications for recruits to a newly defined discipline of history that insisted on the self-discipline of practitioners, who could remove themselves from any subjectivity – from any personality or physicality (or femininity) or values – in order to retrieve those elusive truth-revealing 'facts' secreted in the archives.[51] It seems that the training required for historians corresponded closely with – or perhaps was even identical to – that (alluded to in the preceding section) required for imperial administrators. It was concerned, in however concealed a fashion, to maintain rather than to question existing structures; and that was the case not least in relation to the discipline of history itself.

6 Conclusion

What the two case-studies in Sections 4 and 5 illuminate is how history can follow, or simply *embody*, hidden agendas – how its claims to reveal 'truth' have themselves to be assessed and understood historically; and that implies assessment too of the context in which such claims have been made, with all the attendant presuppositions, aspirations, and values which that (or any other) context implies. For historical truth, like any other form of, or claim to, truth is, as Nikolas Rose (in Foucauldian vein) has said, 'always enthroned by acts of violence'.[52] That is to say, truth can be established only by repelling other claimants to that prestigious title; it's only 'truth' within one of many possible alternative contexts. So it's achieved by excluding whatever fails to fit. Just as we say that some faces don't fit (don't suit a certain social context), so some historical data can't be made to fit the rules of evidence, or the linguistic usages, or the interpretative models that the prevailing discipline demands. What, for example, is actually allowed to count as 'evidence'? Do we trust oral reports, or personal diaries, or political memoirs, or the word of a criminal or witch? (All of those might propose alternative versions of the truth – but which, if any, in history's law-court are to be admitted as permissible evidence?) There's no room for everyone at the centre; so some viewpoints, some interpretations, some versions of the past, must be marginalised – pushed to the periphery, denied validity, excluded from the domain of 'the true', dethroned 'by acts of violence'.

Inevitably, therefore, history works to an often hidden agenda: definitions of 'professional' and 'amateur', 'evidence' and 'relevant', 'mythical', 'acceptable', and 'true', perform a regulatory function. They serve to facilitate distinctions between a past that has been professionally sanctioned (cordoned off as 'history'), and those bits of the past (including people) which are to be deemed marginal, 'eccentric', or off-centre. They constitute what Rose (following Foucault) calls a 'régime of truth', and importantly 'play their part in establishing a division between the sayable and the unsayable, the thinkable and the unthinkable'.[53] In this way, then, histories can be seen, not as unearthing or revealing the past, but as actually *defining* its supposed 'reality'– a reality that impinges on, and helps to shape, the future.

That's one of the things, in short, that history has (knowingly or unknowingly) been *for*. And the question does arise as to whether historians' time would be better spent on other things – working to other (perhaps less conservative) agendas. We'll be considering that in the following chapters, but let's briefly note here Rose's own proposal – that rather than, from our own self-interested standpoint in the present, policing the past and marginalising certain aspects of it, we might be better employed in first questioning our own position, and thence investigating how marginalisation actually occurs: 'we might do better to question the certainties of the present by attention to such margins and to the process of their marginalisation.'[54] We have to accept some conventions to enable us to tell a story of the past at all, but it may be better not to leave those conventions and their implications hidden. We may prefer to be aware that those conventions are there, to be aware of where they're likely to lead, and to be aware of why we've accepted them – with what agenda in mind. And, above all, let's remain aware that they are only conventions (not something that's actually there in nature, fixed and unchangeable), so that we do still have a choice.

Chapter 5

Life and needs in postmodernity

I Introduction

Having considered some of the uses to which history has, whether deliberately or inadvertently, been put in the past – up to the period of modernity, which (in the terminology I'm adopting) culminated in the later twentieth century – it's now time to move to the present and to our situation in postmodernity. For as times change, and we with them, so do our conceptions of the nature and purposes of history.

In particular, as we've seen, some previously proclaimed purposes for history presupposed the existence and the ultimate attainability of 'truth' – in history's case, the truth about the past. That truth, it was assumed, just lay there, deeply entombed in archival deposits, but only awaiting discovery and the kiss of life by worthy knight-errant historians. Perceived as something sacrosanct, absolute, an end in itself, it was the historian's job to represent (literally re-present) it. What has now changed everything is the demise of that belief in 'truth' – or of any truth of that kind. Its replacement by a more pragmatic concept of truth – a truth that has no ultimate external reference, but serves satisfactorily for human purposes in a particular context – has necessarily changed attitudes towards any subject claiming truth (of whatever kind) as its goal; and that, most importantly of all perhaps, includes history. In the absence of historical truth (as previously understood), what on earth can the subject be – and in particular (for us here and now) be *for*? And while some – promoting yet another 'end of history' – have denied it any point at all, others have pointed to newly revealed windows opening on to vistas unbounded by previous confines and constraints; for as the historicised past has become increasingly unstable, and we've become less sure about how properly to handle it, so have its potentialities become extended. And it's that more positive view of history's new purposes in postmodernity that I want to present here.

My aims, then, in this chapter are to outline some characteristics of actual life in postmodernity, and to indicate some possible *needs* that we might feel – needs that might (as we shall go on to indicate) be answered at least in part by history. In other words, this chapter is a necessary step – as outlining our present situation and requirements – towards answering the central question of what, in our own time, history is, or might be, *for*.

2   Postmodernity

> Postmodernity is modernity coming to terms with its own impossibility; a self-monitoring modernity, one that consciously discards what it was once unconsciously doing.
>
> (Zygmunt Bauman)[1]

We need first of all to attempt some definition of the problematic term 'postmodernity', or at least to clarify how it's being used here. It's a notoriously elusive concept, but for me it simply denotes an historical epoch – the one that comes after 'modernity'. So it's the period that we are all living in now, in the early twenty-first century. What is it, then, we might go on to ask, that characterises life in our time, and what are our specific needs? Is our condition any different from that in previous times? Is Barry Smart justified in his assertion that 'there appears to be a considerable degree of concordance that things are no longer quite as they might once have seemed to be'?[2] What on earth does Zygmunt Bauman mean by his definition of postmodernity in the quotation above?

When we ask such questions, we may seem to be referring to the idle musings of an élite, a 'chosen' few – a few self-reflexive 'intellectuals', chosen by us for particular attention. But one of the most noticeable characteristics of postmodernity is 'globalisation' – the ever accelerating erosion of conventional boundaries, social and national; so that what seems to be the case in isolated pockets of western Europe or southern California one day may have acquired relevance and inspired resonance in distant and unexpected places not long after. So while our field of reference may initially seem narrow, it's potentially – and maybe imminently – much broader. We're talking here about ourselves.

Now, when Zygmunt Bauman describes postmodernity as 'modernity coming to terms with its own impossibility', he implies the acceptance of some sort of failure – the failure of what has been described as the 'project of modernity', or (on the assumption that modernity stems from eighteenth-century thought) the failure of 'the Enlightenment project'. And to characterise that project very briefly, we might say that (as self-consciously adopted 'projects' tend to do) it included, above all perhaps, a belief in its own rightness – in this case, a belief that, by applying the power of their intellect, humans could at last attain their long-standing objective: they could finally come to understand, and hence control, not only the external natural world, but even their very human selves (and other people); and they could, not so much in religious as in human terms, reach truth. From an unquestioned centre (themselves), they needed only to apply the right (reasonable) methods to set society and the world itself to rights.

It's the basis of that Enlightenment optimism – standing as it did in part on hidden (unconscious) presuppositions derived from Christian beliefs in the progressive development of a species uniquely favoured by God – that has now, as Bauman explains, been consciously discarded. In the mid-nineteenth century, John Henry Newman as rector of Dublin University could still confidently re-affirm 'a great and firm belief in the sovereignty of Truth', which enabled him to deduce that, despite the possibility of some setbacks, 'knowledge on the whole makes progress'; any problems or errors are just minor blips in the way of a science that 'impercep-tibly all the time ... is advancing'.[3] Those Victorian architects and builders who inscribed 'Progress' on the walls of public buildings (such as Shoreditch Town Hall: Figure 4) knew where they were going. But since Newman's time, such confidence has been eroded. Secularising tendencies generally have, for many, removed any pretence of providential ordering (development in a direction ordained for our benefit by God); and many others have more recently lost faith in humans' ability to make much progress in any direction at all. To compound twenty-first-century disillusionment, earlier presuppositions concerning humans' own uniqueness and centrality in nature have been confounded by Darwinian and subse-quent biological theories; and the stability even of any such essence as 'human nature', and the individual human 'self', has evaporated in the heat of multidisciplinary attacks, led by anthropology, psychology and (Foucauldian) historical study itself. So Bauman's

Figure 4 Victorian certainties:'Progress' on Shoreditch Town Hall, London.

point is that we are now, in postmodernity, having to come to terms with the actual impossibility of achieving the modernist agenda; and in newly self-reflexive mode, we are inclined to repudiate some of those agenda items to which we formerly, unconsciously, subscribed.

Most (or at least very) important is the acceptance of the loss of order – an acceptance, that is, that the modernist agenda of the imposition of universal order, not only on the natural universe, but even on humanity itself (and on humanity's activities), is a non-starter, an essentially unattainable and actually undesirable (if not positively sinister) goal. So that chaotic *dis*-order, which it was modernity's project to overcome and supersede, is in postmodernity to be accepted as both inevitable and positively welcome; it is something, with all its ambivalence and insecurity, that is not to be feared but celebrated.

Writing of the social sciences, then, Barry Smart has claimed that 'Pluralism and polycentrism ... have increased the level of disorder ... blurred the boundaries with related disciplines, and ... rendered the object or focus of ... investigation less distinct'; and he has reminded us that in his own analyses Michel Foucault explicitly eschews that ordering finality (definitiveness), so much admired in modernity, and instead actually *intends* 'to be inconclusive and open-ended. The objective is to pose questions which "may well open the way to a future thought'". And there is of course a moral and political point to that replacement of order by open-endedness: intellectual activity (which should surely importantly include historical enquiry), far from consolidating any *status quo* (as we have seen in Chapter 4 to be the case of history) can positively contribute 'to processes of *questioning, challenging, and transforming* existing social institutions, social practices, and prevailing forms of identity'. One of sociology's purposes then becomes to foster an ability 'to disengage from prevailing forms of experience and thereby *constitute new forms of life*'.[4] And if that's to be an aim of sociology in postmodernity, why not of history too?

3   Centres and certainties

Another major characteristic of life in postmodernity is the loss of any agreed centre from which authoritatively to view and assess the external world – the loss of what Antony Giddens has described as 'anchoring reference points'.[5] And more recently, a much more general awareness of that loss has fuelled the uncertainties which presumably have always lain at the heart of the human condition. For it goes with a recognition that any order – whether psychological or social – that we do enjoy, is enjoyed at the cost of forgetting its contingency, its fragility, its dependence on insecure foundations. Once we question the stability of those conventions by which we order our lives and our selves – those conventions which afford us the security we need for personal and social life – we are forced to concede that instability is all there is. And where there are no secure foundations, there can be no confidence in any superstructure. A superstructure can hang together for a time, like a scaffolding frame or brick-built edifice, by virtue of its own complexity and interlocking mutually sustaining parts; but its ultimate fragility, once diagnosed, hangs over us as an ever threatening presence – a sword of Damocles suspended by a thread.

A recognition of imminent catastrophe, of standing on the edge of a precipitous return to chaos – this has always constituted a part of the gloomier philosophies; but it now seems to constitute more generally a part of life in postmodernity. 'Doubt', as Giddens believes, 'permeates into *everyday life* as well as philosophical consciousness, and forms *a general existential dimension* of the contemporary social world'; and that all-pervasive doubt necessarily 'is existentially troubling for ordinary individuals'. For if doubt – the loss of any certainties – runs right through life, impacting not only on previously accepted beliefs about the external world but also on our carefully built up structures of beliefs about our selves, then real problems are revealed concerning any sense of direction in our lives. It makes sense to talk of 'direction' only on the assumption of a standpoint, of a centre from which to proceed; and a direction can be chosen only on the basis of (possibly various, but nevertheless accepted) criteria for choice. In other words, an individual needs to have some sense of 'self' – some idea of being an autonomous entity capable of making decisions – and needs also to have some standards or values by which 'better' or 'worse' directions may be evaluated. Without that centre and without those standards, the whole concept of 'direction' is lost; and we flounder around, not knowing how to proceed – or where or why. Any idea of a meaningful identity and purposeful life is lost; and, as Giddens concludes, 'Personal meaninglessness ... becomes a fundamental psychic problem'. Indeed, it is in part 'the looming threat of personal meaninglessness' that characterises life in postmodernity.[6]

That meaninglessness is only confirmed by what we might call chronological disruption – an opening breach or disjunction between past and present and future. The past, in the form of film and television histories – 'histories' presented in neat narrative form for general entertainment – may well be accepted in its own terms as a story, but only as a story that has little connection with our own disjointed present; and many aspects of the past (not least moral and political values identified with earlier times) are perceived (and sometimes not without 'official' encouragement) as now irrelevant – as 'unhelpful', un-trendy and outmoded. And the future, about which dire predictions accumulate – political, military, environmental, climatic – seems even less within our control. In postmodernity, we are taught to expect the unexpected in the future, and in that expectation we're seldom disappointed for long. So it's hardly surprising that, in their disorientated present, individuals look in new directions for their certainties and centres.

That serves to account, at least in part, for the resuscitation and rise of 'fundamentalist' religions; but with the loss, for many (if not most), of any religious or spiritual guidance, those new directions can include such alternative activities as sport. Hence, for example, it can be claimed of Britain in 2002, and without any appearance of irony, that 'Football clubs are the social and spiritual centres of most communities now'. Decades ago, the French philosopher Albert Camus proclaimed with self-conscious provocation: 'All that

I know most surely about morality and obligations, I owe to football.' Those words are now emblazoned on shirts in England, substantiating recent claims that the most notable focal point of English culture is now the national football team.[7]

Those for whom such centres are unlikely to provide the social and spiritual guidance or certainties they're seeking may well, then, feel deprived – and experience, in Bauman's words, some 'anxiety, out-of-placeness, loss of direction'. Indeed, those negative emotions are virtually bound to be experienced by anyone who continues to take epistemological, moral, and aesthetic problems seriously; for any hope of solving those problems fades in the foundationless world of postmodernity. Without any universally accepted starting-point or centre or foundation, there can be no 'authoritative solution to the questions of cognitive truth, moral judgement, and aesthetic taste'; for there are no criteria by which competing solutions to such questions can themselves be assessed, judged and evaluated.[8] In a world marked by relativism in all branches of what has hitherto been 'knowledge', marked by the dissipation of any meaningful concept of 'objectivity', and of any unquestioned intellectual and moral 'foundation', we are left in postmodernity with the need somehow to cope with far-reaching and radical doubt. We've lost our centres and our certainties, and we'll need to consider later whether history can compete with the comfortingly rule-bound game of football in providing any remedies – whether that might be a part of what it's *for*.

4 Order

> She comes! she comes! the sable Throne behold
> Of Night primeval, and of Chaos old!
> Before her, Fancy's gilded clouds decay,
> And all its varying Rain-bows die away.
> (Alexander Pope)[9]

The threat of an imminent return to 'Chaos old', with its associated primeval night and the dissolution of imaginary lights and colours, is another characteristic marker of postmodernity – though, as Pope's verse shows, not without its earlier manifestations. The idea of order, writes Barry Smart, 'order as a task, as a practice, as a condition to be reflected upon, preserved and nurtured is intrinsic to modernity';[10] and the insistence on order – on the aim to impose *order* on incipient chaos and the belief that that is possible – is one of the unquestioned premises of modernity, with whose impossibility postmodernity is having to come to terms.

The orderly aim, of course, long predates modernity itself: it's the very stuff of which philosophy is made from the earliest times, when primeval chaos succumbs to the structures of the human intellect. The sun that appears daily and miraculously to traverse the horizon can be explained (as it was in ancient Egypt) by reference to a man-like god carrying the shining orb on his chariot; the appearance of twinkling stars (as the presocratic Greek philosopher Anaximander explained) has its parallel on earth, when we look through the vents of a furnace at the fire within. It's not enough to marvel at nature: it has to be explained – and explained in earthly, human terms. And with modernity and the development of modern science, that aim becomes more insistent, more urgent, more intrusive. Nature can be seen to become increasingly understood, tamed and successfully exploited by proponents of early modern science, which cast its tidy net over the most elusive phenomena, reducing an essentially inexplicable and chaotic complexity to such mechanistic order as made everything clear and comprehensible. And so optimism grew that those mechanistic techniques might prove truly universalisable, and that the whole world, the whole of human experience, might be encompassed within the constraining bounds of the new procedures. The triumph of modernism would be the final eradication of everything that had hitherto challenged human ordering: we'd at last, in Alexander Pope's words again, 'See Mystery to Mathematics fly!'[11]

The assimilation of mystery to mathematics has a long-standing theological pedigree. From the time of Pythagoras in the sixth century BC, mystics have proclaimed the essentially mathematical structure of the cosmos; and as an ingredient of Platonism, that belief in universal order found its way not only into science (in the work of Newton, for example) but also Christianity. So it was virtually taken for granted by such nineteenth-century thinkers as John Henry Newman and Matthew Arnold. Arnold himself notes that 'the feeling after the universal order' derived from both Greek and Hebrew traditions, and could be equated with, 'in a word, the love of God'; and it actually then becomes 'the will of God' that humans attain their happiness through aiming 'to draw towards a knowledge of the universal order'.[12] For as Newman similarly believes, it is God who has created everything, so that any knowledge we acquire must be knowledge of his ordered creation. All the parts of that creation together form a whole, and it is the philosopher's task to comprehend that whole and the way in which all the parts contribute to it. Indeed, it remains the mark of a slave or child not to know how the parts of the whole relate to each other: philosophy can boast to have 'mapped out the Universe'; so that, for the philosopher:

> the elements of the physical and moral world, sciences, arts, pursuits, ranks, offices, events, opinions, individualities, are all viewed as *one*, with correlative functions, and as gradually by successive combinations *converging, one and all, to the true centre*.[13]

Those words beautifully characterise the optimistic modernism that persisted well into the twentieth century; and it is interesting that Newman himself links his (theologically derived) epistemological point with morality and with what is one of our concerns here – therapy (or what to do about human distress). For, he believes, the truly educated person must see things as a unity – see how each interdependent particular relates to every other and to the ordered whole; and with that vision, he will (unlike those one-sided people 'whose minds are possessed with some one object' exclusively, and who live 'ever *in alarm*') derive from his knowledge an equanimity, a balance, a peace of mind – in other words, that 'ataraxia' (or freedom from stress) envisaged by the Hellenistic philosophers alluded to above in Chapter 1. For:

> such an intellect cannot be partial, cannot be exclusive, cannot be impetuous, cannot be *at a loss*, cannot but be patient, collected, and majestically calm, because it discerns the end in every beginning, the origin in every end, the law in every interruption, the limit in each delay, because it *ever knows where it stands*, and how its path lies from one point to another.[14]

Any belief in that 'clear, calm, accurate vision and comprehension of all things' is precisely what has been lost in the renewed intellectual and moral chaos of postmodernity. As we saw above, the loss of any 'true centre' to which all things converge has left thinking individuals today in the very opposite state to that described by Newman: that is, very much 'at a loss', very far from 'majestically calm', and deprived of knowing with certainty about anything 'where it stands' or what its path might be.

Admittedly, there remains in some quarters a naive optimism and reluctance to accept any scientific or human limitations. Some people conceive and have babies, while others cling on to life, against all the odds that 'nature' might once have seemed to impose; and the phenomenon – or industry – of 'crionics' (where the dead are frozen, to await future thawing after the discovery of the cures they need) testifies to some continuing belief in the imminent and ultimate triumph of human science against mortality itself. For such people, nature is no longer seen as threateningly chaotic, but as something that has – at least for the most part – been satisfactorily brought to the heel of human ordering.

But on the other side of that optimistic face lies an anxiety that all might not be as it sometimes seems – that the so-called laws of nature are not laws *of* or *in* nature at all, but are, rather, laws that order-seeking humans have imposed *on* nature and that may be broken at nature's own whim. So that underneath that apparently orderly structure of natural law, still 'chaos lurks' – a chaos that implies a loss of all the order that we customarily take for granted. What holds together falls apart; the closed opens up; 'reality', after all, remains everywhere in question.

In that reversion to chaos, there are no longer any fixed points from which to take our bearings; and that is as much an existential as an intellectual issue. It impinges, that is, not only on the theoretical constructs of academics and intellectuals, but also much more widely on the ordinary everyday lives of people in practice. For just as 'reality' ceases to have much sense in a philosophical context in which the foundation of every judgement concerning our selves and the external world is open to question, so too at a more personal practical level we sense the loss of any markers – of any solidity, any security, that might reassure. Deprived of a secure sense of self and of the world outside us (including other people), we flounder again in a directionless and meaningless chaotic void. To revert to Pope once more:

> Lo! thy dread Empire, CHAOS! is restor'd;
> Light dies before thy uncreating word;
> Thy hand, great Anarch! lets the curtain fall,
> And universal Darkness buries All.[15]

Those words clearly resonate for us nearly three hundred years on, and the question here is whether, in the face of potentially all-embracing darkness in a restored (newly recognised) chaos, history might have some positive role to play.

5 Direction

> I sensed I would have to live a leaderless and difficult individual
> life, I would receive no directives from anybody, no orders and
> commands would any longer be issued to me, no pertinent ordi-
> nances would be there to consult – in brief, *a life never known*
> *before* lay before me.
>
> (Adolf Eichmann)[16]

With Germany's defeat and the end of the Second World War, Adolf
Eichmann's life lost any sense of purpose or direction. Hannah
Arendt has described how he had always been a great 'joiner': he
liked to be a member of a group – a club or gathering or brother-
hood, such as was provided not least by the 'élite' SS. Through his
membership of any group, he would be bound by certain rules; he
could take his place within an established hierarchy; he would be
told what to do – given a function and a purpose. So at his trial in
Jerusalem in 1962, Eichmann represented himself in his wartime
activities as an administrator of the Nazi 'final solution', as a mere
cog in a machine – a man whose function was prescribed, complete
with directives, orders, commands, and pertinent ordinances available for consultation. His life lay before him, as clearly defined and
directed as the railway tracks that led to Auschwitz.

Eichmann realised that, deprived of his wartime position (and
the security of that conferred identity), he faced 'a leaderless and
difficult individual life'; he was on the threshold of 'a life never
known before' – heading in a direction he no longer knew, nor
for what purpose. And in that existential predicament, I would
suggest, he resembled many who similarly now find themselves
alone, without traditional supports, in postmodernity. They too lack
the comfort of belonging to a coherent society or group in which
their own roles – their identities and functions and purposes – are
conveniently prescribed; they too lack directives and directions, and
face a future 'life never known before'.

Again, more general awareness of that predicament does not
imply that the predicament itself is anything new. In his biographical history of philosophy, Diogenes Laertius tells us that
Pyrrhonians – that sect of philosophers with whom postmodernists
are most closely associated – were variously called 'Seekers', as ever
seeking truth, 'Sceptics', as 'always looking for a solution and never
finding one', 'Doubters', who persisted in suspending judgement,

and (most pertinently for us here) 'Aporetics', as being in a state of 'aporia' or perplexity – uncertain as to what direction to take.[17]

'Aporia' – a term now used importantly to characterise postmodernity[18] – is a word that can relate (in its original Greek) to both places, where it indicates a difficulty of passing, and people, where it refers to doubt and hesitation resulting from a difficulty in dealing with something; so, putting those two usages together, 'aporia' is perhaps best translated as 'impasse'. When confronted by an impasse, we know we can't get through, and we are reduced to being at a loss as to how to proceed; and as a consequence we're often riddled with indecision and anxieties. It's that uncomfortable state, again, that seems for many to characterise contemporary life; and it seems that discomfort is being felt not only by 'intellectuals' but more generally. Anthony Giddens has written of how we increasingly find ourselves 'left with questions where once there appeared to be answers and ... it is not only philosophers who realise this. A *general awareness* of the phenomenon filters into anxieties which press in on *everyone*'.[19]

Those anxieties and that whole condition derive in part from finally (over a century later) taking on board some of Nietzsche's insights. In *The Gay Science*, he observes:

> I should think that today we are at least far from the ridiculous immodesty that would be involved in decreeing from our corner that perspectives are permitted only from this corner. Rather has the world become 'infinite' for us all over again, inasmuch as we cannot reject the possibility that *it may include infinite interpretations*.[20]

Needless to say, the 'ridiculous immodesty' of which he wrote lived on (and still in some quarters seemingly lives on); but at last, in our own time, there's increasing recognition that perspectives other than our own must be permitted, and that we do therefore – and not least in history – indeed face the prospect of a veritable infinity of (equally valid) interpretations, and hence an infinity of possible directions. There's no one single route through either history or life: everywhere, as Zygmunt Bauman has noted, we're confronted by ambivalence – by what's left over from (and so disrupts) the order that we've attempted to impose. The modernist project – with its assumed clarity of definition that outlawed am-biguity, and its rigid taxonomies that defied (and denied) classificatory aberrations – aspired to eliminate the final vestiges of chaos in an all-embracing order that guaranteed control; but the world (both natural and temporal, for science and for history respectively) always resisted the imposition of such tidiness, always evaded that final cleaning up and 'flushing out', always left traces of some residue of what just wouldn't fit. And it's that residue (or our consciousness of that residue) of the anomalous, the undecidable and unpredictable and uncontrollable – the residue, in Bauman's terminology, of ambivalence – with which we have to live in postmodernity.

That prospect is of more than merely intellectual concern: it has very practical implications for our everyday lives, inasmuch as, confronting 'infinite interpretations', we're forced to find some way through the resultant impasse and go on making such decisions and choices as enable life to continue. The increasing difficulty we're likely to experience in making those decisions and choices was presciently noted as long ago as 1970. Years before the advent of post-modernism itself, Alvin Toffler wrote of the psychological problems associated with a rapidly changing society – and it's interesting to note how his analysis and predictions correspond with those of Zygmunt Bauman and Anthony Giddens (which we've considered above). Toffler, then, coined the term 'future shock' to describe the stresses to which people must inevitably be exposed in a situation of constant and accelerating change, and he predicted a 'future-shocked society' which lacks any 'clear picture of where it wants to go'. As has now proved to be the case three decades later, people would, Toffler argued, be simultaneously surrounded by newness and deprived of those familiar psychological cues and signposts on which they've previously depended. They would thus be 'cut off from meaning', and so experience 'bewilderment and distress' – 'a panicky sense that events are slipping out of their control', and 'an inability to cope'.[21]

To those living now in the twenty-first century, that description sounds all too familiar; and it's instructive further to consider Toffler's assessment of the likely results of such a situation. Unable to cope with the number of decisions they must make, in a constantly shifting context of multiple choice and lack of authoritative guidance, people would, he believed, display symptoms of 'confusion, anxiety and hostility', and would seek refuge from their impasse in the four 'classical ways [recognised by information scientists] of coping with overload'. These he refers to as blocking-out, over-specialisation, reversion, and super-simplification. First, then, some people will try simply to block out the discontinuities by which they seem to be confronted: they will focus exclusively on continuities – those things that seem permanent or cyclically recurrent; they'll take comfort from the belief that, despite all the flux, 'history repeats itself' so that things after all remain essentially the same. Others will try to avoid complexity by burrowing into their own specialism, confining their own world (whether at work or home) by adopting a self-imposed tunnel-vision and avoiding the complication of anything that might intrude from outside its narrow field. Others again will revert to an earlier position: confronted by what seems to be out of their control, they will appeal to a 'politics of nostalgia' – desperately seeking to apply old solutions to new problems. And others, finally, will try to cope by reducing the complexities, by which they're terrified, into inevitably over-simplified terms. They'll fasten on to some ideology or intellectual fad – some 'over neat set of dogmas' – by which they can believe that everything can be tidily taken care of.

All four of these escape routes can be seen to be in use today, and all four have particular implications for historical study, and for what it is and might be for. In relation to our confrontation by an 'aporia' or impasse – whether seen in Alvin Toffler's terms of 'future shock' or those more generally of life in postmodernity – history's potentially positive (even 'therapeutic') role will be considered below. But let's quickly note here that the deliberate repression of some memories, the acceptance of a narrowing focus that inevitably derives from specialisation, the attempted reversion to some comforting heritage of an idealised past, and the voluntary submission and commitment to an over-arching ideology – all these responses to 'overload', all these defensive positions adopted in the face of 'aporia' or of 'a life never known before', have implications for the direction in which we wish to travel, and impact upon our notions of what history is for.

6 Problems of identity: selfhood and others

> Homo duplex, homo duplex!
>
> (Alphonse Daudet)

There's nothing new, or specifically postmodern, about problems of identity. Early in the twentieth century, the American philosopher William James specifically identified a condition that has subsequently been much studied by psychologists and is now (perhaps increasingly) recognised as widespread, if not ubiquitous – the condition of 'the divided self'. James quotes the nineteenth-century French writer Alphonse Daudet (whose words are quoted above), who had written interestingly of how, at the age of fourteen, he had become aware of his own double nature:

> The first time that I perceived that I was two was at the death of my brother Henri, when my father cried out so dramatically, 'He is dead, he is dead!' While my first self wept, my second self thought, 'How truly given was that cry, how fine it would be at the theatre'.[22]

That 'horrible duality', as Daudet goes on to call it, has probably been recognised in ourselves by most of us: even in the most tragic situations, another 'self' seems to look on at what we're experiencing; and the detachment that that implies can sometimes cause concern, and even feelings of guilt.

Such guilt has often been recorded in a religious context, when two competing selves are seen to do battle as forces of good and bad, spirituality and carnality. As an early Christian, St Paul lamented his own weakness – of how his better self was bettered by his worse, so that he did what he knew he shouldn't do and omitted to do what he knew that he should. In that same tradition, St Augustine confessed to his own guilt, when 'two wills within me, one old, one new, one the servant of the flesh, the other of the spirit, were in conflict and … tore my soul apart';[23] and recognition of such inner conflict between competing selves has been a frequent motif in religious writings through the ages.

But in secular postmodernity, it's more a matter of neither knowing who we are at all, nor even knowing what we would be if we could. There's no longer any final goal or ideal of what a human being should be – no universal model to which it is agreed we should aspire. So it's hardly surprising if no final winner among competing potentialities ever emerges, and lives become, in William James's words again, 'little more than a series of zig-zags, as now one tendency and now another gets the upper hand'. For James himself, there remained a 'normal' development – a 'straightening out and unifying of the inner self', an emergence from inner 'chaos' into 'a stable system of functions in right subordination'.[24] But such a view now, a century on, sounds curiously dated. For since James the problem of identity (of self-definition) has been exacerbated, not least by increased awareness of the complexities of our own psychological make-up.

That problematisation of 'self' has been illustrated by such visual artists as the American photographer Cindy Sherman, who has taken literally hundreds of photographs of herself since the 1970s, each representing, as it were, a different identity. By dressing herself in a variety of costumes, both historical and contemporary, by applying different make-up (including that of clowns), by adopting different physical positions in a variety of contexts, Sherman, far from revealing any particular identity or selfhood, actually (and intentionally) conceals it. Acting as both photographer and model, she deliberately ensures that not one of her representations of herself is 'really' *her*: she is not, she claims, aiming to produce self-portraits, or to reveal any essential 'truth' about herself, in the manner of some other portraitists; but rather she intentionally reveals the ultimately elusive, if not illusory, nature of self-hood. One looks in vain for some common denominator, some essential characteristic that will somehow unify the seemingly infinite variety of personae by which we are confronted; but we are left looking at a range of diverse, ambiguous, and sometimes seemingly contradictory images. Male or female, sixteenth-century or contemporary, aggressor or victim, duchess or prostitute – we're no longer quite sure. With Cindy Sherman, we're back with 'aporia' in relation to the self.

Our own confusion is exacerbated by our evident lack of criteria by which to assess 'normality' or 'rightness' in any functional hierarchy. As the Elizabethan poet Michael Drayton said of his own time, and no doubt would say of ours: 'Certainly there's scarce one found that now/ Knows what t'approve, or what to disallow.'[25] There's no external or acceptable authority to help us make our evaluations, and that is the case even in relation to those 'others', by reference to whom we define ourselves. 'We have,' wrote Coleridge, 'imprisoned our own conceptions by the lines which we have drawn, in order to exclude the conceptions of others';[26] and however much we may sometimes wish it, we seem incapable of formulating any conception of our selves without having some resort to others, whose conceptions we may deliberately exclude. It's only through our relationships with others that we define – and thereby no doubt, as Coleridge implies, circumscribe or even 'imprison' – our selves. For self-definition (like 'truth', as we have seen) necessarily involves *exclusions*: it's by excluding some 'other' that we differentiate our selves; it's by seeing the rest of the world as background that we foreground ourselves, and it's by cutting ourselves off from that background – seeing ourselves as separate entities – that we are enabled to constitute our own identities.

But instability pervades, not only the unresolved identities of Cindy Sherman, but even the physical 'other' of our surrounding environment, where often we can't any longer be quite sure of what it is – let alone of where (and who) we are. That's not just because everywhere increasingly looks the same, with one shopping-centre resembling any other, but because familiar markers disappear, or change their own identities, with increasing speed. Buildings themselves can carry markers of their previous incarnations, embedded relics of earlier times that can still be remembered: the tiles of stations on the London underground confusingly bear witness to place-names now (and long since) superseded. And yet more disconcertingly, architectural identities are totally transformed: in only half a lifetime, churches and railway stations are converted into dwellings; derelict industrial warehouses become trendy apartments; schools become offices; public libraries, bars; banks, bookshops; and that one time epitome of civic pride, London's County Hall, transmogrifies into an aquarium and fun-fair (Figure 5). All this constant upheaval of their external environment, and redefinition of their civic 'other', can only exacerbate the insecurity of the already insecure.

And the problem of identity can be seen, not only in the context of personal psychology, but also at the level of nationalities. Britain is a case in point, where political and social change over the last half-century has paralleled and confirmed contemporary intellectual developments. That is to say, there have been remarkable consistencies and overlaps between postmodernist theorising and the practicalities of 'real life' (as recognised even by men and women in the street). For if, as has been argued,[27] British national identity was forged in the eighteenth century and confirmed in the nineteenth, it seems that the latter half of the twentieth century has witnessed its disintegration and dissolution – leaving a nation in need of, and in search of, its nationhood (or some defined identity).

Thus, Winston Churchill's confidence, as late as 1952, that 'We [British] stand erect both as an island people and as the centre of a worldwide Commonwealth and Empire', now, some half-century on, stands as little more than some historical curiosity on a par with the patriotic proclamations of Shakespeare's Henry V. These may still evince nostalgia from the older generation, but they bear little relation to current actualities. The 'island people', who were once

Figure 5 Unstable identities: County Hall, London.

both naturally (and providentially) defended from external threats and also able to define themselves against those continental 'others', with their erratic politics and gastronomic oddities, have become (or are at least becoming) more or less assimilated into a cosmopolitanism against which the 'English' Channel provides little defence; and centrality, in relation to 'a worldwide Commonwealth and Empire' – a world-wide 'other', in contrast with which identity again could be confirmed – sounds as dated as the earth-centred universe of pre-Copernican astronomers.

Unable, then, to define themselves in relation to any alien (or, with periodic exceptions, any specific hostile) 'other', and themselves incorporating a huge diversity of cultural influences, the British (and especially perhaps the English, from whom the Scots and Welsh are now at least partially 'devolved') are now regularly diagnosed as suffering from a crisis of identity.[28] And in national, no less than in individual terms, that implies a loss of meaning and purpose and direction – and a very real need.

Even if, as individuals or nations, we manage to locate an 'other' by reference to which we may define ourselves, there is increasing uncertainty about how we should relate to it. For the attempted process of individuation leads us towards a potentially ambiguous relationship with the external world (including, for historians, its past). In terms of modernity, on the one hand, that attempt requires us to view that world (and past) as something quite separate, quite distinct from ourselves – and it's that very detachment from the 'other' that facilitates 'objective' study; it's our removal from its object that makes any 'knowledge' possible, and facilitates our adoption of the superior role of knowing (or at least appraising) subject. On the other hand, though, if we revert to an alternative perspective (and an alternative intellectual tradition), that isolation is precisely what precludes the possibility of knowledge: by cutting ourselves off from an object – whether another person, or anything else (including, once again, the past) – we remove our ability to *reach* it; and either way, our attainment of an 'other' by which to define ourselves seems threatened.

The two proposed (and mutually inconsistent) routes to knowledge are noted by Coleridge, who writes of the 'intuition of things which arises when we possess ourselves *as one with the whole* ... and that which presents itself when ... we think of ourselves *as separated beings*'; and D. H. Lawrence similarly identifies the two approaches as 'apartness' and 'togetherness': 'the two ways of knowing, for man, are knowing in terms of apartness, which is mental, rational, scientific, and knowing in terms of togetherness, which is religious and poetic.'[29]

In historical study, this translates into two very different approaches – the validity of each depending on what history is thought to be *for*. The 'other' in the case of history is simply presupposed: it's that other time and country of the past. But historians are still left with the question of how to define themselves in relation to that past (of how to resolve the problem of identity) – of whether (in the amateur, 'feminine' tradition alluded to in Chapter 4) to see themselves 'as one with the whole', aspiring to empathetic 'togetherness' with the object of their study, or (as a 'scientific' professional) to insist on 'apartness' and remaining 'as separated beings'.

The nature of their relationship (and thence their selfhood) must depend on what they (what *we*) want – and need – to get out of it; and it's time to summarise some of those needs that we've identified in postmodernity.

7   Conclusion

It's not for nothing that one of the most reproduced and best-known paintings of our time is the Norwegian Edvard Munch's

terrifying representation of *The Scream*, painted in 1893 (Figure 6).
Two possible sources for the painting have been identified: first,
the dramatist Henrik Ibsen's portrayal of the Roman emperor
Julian as suffering from a vision of himself alone on a vast, motion-
less ocean; and second, the philosopher Søren Kierkegaard's earlier
description of anxiety as a 'dizziness resulting from freedom' – a
dizziness akin, perhaps, to the disorientation felt in the face of a
surfeit of choice today, in postmodernity. Like us, confronted in the
supermarket by too many types of biscuit, Munch's screaming
figure is immobilised – unable to go on along the road on which
we see his friends proceeding calmly. Their road, it has been
noticed, has been painted in terms of conventional perspective,
receding from foreground to background as we would expect. But
the rest of the landscape is not confined in that way: it 'swirls irra-
tionally ... free from the rules of conventional picture-making',
and suggests a landscape in which anything might happen, a landscape in which we might well feel dizzy and fearful – and ready to
scream.[30]

The landscape of modernity – its irrational swirling and ex-
centric disorder – can't itself be changed: once the innocence of
Adam and Eve in their Garden of Eden has been forfeited, it cannot
be restored. So we have to come to terms with that impossibility,
and contrive to live in our new landscape, and find our own way
through it. What's needed is a compass, something to indicate
direction through the chaos on a route that has some meaning for
us – that gives some sense of purpose, and that conveys some sense
of self-identity.

These are not new requirements, specific to those privileged (or
condemned) to live in postmodernity: they're of the very essence of
what it is to be a human being. But what's new, as we've seen, is a
much more widespread recognition of the inadequacy of past
answers – the answers of such traditional bestowers of direction
and meaning as religion, patriotic nationalism, and overall belief in
progress. It's the democratised (if not yet universalised) self-reflexive
recognition of (now unanswered) needs – a self-awareness about loss
and lack – that characterises life today.

The question, then, becomes whether history can help in the
postmodern project of somehow alleviating the postmodern
condition. Can it contribute to an understanding of our own self-
consciousness, of our own precarious position in outdated
intellectual superstructures that lack foundations, of the inevitable

Figure 6 Emblem of postmodernity? Edvard Munch, *The Scream*, 1893.

uncertainties and ambiguities that characterise our relationship with those 'others', whether nature, or the past, or other people, that constitute the external world? Can it address and illuminate problems of language, with all their implications for reference, representation, and communication? Can history, in short, assume a therapeutic function for those who might otherwise resort to screaming?

I want to go on to suggest in the following chapters that it can — and that, at its best, it does so already. That's not to say that in some simple way all our needs can be answered or satisfied by some sort of 'therapeutic' historical study, but it is to suggest that those recognised needs may provide a convenient point from which to consider what, in postmodernity, history might be for.

Chapter 6

History in postmodernity

Future prospects

I   Introduction

> What is peculiar to our own age is the abandonment of the idea
> that history *could* be truthfully written.
>
> (George Orwell)[1]

Orwell was writing decades ago, but again it has taken time for the
rest of us to catch up, or to grasp his point in the quotation above.
That point now rings true in postmodernity, for it has taken postmodernism finally to make clear that any talk of historical 'truth', as
implying some exact correspondence between historical narratives
and the past events that they purport to describe, is meaningless –
that any claims to such absolute historical truth are as foundationless
as pre-Nietzschean claims to uniquely privileged perspectives.
Nietzsche's insistence on the need to take account of alternative
perspectives already implies the conclusion drawn by Orwell – that
no history or historical truth can be claimed as uniquely privileged;
so that the very idea of any one history being 'truthfully written' (in
the sense of it accurately mirroring 'the past') has to be abandoned.

Historians themselves (or some of them) have long since been
aware of the theoretical complexities inherent in their subject – of the
subjectivity involved in assigning causal connections, for example,
and the inadequacy and contingent nature of their own analytic tools.
In Christopher Hill's words: 'wisdom lies, I think, in recognising the
complicated interconnexions [in historical events] and not allowing
ourselves to be unduly influenced by the categories of analysis which
we *invent for our own convenience*.'[2] But as previously indicated, it's the
changed understanding of what we mean by 'truth' that is crucial in
this context. In modernist terms, historical truth, like scientific truth,

consisted of a correspondence between one's representations of the past (or in the case of science, one's representation of nature) and some supposed objectively existing external reality – the past as it had been (or nature as it simply is). The unproblematised belief both in 'the past' as an identifiable and describable entity, and in our ultimate ability to apprehend and re-present that past, made possible the idea that 'history could be truthfully written'. However difficult, that remained for historians as a meaningful aspiration and objective, and went in some cases with a fair degree of professional confidence (not to say, dogmatism): as Richard Evans writes of that twentieth-century disciplinary role-model Geoffrey Elton, 'there were indeed few things about which he had doubts'.[3]

The simple model assumed by the more bumptious empiricists has, of course, been challenged periodically from antiquity on; but its total abandonment, as Orwell notes, is 'peculiar to our own age' – or to the twentieth century when he was writing, and the early twenty-first when we are reading. That abandonment was already implied in the thought of the American philosopher John Dewey (1859–1952), who rejected the long-lived (and admittedly in many ways attractive) idealist notion of an absolute truth, and proposed instead a more pragmatic approach whereby truth becomes identifiable with what works – that is, with what is satisfactory and helpful within a given context. The very idea of a perfect correspondence between some external entity 'in itself' (whether that entity is nature or the past) and our representations of it is, in his terms, meaningless (and anyway unhelpful): its complexity (whatever it is) is too great to be subsumed within any single definition; and, even if we aspire to do so, we can never in practice detach our selves, with our own subjectivities and intellectual and perceptual limitations, so as to be able to claim that much vaunted (by scientists and historians again) 'objectivity'.

So rather than engage in some futile (and ultimately useless) quest (as for some Holy Grail), why not redefine 'truth' in such a way that, instead of being just an abstract and theoretical concept, it can actually become of some practical use? Instead of trying endlessly to approximate to some assumed external reality, why not call 'true' (as Richard Rorty summarises) 'whatever belief results from a free and open encounter of opinions?'[4] That way, there's no need to refer to any problematic essence or externality; and truth – and we ourselves as human beings – can be geared instead to a future that we want to achieve. The old theoretical 'quest for certainty' is replaced by a new practical *hope* for a better future: the true becomes what it was for William James – that is, 'what would be better for us to believe'; or as Dewey himself writes, 'The time has arrived for a pragmatism which shall be emphatically idealistic, proclaiming the essential connection of intelligence with the unachieved future'.[5]

A number of words in that sentence of Dewey might seem to indicate that what he's saying is totally irrelevant to history. 'Idealism', for one, has long been out of fashion amongst intellectuals generally, and runs counter to the prime concern of historians in particular, whose business is to focus on what actually (really/in fact) went on. And the proposed connection of their intelligence 'with the unachieved future' runs counter to their whole agenda: historians' disciplinary rules apply to what *has been* achieved and, with their focus on the *past*, preclude consideration of any hypothetical as yet unachieved *future*. But if history, as a typically modernist truth-seeking activity, is no longer feasible, if we're forced with Orwell to abandon the very idea that history could ever, in principle, be 'truth-fully' written, then perhaps it's worth considering the subject anew, with Dewey's conception of truth and Dewey's idealistic agenda in mind, where, as he proposes, 'Growth is the only moral end'.[6]

There are, of course, very real dangers along the way – and not least the apparent implication that, once the traditional conception of truth has been abandoned, history can be anything at all that we want it to be. Orwell himself was well aware of the potentially sinister implications of that position – realising, as he puts it, that it could lead to 'a nightmare world in which the Leader, or some ruling clique, controls not only the future but the past'; and we've already seen in Chapter 4 how stories of the past can indeed be (and have often been) moulded to suit ideological purposes. So we have to clarify that history cannot be just *anything*: the public past is not, any more than our personal minds, a 'tabula rasa' – a blank sheet on which we can make or unmake any impressions as we feel inclined. Something happened: we stole a car; the events that constitute the Holocaust did occur – and there is evidence, oral and documentary, to substantiate (or repudiate) claims that historians might make about our private misdemeanours and more public happenings.

But, to take the easier personal example, it's not particularly illumi-nating, historically speaking, to know simply that I stole a car: what would be more interesting would be to offer some explanation for that anomalous behaviour – to construct some sort of story in which that theft made sense, where I continued to appear as a reasonably coherent character, and the past seemed to re-acquire some meaning. That sort of story might have some use in relation to the future – my future and that of potentially vulnerable car-owners. And even in that very simple example, the point, surely, is that there's no one story that will tell it all – no single standpoint from which a definitive history can be 'truthfully written'. One might refer (or aspire to refer) to my whole psychological make-up (the genetic and environmental factors that might have influenced my action); and an attempted 'contextualisation' of the episode would reveal another infinity of potentially relevant considerations (such as the breakdown of my own car, my desperate need to get to a hospital with my sick child, the absence of taxis and any public transport). Different interpretations of my action would result from the inclusion of different factors in that history; and just as in a court of law, evidence would be weighed, witnesses interrogated, probabilities considered, and tentative conclusions drawn. It's not some hypothetical 'essence' of a supposedly 'truthful' past that matters, but rather what we do with it – how we 'emplot' it (making our story tragic or comic or satiric, or whatever); and that depends on what it's *for*.

If it's what we do with the past that matters, and if what we do with it depends on what it's for, how does that leave us in relation to the needs identified in Chapter 5? What we considered there were some losses suffered in the context of postmodernity – losses to do with centres and certainties, with order and direction, with identity and selfhood. These are all interconnected, and we'll consider in the following sections how a refigured history might play a therapeutic role in respect of what, though perceived in a modernist perspective as 'losses' (as, to return to Bauman, a conscious discarding in postmodernity of what modernity 'was once unconsciously doing'), might be more positively construed as gains.[7]

2 Closure and openness

> History can be seen ... as the forgetting of the complexity of possible closure.
>
> (Hilary Lawson)[8]

Historians have generally advocated 'closure' – which is to say that they have preferred an account that tidies up some aspect of the past, that seemingly solves some problem of causation or explanation, that aspires to being 'definitive', or something that will stand the test of time and the assaults of their colleagues. Geoffrey Elton wrote of how historical 'work must be carried out *in a cage* set by certain *inescapable* conditions', and it 'must concentrate on one thing' – the search for truth 'within the confines of its particular province'. Arthur Marwick more recently has reiterated his insistence that *'ambiguity is always to be avoided* in historical writing', and has claimed, remarkably, that his own hard work has resulted in 'prose which *expresses precisely* what one wants to say'.[9] In such respects Elton and Marwick, as representatives of proper professional history, are only following their scientific models. For scientists are the great schematisers: they are the makers of categories, the insistent classifiers, the authors of order. In its 'purest' form, science aspires to the condition of mathematics – a subject and a method where ambiguity, ambivalence, inconsistency, and shades of grey are outlawed (denied by the rules of the game), and where pristine clarity is believed to indicate arrival at what is effec-tively a higher order of 'reality', a reflection (as we've seen in the case of Stephen Hawking) of the very mind of God.

That mathematically orientated scientific model has served its users well. If we are going to play a game, we do need rules, and science itself – and the particular way of viewing nature implied by science – has proved in many ways a winner. Most importantly for most, it has facilitated humans' greater control of the natural world – has provided the knowledge which has in turn, as its earliest advocates envisaged, conferred enormous power. Few of us, as it has often been observed, would wish to rely on the dental treat-ments of a hundred (or even fifty) years ago; and few of us are prepared to forgo the numerous technologically based benefits that science has made possible. But that very success of science – the obvious mat-erial progress that it has brought – has sometimes resulted in an unwillingness to consider alternative goals, with alternative routes; and as persistent followers of intellectual fashion, historians themselves may have over-emphasised the supposed bene-fits and virtues of what they have taken to be a 'scientific' approach.

It may, at least, be time to call time on the game of history as it has been played for the last hundred years – be time for historians to consider embracing alternative goals, via no doubt alternative routes? And one possibility might be derived from Hilary Lawson's recent discussion of 'closure'. His main point is that, in order to be effective at our chosen game, we all – and that includes both scien-tists and historians – have to operate within 'closed' systems of rules and beliefs, but that there is nonetheless virtue in retaining an openness to alternative possibilities – openness to that 'complexity of possible closure' which, as he suggests in the quotation above, tends (inevitably, perhaps, within the constraints of traditional procedures) to get forgotten.

Lawson's main idea may best be summarised by using his own example, where we are invited to consider a page on which is inscribed a random pattern of dots. When asked to describe what we see, we scan the dots and search for a pattern in them that is not random; and we succeed in seeing, perhaps, the image of a face. Once we've identified that face, all the dots assume some function in relation to it – some serving as the outline of the nose, others as the mouth, and others fading into an inconsequential background. We have succeeded in making sense of what's in front of us, by closing down the possibility of other interpretations and focusing on our own; we have, in Lawson's terminology, achieved 'closure'. And no doubt we feel all the better for that: it's hard to confront with equanimity what appears to be just a meaningless jumble of 'data'. But the corollary – the price of our satisfaction – is, of course, the exclusion of a host of other possibilities: those dots might have been interpreted in innumerable other ways, and we are no longer open to them; to make sense of them, we have had to forget their underlying complexity.

The question is, then, how we might retain our openness, and that ability (to remain open) is more usually associated, not with science or scientific history, but with art. Indeed, the very goal of art, as identified by Lawson, is to challenge 'closure' – to challenge our habitual modes of perception and our confinement within existing categories. Works of art, he suggests, admittedly have to offer some prospect of closure, if only to attract our interest. But they need then, in order to retain our interest, to go on to deny its possibility: they need to keep us guessing – to embrace uncertainty and ambiguity. Those artists of whom he obviously approves, then, 'serve to unsettle our habitual closures and offer an alternative not as a replacement but as a means of looking out from our current closures and escaping their grip'.[10] Their images are not intended to be 'definitive' – to be clearly defined, or the last word (or brushmark) on their subjects; they are not meant to be complete, or provide us with any conclusive certainty. On the contrary, their intention is to induce doubt and to unsettle, to highlight ambiguity and encourage further questioning; to indicate that no final solution to the problem of representation is ever possible.

It is, for example, the essential ambiguity in the smile of Leonardo da Vinci's *Mona Lisa*, achieved by an indefiniteness and blurring of lines in the face's representation, that accounts for the enduring popularity of that image. We are confronted by something – by someone – that we can never finally interpret and assess; we are never quite sure what the girl is thinking or how we should react to her. As soon as we think we've grasped her, she moves on once more and eludes us; and, as in real life with real people, it's her ambiguity (denying us the achievement of any final closure) that keeps us awake and interested, intrigued and determined to continue with our quest for understanding.

What Leonardo and other great painters teach is that the possibility of any perfect representation is forever deferred. The French impressionist Cézanne, who painted many studies of the 'same' scene (the same mountain or haystack or cathedral) explained that 'nature reveals herself to me in many complex ways'.[11] He realised that 'just by leaning a little to the right and then a little to the left', he would be confronted by a totally different picture of the scene before him, so that he could work away for months at the same subject. There was, of course, nothing to indicate what was the 'right' point from which to view the scene; so that, as Andrew Graham-Dixon has explained,

> he destabilized the traditional single viewpoint ... by giving the forms in his pictures an unsteady or doubled outline, as if to combine both views of what a person might indeed see if they moved their head 'a little to the right and then a little to the left'.[12]

He could never hope (or fear) to reach any final and definitive depiction of what lay before his eyes. No two of his versions of any subject are ever the same – far from it – and who is to say that one is more 'true' or 'faithful to reality' than any other? No artist, surely, would ever claim to have presented the last word, or the perfect representation, of any matter; nor, of course, would any scientist or historian be so presumptuous as to do so. But the point here (that we might derive from Lawson) is that historians might align themselves with artists, in *deliberately* avoiding final closure – in deliberately leaving blurred lines (as in Leonardo's use of 'sfumato') and provoking further thought about alternative interpretations; so that, for instance, instead of presenting their work in the form of a water-tight argument, concluding with the triumphant QED (I've proved what I set out to demonstrate) of the ideal geometer, they might instead end with a question-mark?

As well as in the visual arts, that sort of questioning has been deliberately provoked in and by forms of postmodernist literature. The genre of so-called 'historiographic metafiction', for example, deliberately mixes 'fact' and 'fiction' – placing 'real' historical people in obviously anachronistic contexts, thus enabling them to meet others whom they could never have actually encountered; or they make claims for historical influence that are so preposterous as to subvert the very idea of conventional causation. Salman Rushdie's character Saleem Sinai, in *Midnight's Children*, makes the impossible claim that he was 'directly responsible for triggering off the violence which ended with the partition of the state of Bombay'; and, in a further challenge to conventional historiography, he affects to be so unconcerned about his own mis-dating of the assassination of Mahatma Gandhi, that he can simply shrug off the fact that 'in my India, Gandhi will continue to die at the wrong time'.[13]

That use (or, as some might argue, abuse) of actual historical events, linked with an explicit repudiation of conventional disciplinary procedures concerning how properly to handle and 'place' such events, may well lead the reader to question the whole professional apparatus that is normally just taken for granted. Historiographic metafiction, as Brenda Marshall writes, 'openly fictionalises its own given history, and in the process subverts the concept of *innocent* historiography'. As Salman Rushdie's character concludes:

> I have been only the humblest of jugglers-with-facts ... in a country where the truth is what it is instructed to be, reality quite literally ceases to exist, so that everything becomes possible except what we are told is the case.[14]

Another country where, with juggled facts, 'truth' and 'reality' become similarly elusive, is the Mexican writer Carlos Fuentes' *Terra Nostra*, which presents an *alternative* history of Spain and Spanish America. Again, 'real' historical figures such as Philip II of Spain and Elizabeth I of England are introduced, but in a revised and anachronistic context – so that, for instance, Philip actually marries the Virgin Queen (of conventional historiography), and the discovery of the New World, having been deferred by a century, provokes political and economic consequences that unfold in days rather than decades. Once more, lines are left blurred, with disciplinary methods and chronologies deliberately overturned, and a narrative proposed in which a supposed account of 'what *actually happened*' is replaced by 'the memory of what *could have been but was not*'.[15]

Such alternatives are projected in the so-called 'Theatre of Memory' of Valerio Camillo. There, we are advised, values prevail that are the very opposite of those to which we are accustomed; so that, for example, contrary to 'normal' belief, 'the world is *imperfect* when we believe there is *nothing lacking* in it; the world is *perfect* when we know that *something will always be missing* from it'. So the audience is presented with what has been missed – with 'counterfactuals', the 'memory' of what might have happened but never actually did: the notoriously excitable Cicero exhibits 'patient silence' in the face of Catiline's conspiracy which in fact he violently attacked; Caesar's wife Calpurnia convinces him not to attend the senate on the fateful Ides of March (when in fact he was assassinated); the Greek army at Salamis (instead of their great victory) suffers defeat; Jesus Christ is born as a girl, and is later pardoned by Pontius Pilate; Socrates declines to drink hemlock; and Noah's ark sinks. These (counterfactual) images 'bring together all the *possibilities* of the past', and so 'represent all the *opportunities* of the future; for knowing what was *not*, we shall know what *demands to be*'. After all, it's precisely because we are not aware of such alternative possibilities that 'history repeats itself'.[16]

However bizarre they may seem within our own disciplinary frameworks, such alternative histories of *what might have been* may serve to open our eyes to the constraints and limitations of our own (premature?) closures; and, with its importance for envisaging an alternative (and maybe better) future, a *questioning* of past closures becomes a central part of what history in postmodernity might be for.

3 Self, narrativity, and meaning: personal and national identities

> History is the 'Know Thyself' of humanity – the self-consciousness of mankind.
>
> (Johann Droysen)[17]

As we were considering in the previous chapter, whether in personal or national terms, there's nothing new about ontological insecurity – about being anxious about who or what we think we are, about being insecure in our identities. But that malaise – if malaise it is – has become exacerbated, or more widely experienced and admitted, in our own time. The old supports have broken down: nationalism and other ideologies, religious certainties, stable social classes and hierarchies – all those aids to personal definition – have evaporated; so that as one contemporary social theorist concludes, 'The self in modern society is frail, brittle, fractured, fragmented'[18] – in need of a bit of supportive therapy, in fact. And that diagnosis for individual selfhood is replicated at a national level, where the issue of identity, or nationhood, in our cosmopolitan 'global village' is a recurring theme in contemporary politics.

At both personal and political levels, there is a perceived need to get some sort of grip on selfhood – to assert an identity, a set of values for ourselves; and in order to do that, some meaningful narrative in which to locate ourselves seems needful – in other words a history that leads to where we are (or where we want to be), confirming and validating, and reassuring. For the deracinated, it seems, do come to feel a need for roots; all but the deeply planted are liable to be blown away in the storms of uncertainty. 'It's not,' as one of James Hamilton-Paterson's characters explains, 'that I so love the past I can't bring myself to leave it. It simply gave me all the bearings by which I know I'm me'.[19] So while youth and novelty may officially be all the cry, what's privately sought is something older to hang on to – preferably something that's deeply and firmly embedded in the past. We need the sort of history implied in the quotation from Johann Droysen above – a history that will enable us to know our selves.

So it seems – and especially perhaps as we become increasingly aware of the reality of our own mortality – that we feel some need to make contact with those who have died before us. Death itself is something from which humans in modernity (unlike, it seems, the Middle Ages) have tried to distance themselves, and in the twenty-first century we banish death so far as possible from polite society, trying to forget it. But when forced to recognise that we too will soon be past, we may be more inclined to ascribe a value to that past, and assert (now from personal self-interest) that some consideration and care is due to that past, from the present: we must do today as we hope to be done by tomorrow, and recall Jules Michelet's reminder (noted earlier) of memory's demand 'that we care for it'.[20]

History is thus revealed again as having a therapeutic function, in that it's taken to respond to everyone's demands to have their memories taken care of. And that can be the case at both personal and public levels. For as Michelet's own recent biographer, Arthur Mitzman, records of him: 'He recalled Caesar's dream of a weeping, beseeching army of the dead, and how, when waking [he] ... wrote down the names of two lost cities, Corinth and Carthage, and rebuilt them.' And for him, again significantly, that rebuilding of (public) cities, at the instigation of the pleading dead, was comparable to (personal) resuscitation by 'the historian, who also resurrected the dead'.[21]

Such resurrections involve huge responsibilities: the giving of renewed life is no less weighty a matter than its taking. For in each case selections have to be made – choices of those deemed worthy and worthless. And of course preferences are liable to change: we now seek to resurrect some dead who had previously been long ignored, or deliberately turned down as unworthy of our life-giving attention – the un-heroic, ordinary men and women (with whom we may identify more readily?), the minorities and the subjugated (to whom we may wish to make belated reparation?). So it's hardly surprising that our new excavations of the past have unearthed some worm-filled cans, from which unsettling thoughts may slither their way into our own consciousness. For whenever we look back on (or from) an alternative perspective (a perspective new to us), we are liable to be presented with (have imposed upon our present consciousness) some people and events we've previously, either deliberately or inadvertently, neglected. And as these lurch to life again, their new-found presences can prove disconcerting (literally disconcerting, or disruptive of our harmonies) – and threatening not least to our own conceptions of our selves.

So Raimond Gaita has written of the Australian Aborigines who, he insists, deserve some form of reparation and apology, some recognition of the historic wrongs they suffered at the hands of newcomers who failed to recognise or appreciate their rights – their entitlement to land and to the preservation of their ethnic identity or, in brief, their entitlement to being treated as humans like ourselves. Their ways of holding land and using it, and their actual ways of life, may have been quite different from those of the incoming Europeans, but they were (as we now newly see) no less valid; so that the conveniently adopted assumption that they didn't exist – that the land was uninhabited – is, when challenged, bound to provoke an historically induced shame that requires expiation. So too does the revelation that, throughout the twentieth century right up to the 1960s, children were forcibly removed from their families and fostered elsewhere, in an attempt to assimilate indigenous peoples with the white population, and thereby effectively eliminate their whole culture. The official report on that policy, *Bringing Them Home*, concluded *inter alia* that 'the predominant aim of Indigenous child removals was the absorption or assimilation of the children into the wider, non-Indigenous, community so that their unique cultural values and ethnic identities would disappear'; and that, as Gaita argues, is a policy that qualifies as a form of genocide.[22]

Pasts both personal and public, then, are unlikely to be thoroughly investigated without discomfort – without some consequent feelings of guilt, where we ourselves feel personally responsible for actions taken even before our own lifetime. For our identity, again, can't easily be confined within chronological boundaries: it necessarily derives from earlier generations, and our genetic and cultural inheritance doesn't stop at the limits of our own remembrance. Looking back far enough, there are almost bound to be skeletal remnants in our ancestral cupboards – aspects of our identities that we'd rather be without.

So the question becomes what to do with such unwelcome resurrections. One answer is suggested by the Australian Prime Minister, John Howard. Confronted by spectres from his national past, and though criticised by others for so doing, he offered a personal apology to the Aborigines. In another national context, Germans have reacted variously to the historical resurrection of their Nazi past: some have refused to face it; and the inability of others to cope with it has been manifested in their parallel inability to write creatively any longer in the German language.[23] Elsewhere, and yet more recently, South Africans have sought to come to terms with their past in a formal quest for truth and reconciliation (reconciliation – a new getting together); and more generally it seems that some repudiate their past, others embrace it with pride, while yet others feel shame. But all are compelled to make some response to it: it won't just go away. And the task of the therapist (or therapeutically inclined historian) is, in the light (or the darkness) of that past, to facilitate a good life in the future.

That is precisely why we need to sort out what we believe a good life actually is, for it's only after having resolved that question (however provisionally) that we'll know what characters and events from the past we need to recruit to enable us to get there – or at least to head in the right direction in order to achieve our goal. Barry Smart has asserted what is in a sense obvious but does tend to be forgotten, that we do need to be able 'to differentiate between acceptable and unacceptable practices and positions, the appropriate and the inappropriate'; and we'd really like some answers (however provisional, again, and conditional) to some fundamental questions.[24] So one of history's (therapeutic) functions might become to provide us with the confirmations that we need for some provisional establishment of our own selves. No more than any building can the human being be constructed on nothing: without foundations, we collapse – not immediately perhaps, but when put under pressure. So in Carolyn Steedman's words:

> In the project of finding an identity through the processes of historical identification, the past is searched for something (someone, some group, some series of events) that confirms the searcher in his or her sense of self, confirms them as they want to be, and feel in some measure that they already are.[25]

That's not to imply that our identity is just *given* once and for all: in Anthony Giddens' words, it's 'something that has to be routinely created and sustained in the reflexive activities of the individual'.[26] It's an ongoing *process*, in other words, but a process in which we need the help of history – a history that provides us with some narrative. That narrative, again, is not something fixed (as some traditional historians might have wished) but is itself constantly revised and renewed, as we continue to respond to and adapt to changing circumstances; it is, in other words, itself an ongoing *process*. And our autonomy as individuals depends on our ability to continue self-consciously making those adaptations and those revisions to the story of the past that underpins us. That's what makes us free.[27]

Self-conscious acceptance of the endlessness of that process, though, might have further implications – implications both for our sense of personal identity and for our arguments concerning history's therapeutic role. For Foucault has suggested another way in which history's 'task is to become a *curative* science'. What may be required, he suggests, is something that, far from stabilising our identities, might actually do the reverse, unsettling and disrupting them; and in that case, history should go against the grain of convention. Whereas it has traditionally been expected to reveal the roots of an identity – whether for individuals or societies – history's function might be instead to renounce such confirmation as overly simplistic, and to expose a much less coherent pattern in the past, uncovering, as Foucault suggests, 'a complex system of distinct and multiple elements, unable to be mastered by the powers of synthesis'. That gives a new purpose to history: 'not to discover the roots of our identity but to commit itself to its dissipation'. It's of our much vaunted settledness and self-assurance that history may provide the cure in postmodernity.[28]

Whatever past we choose for resurrection, and for whatever motives, history's particularly important function now, in relation to our personal and public selves, derives from its ability to provide that 'other', without which self-definition seems not possible. As we lose those *geographical* and racial 'others' of whom we previously made use (those alien 'foreigners' across the Channel or the ocean, those slaves and primitive 'colonials', by whom we measured our own superiority), we may need now to seek *chronological* 'others' – others in the past, other past people and values, in contrast with whom and with which we can continue to define our selves. And in that case, we need history to provide us with models, not so much to emulate as to repudiate – models in *contrast* with which we can see what we are and should be. That is one way that history can still enable humanity to know itself and make itself – and contribute, as Droysen required, to 'the self-consciousness of mankind'. That is the way that history, again, may feed our hopes.

It's not, though, only contrasts with the 'other' of which we need to take account: somehow authentic 'engagement' with that other is required; and that may require in turn an openness on the historian's part which goes against some grains. It's easy enough to accept evidence and to believe witnesses from the past that confirm our beliefs and expectations, consolidate our definitions of what's 'obvious' or 'common sense' (or what we lazily assume that *any* 'reasonable' person, like ourselves, would naturally accept – or simply accept as 'natural'). The challenge comes in promoting change – or hope for something better in the future; for that requires, as Kelly Oliver has insisted in a recent paper,[29] 'a vigilance, an insomnia, that refuses to sleep the dogmatic slumber of historical facts inhabiting a determinant world where the past has already caused the future and the future is just like the past'. It requires a rethinking of the past and of what would have been possible in that past; for by opening up such possibilities for *then*, we make them possibilities for *now* – for us now in the present. And we can then extrapolate and show how apparent impossibilities in our own present can become practical possibilities for the future. We open up the possibility of alternatives – we give cause for hope – 'by reading the conditions of the possibility of that future into the past'; and history thus becomes, once more, a path to a more hopeful future. That's an important part of what it might be *for*.

Related to that important potential is another contribution that history can make, in relation to the language that we use, and the linguistic restraints imposed on the construction of our selves. As Nikolas Rose has clarified, 'we can experience ourselves as certain types of creatures only because we do so under a certain description': our identities, in other words, or the ways that we define ourselves, are necessarily constrained by the words (and so the concepts) that are available (or not available) to us at any given time; our nature – human nature – is itself contingent, an *historical* (and historicisable) phenomenon. Thus, for example, we in the twenty-first century rely heavily on such newly formulated (but now seemingly ubiquitous) psychological categories and concepts as 'winner', 'survivor', 'victim', 'trauma', and 'stress': it is from that sort of psychologically orientated vocabulary that we derive our own characteristics, and make our own self-identifying assertions about our selves. And those terms are themselves not static, but have their own origins and developments, as well as their own validating contextualisations; their 'truth', to be a truth, needs some authority – and the basis of that (or any other claimed) authority is properly the subject of *historical* investigation and analysis. 'What humans are – perhaps better, what human beings are capable of, what we can do – is variable, *historical*, situational – not an originary "being" but a mobile "becoming".'[30] History, then, as Droysen saw, becomes again a central means of promoting 'the self-consciousness of mankind'.

For it's to do with what our hopes are for the future – with what, being the sort of person we construct, we see as our own telos or end. Neither our personal nor our national identities are prefigured in such a way as to define what it is that we want to be (or want to hope for) in the future: our futures, rather, are for us (within limits, of course, but to a great extent) to determine. The whole modernist goal of a stable personal and public identity, for all its comforting securities, has been replaced by such recognition of diversity – such openness to difference – as to require that personal and public histories be subject to constant modification, as aspirations change. Our memories and forgettings will depend upon the relationships we wish to have with those 'others' who, as we now see, constitute not something separate and apart, but actually another aspect of our selves. And the moral choice is to do with which parts of our selves we wish to identify, and therefore wish to have incorporated in our histories.

4 Historic moments and empowerment: making choices

> At the heart of their [i.e. postmodernists'] vision lies the rejection of authority, including the authority of circumstance – often known as reality or necessity.
>
> (Elizabeth Fox-Genovese)[31]

A pragmatic acceptance of 'reality' can sound like a virtue: it makes good sense, after all, to take things as they are (rather than as we would wish them to be); there's no point in fantasising about hypotheticals. As an historian himself, Geoffrey Elton was in a good position to note how sensible – how adult – historians were in that respect, 'willing to accept life on earth with all its imperfections'.[32] And the quotation above suggests that Elizabeth Fox-Genovese agrees with him: there is obviously an implied criticism of postmodernists' alleged 'rejection of ... reality or necessity'.

But my response (whether 'postmodernist' or whatever) to what she claims as postmodernism's central vision is: 'You bet!' For what 'authority' determines 'circumstance', or 'reality', or 'necessity'? These things are not natural, in the sense of being given in nature: they're what we make of them. It's how we respond to circumstance – whatever lies around us – that's important, and that defines what, for us, 'reality' is. As John Dewey puts it, '"reality" is a term of value or choice'.[33] Admittedly some things constrain us: responses to illness may and do affect the outcome of illness, but death is ultimately unavoidable. But as a principle, it's surely defeatist rather than 'adult' simply to accept what confronts us as 'necessity'. It's also profoundly conformist and conservative, which are other supposed virtues often associated with historians, but which are vices in the context of aspiring to a better future.

They are vices, too, in the context of seeing a possible function for history as actually 'therapeutic'. For the very notion of therapy implies that something could get better: rather than leaving everything as it is – as it's currently presented to us – there's an assumption, a belief, a confidence even, and certainly a hope, that things could be better, that we could become better people, that our world could improve. And that more optimistic approach comes from a realisation that we *do have a choice* about our direction – a *choice* of the historical narrative in which we locate ourselves. Life itself, after all, as Oscar Wilde noted 'is terribly deficient in form':[34] the imposition on it of some form is up to us – it's our responsibility and the outcome of our choice. And our realisation that that is indeed the case – that, yes, the choice is ours and, yes, we're justified in having hope – itself derives from looking at the course of history (at how change has been effected) in the past. As Nikolas Rose has said: 'Human beings must *interpret* their past, and *dream* their future, as outcomes of personal *choices* made or choices still to make.' He goes on immediately to clarify that those choices are necessarily made 'within a narrow range of possibilities whose restrictions are hard to discern'; and they are hard to discern because they actually 'form the horizon of what is thinkable'. And it thus becomes the horizon of what is *thinkable* that needs to be extended; and our understanding that it can indeed be extended (that it's not natural but contingent and so changeable) is precisely what can be encouraged by a therapeutically inclined history. For such history, as Rose goes on to suggest, 'is one that helps us think about the nature and limits of our present, about the conditions under which that which we take for *truth and reality* has been established'.[35]

Looking back, then, it may be possible to construct numberless persuasive accounts of what has happened; but what we can choose is an account that gives priority to human agency. Past interpretations have often relied on providential intervention: God can be made to account for any outcome whatever, however unexpected, however contrary to what we might have wished. Or we can replace old gods with a new intruder to the pantheon called economics, and we can then attribute political and personal and social change to that much more material base. But, rejecting providential or economic or any other form of determinism, we can just as well construct our narrative around individual human volition: that is, we can look back and see individuals who have somehow contrived to change the course of history as it has affected them – and in a direction that we think would be desirable for the future. This doesn't by any means imply a return to Carlyle's organisation of history around the deeds of a few heroic figures, but it does imply one possible focus as being upon the ability of individual men and women to take control of their own destiny and perhaps the destiny of others. Historians might then put emphasis on historic moments of choice – not those historic moments confronted by great world-leaders at conventional 'moments of destiny', but on significant choices made by more 'ordinary' individuals. Such individuals could be shown not to have been swept along by any 'course of events' that seems to be unfolding all around them, but rather to have acted *against* the apparent flow of history, *against* 'the authority of circumstance', *against* the prevailing perception of what constitutes 'reality or necessity'.

As an example of one individual who has managed, at a very personal level, to do just that, and who therefore in my view represents a role-model of empowerment, I would cite the American helicopter pilot, Hugh Thomson.[36] During the notorious raid on My Lai in Vietnam in 1968, Thomson refused to join in what was later seen as a massacre, but instead used his helicopter to rescue wounded villagers. That may sound a simple tale, with Thomson doing only what any moral person would. But it isn't: it must have been extraordinarily difficult in the confusion of battle to resist 'the authority of circumstance' and, in the face of that, to make his individual contrary stand – to make his choice. All the external pressures must have been for him to join in what everyone around him was doing, but he had the ability to see things differently – by extending at that moment what was thinkable. And he also had the moral strength to align himself quite differently (and perversely in the view of others) with what he saw – with that compelling 'authority of circumstance' again.

At My Lai, in retrospect, we can see that Hugh Thomson faced an 'historic moment' – a moment of decision to which his past had brought him. Had he seen the course of past events as leading to a situation in which he would play an inevitable (unavoidable) part, as (like Adolf Eichmann) a cog in a military machine, he would simply have joined in with everyone else. But he must instead have viewed (or at least utilised) those past events as leading up to a specific moment – the moment at which he found himself, which (like every other moment) was a moment of which he could take charge; it was a moment at which he had a choice, at which he could conform or resist – a moment at which he was personally empowered to change the course of history. And in the event that's what he did.

It's in part by resurrecting stories like Hugh Thomson's, then, that historians can play a therapeutic, hope-inspiring role – by clarifying the individual's power to act in defiance of what seems to be the habitual or the inevitable. Such stories have to do with maintaining the ability to see things differently. The poet Coleridge writes of the Romantic aspiration of his friend Wordsworth to pierce 'the film of familiarity', and to awaken 'the mind's attention from the lethargy of custom'.[37] And that aspiration need not remain confined to the realm of poetry. The Victorian critic Walter Pater referred more generally to 'speculative culture' (which surely could and should include history) having a special 'service ... towards the human spirit': namely, 'to rouse, to startle it to a life of constant and eager observation'. The formation of habits, he suggested, actually constitutes failure: 'for, after all, habit is relative to a stereotyped world' – it denotes conformity, and detracts from our ability to discriminate as we should, making (always different) people, things, and situations look alike.[38]

In that respect, the case of Hugh Thomson, who personally exemplifies an ability to break through the habitual and familiar and customary, demonstrates that history too can play its part in fulfilling the therapeutic function of keeping us alert – burning, as Pater famously puts it, with a 'hard, gem-like flame' – at every moment. For what we're talking of here is a form of creativity – what Anthony Giddens in a different context refers to as 'the capability to act or think innovatively in relation to pre-established modes of activity'. It implies a preparedness to embrace new experiences; and what Giddens goes on to suggest is that that openness derives in some sense from *trust*. Before we're able to make any leap into the unknown (which must always be an act of faith), we need to be firmly anchored in our own selves. For the sort of historic or 'fateful moments' by which, for example, Hugh Thomson was confronted, are 'threatening for the protective cocoon which defends the individual's ontological security'. We need, that is, to be very secure in our own internal beliefs and selves before we can hope to stand against a collective external challenge; and that security is dependent on a 'mantle of trust'.[39]

This has enormous implications for individuals in postmodernity, when emphasis is placed on recognising our position in such historic or fateful moments all the time – when, that is, we're *constantly* confronted by the need to choose what action to take, in the face of 'aporia'. In this context, Hugh Rayment-Pickard has drawn attention to the proto-existentialist philosophers Nietzsche, Kierkegaard, and Schopenhauer. Nietzsche, he notes, depicts any moment as a gateway, at the intersection of two paths – one leading back to eternity, the other forward to 'another eternity'. Kierkegaard similarly describes such a moment as 'the intersection of eternity and temporality' – an occasion for 'existential decision and resolution'; while the 'present alone,' insists Schopenhauer, 'is the form of all life' (it's in the present that we determine what we are). For all three, then, as Rayment-Pickard concludes, the present moment can be seen to be defined, 'not as a unit of time, but as a kind of *opportunity* or *opening*'.[40] The revelation of the omnipresence of such opportunities and openings, might constitute an important part of what history is for?

5 Colonising the future: towards a better world

> If your main aim is to shape the future, then it is not a good idea to devote your life to studying history.
>
> (Richard J. Evans)[41]

> Is not the close and bounded intellectual horizon within which we have long lived and moved now lifting up?
>
> (Matthew Arnold)[42]

It's surely sad that the first of those quotations was written well over a hundred years after the second. Whereas Matthew Arnold in the nineteenth century was optimistic about the opening up of intellectual horizons, Richard Evans in our own time is careful to close them down. For Evans, as probably for most other historians, history is to do exclusively with the past, and it is thereby excluded as a suitable study for those whose (admittedly 'main') aim is to do something about the future. But what young person, who looks around at the present – at 'the authority of circumstance' – does not feel impelled above all to help 'to shape the future'? My recipe for history would enable them quite properly to do just that. For if postmodern thought has taught us anything, it's the contingency of our categories – the fact that supposedly rigid distinctions between such words as 'past' and 'present' and 'future' are imposed by us on

our world, and on our experience of that world, in ways that (
be quite different, and in ways that can be changed at any time
a blurring of chronological categories liberates historians (or historians who so wish) from self-imposed restraints, leaving as central
to their task the shaping of the future.

Arnold's point was that an examination and retrieval of the past –
and particularly of what was 'best' in it – must provoke questioning
about our present. He saw his own society as confronting similar
problems to those we face today, not least in what he saw as the
potentially anarchic consequences of a heightened individualism.
'Freedom', he believed, had become an end in itself, and was
'worshipped in itself, without enough regarding the ends for which
freedom is to be desired'; and with the dissolution of any traditional
notions of deference, and the assertion of the right of individuals, in
the name of 'personal liberty', to do exactly as they like, the threat
of anarchy was looming. As in our own time, it made sense to write
of 'our disorders and perplexities': 'Everywhere we see the beginnings of confusion, and we want a clue to some sound order and
authority.'[43]

Arnold himself looked to what he saw as traditional culture to
provide a solution. 'Culture' he defined as 'a pursuit of our total
perfection by means of getting to know, on all the matters which
most concern us, the best which has been thought and said in the
world'. From our own standpoint, that is obviously full of problems: 'total perfection' has become a meaningless goal for those
who are unable or unwilling any longer to assess what is better or
worse in matters that concern us, let alone whatever in the world is
to be accounted 'best'; and Arnold's ultimate aspiration 'to see
things as they really are', though still sometimes retained as an
idealistic aim in historical study, has long since lost any actual
meaning. But the implied resort to history is still not without
some point even for the cultural relativist: the main point of
looking back for what is 'best', is to encourage reconsideration of
those presuppositions and habits which we thoughtlessly accept –
even convincing ourselves of the virtue of that thoughtless (and
actually vicious) acceptance. Arnold writes of 'the iron force of
adhesion to the old routine' – a routine beyond which people have
'no power of looking'. But historical knowledge of alternative and
superior models from the past enables us to turn 'a stream of fresh
and free thought upon our stock notions and habits' – habits
'which we now follow mechanically, vainly imagining that there is

a virtue in following them staunchly which makes up for the mischief of following them mechanically' – which of course it doesn't.[44]

That sort of unsettling of our intellectual habits was the educational ideal proposed in classical Athens by Socrates, and Arnold believes that everyone carries with them 'a possible Socrates' – by which he means that we carry with us the potential of 'detaching ourselves from our stock notions and habits'. The point, however, is not to replace one mindset, or philosophy, or system of belief, with another: rather – and this is where Arnold's thought, so long discredited, may still resonate for us – the point is, far from substituting some new dogma ('some rival fetish'), rather 'to turn a free and fresh stream of thought upon the whole'.[45] The mechanical followers of fashion, as obtrusive in our own time as in his, are forever banished.

That then links with Arnold's educational and cultural goal of 'the study of perfection' – and that too, paradoxically as it might now seem, is not to be instantly disparaged and dismissed. For his point is, as in the classical Greek tradition again, to emphasise the importance of developing the whole person. He criticises the practice of his own time, when such concentration is given to one side at the expense of others, that people have become 'incomplete and mutilated'. There was, he believes, an acceptance of 'a limited conception of human nature', from which it was deduced that only one thing was needful, while others could be safely ignored as unimportant; and people were thus deprived of the realisation of their full human potential. What was needed, rather, was a reversion to the ideal of conceiving 'true human perfection as a harmonious perfection, developing *all* sides of our humanity'; and only in that way could all parts of society be similarly developed.[46]

Arnold himself realises of course that, as a state of being, 'harmonious perfection' could never be attained. But, in a manner again with which we can still sympathise, he aspires not to any static state of fulfilment, but rather to a continuing *process* of growth and becoming. His much mocked references to 'sweetness and light' are derived from Jonathan Swift's *Battle of the Books* where, as a spokesman for the 'Ancients' in debate with the 'Moderns', Aesop proclaims the value of the 'honey and wax' of ancient learning, these furnishing humankind with 'the two noblest of things, which are sweetness and light'.[47] Those two qualities, both for Aesop and for Arnold, imply beauty and intelligence: they may never be finally attained, but they remain as goals to which to aspire. So, as 'the disinterested endeavour after men's perfection', culture consists 'not in resting and being, but in *growing* and *becoming*'.[48] We may never get there, but at least for Arnold the favoured direction (unlike our own situation) is still clear.

Any postmodernist, though, might surely subscribe to Arnold's main point, concerning the use of the past in the continuing quest for improvement in the present and for the future. In similar vein, for example, Zygmunt Bauman has written of postmodernism as involving a 're-enchantment' of a world 'disenchanted' by modernity – a bringing back of something that lies further back in the past than we sometimes look when contemplating our own historical roots. And Richard Rorty has proposed the use of history to support (political) philosophy, in the belief that 'historical narrative and utopian speculation are the best sort of background for political deliberation'. It could (or should), he believes, provide the imaginative narrative that is necessary to act as a springboard for take-off into a better future.[49] That is not to predetermine the direction of the dive: postmodernism of itself offers no particular political agenda (which is one reason it confuses and frustrates those critics who aspire to pin-point their targets) but it does, as Barry Smart has indicated, constitute 'a site, space, or clearing for political possibilities'.[50]

Cleared in particular of those rigid chronological categories, which have so long (in the name of disciplinary purity) provided a refuge for historians intent on avoiding any contact with the future (and so with any ideological involvement), history can start to play its proper place in shaping the future. For as Carolyn Steedman has observed: 'all historians, even the most purblind empiricists, recognise this in their acts of writing: they are telling the only story that has no end.'[51] Like the 'emotional dance theatre' performance at Hoxton Music Hall, advertised in May 2002, it 'is a modern fairytale that never ends; it simply stops in interesting places'; and the challenge for both historians and dancers becomes to ensure that where they stop, which is a matter of their *choice*, is in fact an interesting place – a better place – to stop.

In making that choice of stopping-place, there is of course a risk, for the implied involvement with the future in turn implies uncertainty. There can be no more burrowing away in what is thought to be a static past, deliberately regardless of what lies outside – no more taking refuge in the supposed disciplinary virtue of uninvolved detachment. Historians are required self-consciously to assume responsibility for colonising not only the past but also the future – a future that's by definition unknown. Exposure to that sort of risk doesn't come easily to those trained to think of their subject as having little to do with the practicalities of life tomorrow.

But there are of course compensations. In the mid-seventeenth century, when what we call 'science' was radically changing its nature and direction, John Wilkins was at the forefront as an advocate of intellectual change; and, like Francis Bacon before him, he was concerned to emphasise the need for science to be justified by reference to its practical effects. So he wrote: 'those may justly be accounted barren studies which do not conduce to practice as their proper end.'[52] Since Wilkins' time science has become revered for its beneficial human consequences, and one might hope that a practically orientated history might achieve a similar reputation. An example might help to clarify my meaning here, and I'll cite the case of Hugh Trevor-Roper.

Trevor-Roper described how, at a conference in 1950 – when the western world was clearly divided between the conflicting ideologies of 'democracy' and 'Communism' – he had heard a succession of speakers confirming the absolute incompatibility between Communist and democratic societies: 'one must destroy the other: there was no alternative. Therefore, he who was not for us was necessarily against us in the holy war.' Unwilling to accept that Manichaean-style analysis, in which the world was irreparably split between incompatible absolutes ('good' and 'evil'), the young historian (as he then was) felt inspired to go away and write an article on co-existence. It concerned the co-existence of Christendom and the Turkish Empire – 'but,' as he insists, 'it could equally have been on other such ideological confrontations'. In other words, there were instructive parallels – lessons even, about the possibility of mutual toleration and peaceful co-existence. 'All historical parallels,' as he admits, 'are imperfect and therefore dangerous; but those who use them would do well to remember one which, being inconvenient, they too often neglect: the parallel of co-existence, of Europe and the Turk.' His article was intended not only to say something about past confrontations, but by implication to colonise the future with important ideals to which he personally subscribed, and which seemed to him preferable to those that at the time (and increasingly again in our own time) seemed fashionable and even incontrovertible. As our own world in the twenty-first century is once again analysed in terms of 'them' and 'us', friend and foe, those with us or against, and the inevitable confrontation between opposites, it would be well to heed Trevor-Roper's conclusion – that 'the theory that the world cannot be "half slave and half free", that a frontal struggle between opposing systems is sooner or later inevitable and might as well be hastened by an ideological crusade, *is simply not true*'.[53]

It's with an eye similarly focused that another respected historian has recently written of restoring history to life by restoring to it 'its *open future*'.[54] Jonathan Clark opposes a 'postmodernism' that he perceives as essentially a- and anti-historical, but many of his own views are far from incompatible with some postmodernists' agendas. Most importantly, he is concerned to emphasise historical *contingency* and, by examining 'counterfactuals' or alternative past possibilities that were (often as the result of some chance) never actualised (but might have been), to erode any sense of historical *inevitability*. For, as we've considered in the case of national myths, any belief in inevitability is liable to result in – and seemingly justify – a dogmatic and complacent faith in the rightness of one's own position – a position that's apparently (or claimed to be) the culmination (or 'end') of an inevitable historical process.

Professor Clark himself, then, argues (in a way that Hilary Lawson would surely approve) against premature 'closures' – against attempts 'to reduce to order the teeming chaos of fundamental change'. His own consideration of counterfactuals involves, on the contrary, acceptance of 'the vast diversity, variety and unpredictability of the causes which actually operate in the world of events'[55] – an unsettling prospect but, as postmodernists would surely agree, none the worse for that. For it's the erosion of supposed past certainties in that way, that permits a path to be cleared to an '*open* future'.

'History,' wrote A. L. Smith in 1898, 'demands judgement, experience, tolerance; whereas the schoolboy demands ... black or white, angels or devils.'[56] In an age of 'schoolboy' politicians, trying in the face of contrary evidence to restore the appearance of a clearly ordered world, historians' 'judgement, experience, [and] tolerance' is ever more necessary for a hopeful future.

6 Conclusion

> Even historians may cherish hopes.
>
> (H. W. C. Davis)[57]

The past, present, and future are all of one piece: 'Old and new,' as Emerson reminds us, 'make the warp and woof of every moment.'[58] We can never escape from the past – or from history: every moment of our lives – every 'thread' – is 'a twist of these two strands' of old and new, of past and future. And my argument is that, if that is so (as it surely is), then, standing as we do as agents in the present, we should weave those strands (those elements) in a pattern that is not repetitive and dull, but imaginative and (aesthetically and morally) beautiful. For historians, as H. W. C. Davis recognised some three-quarters of a century ago, may not be able to prophesy but, as they intervene in the present between the past and the future, they may at least 'cherish hopes'; and their cherished hopes cannot then surely be completely disconnected from the histories they write. I'll go on now, in Chapter 7, to consider some possible aspirations, and in Chapter 8 to offer some actual examples of how such aspirations may be put into practice and hopefully become realities.

Histories for postmodernity – some aspirations

I Introduction

> After all has been said, we [historians] are still quite safe.
> Nobody can abolish the past.
>
> (F. M. Powicke, 1944)[1]

> That kind of information which, in our schools, usurps the
> name of History ... has not the remotest bearing on any of our
> actions.
>
> (Herbert Spencer, 1859)[2]

Historians may be justified in exuding some complacency. In a time
of fast-moving change, constant educational upheavals, built-in
obsolescence, and imminent redundancy for many, they can take
some comfort from the thought that, however public attitudes
towards their own preserve may fluctuate, at least one thing seems
sure: as F. M. Powicke notes above, 'nobody can abolish the past'.
We've seen that there may well be attempts to do just that – to
abolish the past at both personal and public levels: as individuals,
we may try to suppress those aspects of our past we'd rather be
without; and ideological reasons continue to abound for excising
those memories of a national past that conflict with current political
aspirations. But, whatever attempts are made, 'the past' persists –
eluding containment, seeping through boundaries and barriers into
present consciousness once more, resurfacing against the odds, and
finally resisting abolition.

But though the past can't be abolished, historians' complacency
can quickly go too far; and it's possible now to identify numerous
threats to the discipline of history in its traditional form. The other
country of the past may have long been colonised by historians and

adopted as their own; but there are now many other claimants to that territory, and the age of even academic imperialism has passed. As we've seen, 'professional' historians have always taken pains to expel any amateur or alien intruders from their claimed patch; but the forces lined up against them now – a coalition of 'amateurs' and entertainers, political revolutionaries and revolutionary theorists – are becoming formidable. And their cause is not helped by a continuing perception that the actual point of academic history remains unclear. Herbert Spencer's criticism in the quotation above may sound, some century and a half on, no longer relevant; but a cogent claim could still be made that the sort of history that's taught today 'has not the remotest bearing on any of our actions'.

Writing only a couple of years after Herbert Spencer, the historian Thomas Henry Buckle complained that:

> The vast majority of historians fill their works with the most trifling and miserable details; personal anecdotes of kings and courts; interminable relations of what was said by one minister, and what was thought by another; and what is worse than all, long accounts of campaigns, battles and sieges, very interesting to those engaged in them, but to us *utterly useless*.[3]

Since Buckle's time, historical study has of course been revolutionised, its political and military emphasis superseded by a host of competing interest groups; but in many cases the charge could still be laid that those histories are, for practical purposes, and sometimes quite deliberately, 'utterly useless'. The British educationalist Nicholas Kinloch, for example, has specifically repudiated any social or moral purpose for history, even (or especially) in relation to teaching about the Holocaust. The Shoah, he insists, should be treated strictly *'as history'* – and by that he means that teachers should be concerned (and concern their students) only 'with what happened and why'.[4]

Now that is already an unrealistic, unachievable – if not downright meaningless – task. (What could it possibly *mean* to know 'what happened and why' of such a complex aspect of the past?) But Kinloch goes on categorically to assert that the teaching of such historical events 'does not, or *should not*, involve any attempt at "making the world a better place" ... All teachers can really do is to help students become, as far as they can, better historians'. The clear implication is that, being an historian for its own sake, one must teach history for its own sake; and let that have nothing to do with aspiring to any moral or practical benefit. It is significant that his article is concerned with the question of whether the Holocaust is a 'moral *or* historical question', as if the two were mutually exclusive and we were confronted by a choice of either/or; and it's small wonder that the author concludes elsewhere that 'History itself, and the history of that history, might well induce a certain propensity to pessimism'.[5]

We return, then, to the question of what history is for. Historians can't do it all: they can't really or realistically be expected to embrace the whole of 'what happened and why'. So, granted the need for some selectivity, what – if 'making the world a better place' is deliberately excluded from the outset – are to be the criteria for selection? What can it mean to be a *'better* historian'? In what sense better? Better for what?

To revert for a moment to the nineteenth century, but for a point that is, now in the twenty-first, more relevant than ever, John Stuart Mill noted the uselessness of raw information – of simply 'remembered facts'. Such 'knowledge' of itself, as he proclaimed, is 'not enough'; 'a mere magazine of remembered facts' is nothing but 'a useless treasure' awaiting application. 'Amid the vast variety of known things, there is needed a power of choosing, a power of discerning which of them are conducive, which not, to the ends we have in view.'[6] We can't, again, do it all: we can't remember, or include in our histories, everything. As Thomas Carlyle too noted, we have to select, abbreviate, and forget, since otherwise the treatment of one single hour of our life would be enough to keep us fully occupied. And if we think of memory as light, and oblivion as dark, it's clear we need them both; for 'were it all light, nothing could be read there, any more than if it were all darkness'.[7]

There's some sign now of recognition of those points – the need for plurality and for some purposeful selection – in disciplines other than history. In sociology, for instance, Barry Smart has written of new roles and a 'reorientation' of the subject. The attempted accumulation of a coherent body of knowledge, with its modernist agenda of rational ordering and prediction and control, has given place to an accepted 'dispersion, fragmentation, difference and disagreement'.[8] So one point of history might become to highlight the meaningless nature of Nicholas Kinloch's project. For as Bernard Williams has recently confirmed, 'The past will not make sense unless we make sense of it', and we tend to make more sense of it – to impose more sense on the past, and to ascribe greater rationality to people's actions and motives – than is actually justifable. Far from aspiring, then, to any definitive historical explanations, our study of history should teach us to avoid any facile claims of understanding 'what happened and why', and (in Bernard Williams' words again) 'should itself guard against heading rapidly toward reductive explanations'.[9]

That, perhaps, needs to be remembered, together with Mill's reminder concerning the uselessness of our treasuries, stuffed full as they are with 'remembered facts'. For as we struggle with 'information overload', and burrow ever more narrowly and deeply into specialist bunkers, we contrive to convince ourselves that it's legitimate to reject most of what we're liable to encounter and experience as peripheral and inessential to our immediate task. The broader question – the question of whether that immediate task itself has any point – meanwhile remains not only un-answered but un-asked. So what might history – what might histories – be *for* in postmodernity? What aspirations might we have for them?

2 Realism, pessimism, hope

> Whether a story or a scheme of interpretation is hopeful or not does not provide a *criterion of choice*.
>
> (Bernard Williams)[10]

Some quarter-century ago, the respected cultural historian Peter Gay distinguished between what he termed 'pleasure' and 'reality' principles: 'As he ascends from the self-indulgent and self-centred realm of the *pleasure* principle to the austere atmosphere of the *reality* principle, what he [the historian] sees and what there is match more and more closely.'[11] Ranke's 'celebrated wish to relate the past as it actually happened' is, then, for Gay still a realisable ambition, though admittedly 'difficult'. But there's a price to be paid: just as it's only by repudiating the pleasure of love that Wagner's mythical Alberich gains possession of his gold and power, so it's only by forswearing their own self-indulgent pleasures that historians can ever gain access to the object of their own desires – the truth about 'the past'.

Belief in the feasibility of such bargaining still, remarkably, persists (as we have seen); and though Bernard Williams is well aware that it's we ourselves who have to make what sense we can of a past that may be susceptible to various interpretations, or conflicting narratives, between which it's impossible to choose, yet he too cannot accept that historians be allowed the best of both worlds, or simply be allowed to choose the better. Determined as he is to retain some concept of a 'truth' external to ourselves, he remains insistent that 'we should resist … the idea that we can *choose* the way in which we see the past'. We may have lost our faith in any Holy Grail-style unitary 'truth about the past', but although 'a more hopeful story' is preferable (in serving most of us better), and although therefore we may well hope that such hopeful stories will endow the past with sense and go on being told, still we have to resist any idea that we can simply *choose* such hopeful stories – because at the same time they must be *'truthful'*.[12]

But if, as it has been conceded, we may be left unable to decide between two conflicting accounts of past events – two sense-bestowing historical narratives – and if, having investigated their respective 'veracity', we've been persuaded of the truthfulness (sincerity) of both their authors, then why (we're surely bound to ask) should we not choose between them on grounds of their potential 'hopefulness'? Why should that not provide 'a criterion of choice'?

For that, after all, is what we might well accept on a personal level. Looking back, there are many paths that we can trace through the past to our present – many ways that we can choose to see those events and experiences that have served, at least in part, to determine what we are. To a great extent, we fashion that 'reality' ourselves, looking back with regrets and forward with anxiety, or back with delight and forward with high expectations. Negative autobiographies can be replaced with positive: one therapist has described how her own account of past experiences changed from sounding 'aggrieved, embittered, and victimised' to emphasising 'the strengths I gained as a result of these events';[13] and her outlook on and expectations for the future were no doubt changed accordingly. Similarly, there would have been little point through the Second World War in looking back at the withdrawal of the British Expeditionary Force from Dunkirk in 1940 as the catastrophic defeat that, from one standpoint, it evidently was; far better surely to view it and portray it as the triumphant rescue-operation that it also was – for that latter 'reality' at least had the advantage of inspiring confidence and hope for the future.

Such issues are particularly pressing at times like this (in the twenty-first century), when demands for sense-making narratives become ever more insistent. For it is, as Williams himself makes clear, particularly at moments of crisis – 'when the smooth order of things is disturbed by violence' – that historically orientated questions are provoked: '"Why?" "Why us?" "Where from?"' Such questions have come to the foreground of our current concerns, and such answers as we might find are embedded in the past. So they clearly require some appeal to the past – and 'If it is not to the historical past, then it will be to some kind of myth about it'.[14] And that returns us to the distinction between history and myth, discussed in Chapter 3, §4.

3   History and myth again

The distinction between history and myth is particularly pressing now, at a time when alternative narratives – and even alternative accounts of what constitutes a properly *historical* narrative – are being fed to a public with a seemingly insatiable hunger (visceral need) for a past that resonates for them, and helps to answer those insistent 'Why?' and 'Where from?' questions to which we've just referred. David Harlan has recently drawn attention to what he calls 'the coming crisis of academic history' – a rapidly approaching crisis that is in imminent danger of resulting from a reappearance of that old divergence of 'popular' (amateur) from 'proper' (academic) history – or, as the 'professional' historian might put it, of 'history' from 'myth'.[15]

The 'popular' strand of history in the United States is represented by the work of Ken Burns – a man who gladly confesses to being 'an amateur historian ... a popular amateur historian',[16] and whose popularity is indeed such that Harlan can describe him as currently 'a household name', and even 'the most famous historian in the country'. That position of celebrity does, of course, bestow enormous power: Harlan describes how Ken Burns'

> images, [and] his particular way of seeing the past, have become part of the very texture of American cultural life ... And ... his particular recasting of American history has come to play a central and vital role in shaping the public's sense of who we have been and who we are now becoming.

That role has not resulted as some unexpected and contingent by-product from his historical work: it is central to his self-professed concerns. Burns himself has criticised academic historians for having abandoned their traditional role as 'tribal storytellers who craft tales about the past in which the nation can find its identity',[17] and he has made it clear that 'The animating question of all my work is *what it means to be an American*' (my emphasis).

Such apparently high-falutin' aims, relating as they do to fundamental existential issues, go down ill, as we have repeatedly seen, with proper academic historians; and Ken Burns has been duly attacked for his amateurish pretensions. Like those nineteenth-century women, or those historical novelists epitomised by Walter Scott, he has somehow, by his very success in the popularity stakes, demeaned his subject. He has also sacrificed such stimulus to thought as might be produced by a recognition of complexities and ambiguities, on the altar of such simplicity as is required by his tidy and supposedly inspiring story-line. Far from producing real history, it is claimed, he has reduced historical study to 'a mind-softening, saccharine-like substitute', appealing to the emotions and pandering to the lowest common denominator of people's taste for nostalgia.

Yet, like his 'amateurish' predecessors, Burns (together with other 'popularisers') is evidently providing something people want, fulfilling some basic needs – of the very sort indicated above in Chapter 5. His focus on questions of *identity* is central, and (as I would argue) his provision of some sort of future *hope* no less important. Motivated, as he himself professes, by 'an absolutely undying love of my country', and concerned to achieve 'an emotional consensus', Burns provides a history that is designed to integrate – 'to find a way in which we can include the diverse tributaries of our experience into something that might nourish the whole';[18] so that, as Harlan describes, he wants Americans to think of themselves 'as inhabiting a world that has been shaped and formed by shared cultural values and social ideals'; he aims to (re-)create 'a common American culture'.

That implies further the repair of 'that now-withered link between family stories and national narrative' – a demonstration of how the individual links with the social and political, the private with the public; and it can be made effective only through ensuring that the stories told of the past (as well as their techniques of presentation) resonate in the present and look forward to a hopeful future. Burns' histories don't deny such evils in the past as slavery: indeed, as Harlan claims, they *force* 'white Americans to accept their own complicity'. But (as in the case of personal therapy) that acceptance is not doomed to lead to negativity, but is to be seen on the contrary as a prerequisite for liberation. For Burns, what is to be emphasised in history – what it's *for* – is its 'redemptive possibilities', showing, in the quoted words of Michael Walzer (with my emphasis), '*how we mean to live* but do not yet live'.

We may not all agree with Ken Burns' aims. To some, his fervent patriotism and integrative and consensual goals will sound curiously old-fashioned and reactionary; and he has importantly been criticised for providing an over-simplified narrative that fails to do justice either to minority interests (such as Blacks) or to the complexity of events: his focus on national unity blinds him (and his audience) to such ambiguities of the historical legacy (notably of the American Civil War and Reconstruction) that continue to bedevil relationships within society today.[19] But, as David Harlan indicates, he is currently providing an alternative history, with a self-consciously and clearly defined agenda; and, using television, film, and up-to-date modes of representation, his form of history – however much reviled as 'myth' – is having an enormous and practical effect. He and his kind deserve to be taken very seriously in any assessment of what history, now and in the future, might be *for*. We're talking here about no less than the sort of person and the sort of future that we want.

4   The labyrinth of language

'Language,' wrote Wittgenstein, 'is a labyrinth of paths. You approach from one side and know your way about; you approach the same place from another side and no longer know your way about';[20] and Raimond Gaita has much more recently written of how 'Profound and very difficult matters about the relations of thought, language and truth to one another are now impossible to avoid *for almost anyone who thinks*'.[21] By that Gaita means that the sorts of problem concerning language with which Wittgenstein, and of course earlier philosophers, were concerned are not just airy-fairy theories that historians and other sensible people don't need to bother with: they now, in postmodernity, impinge on any thinking person – who is unlikely then to remain confident of any longer knowing his or her way about, not least in the linguistic labyrinths of history.

There can be few historians who haven't thought that they at least knew their way around their own specialism, but who later, confronted by some alternative approach towards or re-description of their chosen patch, have had their confidence undermined, and come to realise that they barely knew their entrance or their exit – let alone what lay between. For as a text-based study, history is particularly prone to linguistically based problems – problems of translation and more generally of meaning (as, for instance, in the constantly changing meanings of words and phrases through time), problems of reference, equivocation, and ambiguity (as evidenced in our personal conversations daily), problems, in short, of expression and communication by which, whether in our academic or our personal lives, we are constantly and inevitably beset.

So it seems that language must be relevant to historians' aspirations in at least two important ways. First, it's clear that historians themselves might need to take more account of linguistic issues in their own writing, making clear to themselves and others their own rhetorical standpoints. And second, historical study might be commandeered by educationalists as particularly useful in assisting in the promotion of a more general *linguistic awareness* – by which I mean an awareness of how, and for what purposes, language at any time is being used.

To take those points in order, then, recognition of underlying problems in our use of language – problems of direct relevance to our attempted imposition of order on the world or on the past – is of course nothing new. Plato discussed the fundamental issue of whether language referred directly to the external world and somehow described the very *essence* of the objects in that world, or whether on the other hand linguistic descriptions were nothing more profound than *conventions*. And the sceptics, as Sextus Empiricus reminds us, argued that if the former theory was right, everyone would be able to understand what any word referred to: it would be obvious, even to those who didn't speak English, that the word 'rose' referred to what we see in nature as a rose. But that is patently not the case: a rose by any other name would smell as sweet, and would be (is) no less a rose; and that's because 'the significance of names is based on convention and not on nature'.[22] And so, as Wittgenstein later concluded, the order that we establish by our use of language is 'one out of many possible orders; not *the* order'. In other words, we could describe the world in many other, equally orderly, ways: what we do is just choose one such way, 'with a particular end in view'.[23] That's then what our language re-presents, but (as we know from other languages that *do* order the world differently) it could be quite different.

It is indeed clear that *any* language we use (or could possibly use) must remain in some sense deficient, in that it couldn't possibly describe or fully re-present the totality of any event or experience. At the very simplest level, we have to make choices concerning which aspects of events or experiences we wish to discriminate, single out, and describe with the linguistic resources currently available to us; and we are most of us aware of having periodically had resort to words and phrases from alternative languages, and of having been frustrated at our inability to convey to others exactly what we feel. Even for the linguistically sophisticated, it seems that there remain some things that 'can't be put into words', that elude our linguistic nets, and that threaten once more the intrusion of chaos into our ordered universe, including, again, our provisionally ordered past.

To our now heightened awareness of language's labyrinthine quality, philosophers – often decried for their remoteness from real life – have made important contributions. Way back in the 1960s Stuart Hampshire considered our descriptions of such games as chess and cricket. There are, of course, specified ways of enumerating the various moves made in such games, and in one sense these can be said to provide an accurate and complete description. But their validity as such is assured only because their 'terms of reference' have been deliberately curtailed: they are required to record only a clearly defined set of moves; anything else is to be deemed irrelevant. So long as we confine our interest to what such records provide, we can claim to have a complete account of the game, but it would of course be possible to take an interest in other aspects of behaviour that might be manifested in these games; and then, with our focus changed, the bare records of the moves in chess or the score in cricket would fail to satisfy our new requirements, and a whole new description would be needed. So as Stuart Hampshire concluded:

> it becomes plain that any representation or description of [a segment of experience] … in any form is always incomplete, in the sense that there is always more that could be represented or described, and that is left out of this particular representation.[24]

Which may, to some now, sound like a truism, or something so obviously the case that it hardly merits being stated – something that, as we say, goes without saying. But when applied to historical study, as it surely must be, it may still give pause for thought; for it implies once again the *inevitable* incompleteness of any historical representation, and the consequent need (even from this perspective alone) to see history as an *endless* process of enquiry. We can never rest satisfied with our result: it can never ever be 'definitive', but could always be different, and in some sense no less 'true'.

That possibility of difference, necessitated by the contingency and instability of language itself, can be another cause of anxiety: we think we've got the world (and the past) somehow taped – categorised and described in terms of its very essence – but all we've done is describe it in one particular way, a way that suits us for the moment, but a way that can be questioned, challenged, supplanted at any moment from any one of an infinite range of alternative perspectives. So if we lay claim to any hold on orderly 'reality', we have to be aware that that hold is very tenuous: there's nothing absolute or permanent about it; it can be broken – now.

That puts us permanently on the edge of a linguistic precipice, over which we can topple into an abyss of confusion at any moment – a situation recognised by W. G. Sebald's character, the writer Austerlitz. This man suffers some sort of breakdown, as he comes to realise the terrible complexities of linguistic representation, where a sentence

> only appears to mean something, but in truth is at best a makeshift expedient, a kind of unhealthy growth issuing from our ignorance, something which we use, in the same way as many sea plants and animals use their tentacles, to grope blindly through the darkness enveloping us.[25]

For Austerlitz there, language remains a potentially positive tool (as it can be for historians groping through the past), but sometimes, as we've briefly noted in the case of Nazi Germany, it can be used, not so much to enable us to grope through darkness as to envelope us the more within it. Which is worth reiterating here, since it leads us to my second point concerning history's relationship with language, suggesting as it does another crucial role to which historians might aspire in postmodernity: a study of past usages may alert us to present manifestations of linguistic manipulation – may encourage, that is to say, some greater linguistic awareness.

In this respect we are fortunate to have historical evidence in a case-study carefully preserved by Victor Klemperer – a German Jewish academic, who miraculously survived the Second World War partly, it would seem, through his determination to serve as a witness to the linguistic abuses perpetrated in the name of the Third Reich. As a philologist and cultural historian, Klemperer was particularly sensitive to the ways that language was brought into service for totalitarian purposes, and he kept careful notes and records, as well as more personal diaries, from 1933 to the end of the war. And he concludes, in short, that 'Nazism permeated the flesh and blood of the people through simple words, idioms and sentence structures which were imposed on them in a million repetitions, and taken on board mechanically and unconsciously'[26] – an analysis that alerts us to the need above all to remain fully *aware* of our own linguistic environment, of the ways that language is used by those with power, whether political or economic, in our own time.

For (whether this sounds melodramatic or just obvious) language profoundly affects us – the ways we think, the ways we act, and the ways we are. As advertisers, propagandists, and spin-masters of all kinds know, we can be influenced subliminally – 'mechanically and unconsciously' – by constantly reiterated words and phrases, so that we come to act *unthinkingly* in ways that are required. The purpose of language in the Third Reich, as identified by Klemperer, was 'to strip everyone of their individuality, to paralyse them as personalities, to make them into unthinking and docile cattle in a herd driven and hounded in a certain direction';[27] and that docile and unthinking herd contained not only *victims* of violence, as we might at first have supposed, but (as we shall see further below in the case of Adolf Eichmann) also and no less its mechanical and unconscious *perpetrators*.

It could, then, be one useful role for historians to provoke periodic questioning about our own subjection to similar pressures and perversions in our own time? That at all events is one of the obviously intended effects of reading Klemperer's record of his own experience, and some examples will suffice to indicate their continuing relevance.

First, we are advised of the Nazi appropriation of the word 'people' for identification with the ruling party. It is, of course, considered to be good to be one of 'the people', and festivals 'of the people' are duly provided by those representing 'the people's

Fuehrer', who would himself later be instigating a 'people's war'. (British readers will not need to be reminded of their Prime Minister's sanctification of the late Princess of Wales as 'the people's princess'.) Second, as Klemperer records, was a claim upon the future: Nazi deeds and achievements were to be judged not in the shorter term, but (like those of Tony Blair) in the light of history. So with utter conviction of the permanence of their own régime, Nazis endowed the most trifling event or achievement with 'historic' importance (and as I revise this in March 2004, I read of Blair's 'historic handshake' at his 'historic meeting' in Libya with Colonel Gaddafi); so that, for example, their leader's meetings and speeches and edicts were described as having 'historical significance', or even 'global historic significance'.

The universalised significance of the Nazi régime was matched by its eternity – an assumed eternity that invited and enjoyed religious resonance, confirmed by deliberate use of language traditionally associated with Christianity. Hitler himself was presented as Germany's 'saviour', aligned with Christ, complete with his own 'Apostles'; so that, in terms that may not be altogether unfamiliar to followers of more recent fashions, Hitler was duly 'led by Providence' in his 'crusade' or 'holy war', and naturally acted always 'according to the Will of the Almighty'. Re-emphasising the practical importance of such linguistic borrowings in his own time, Klemperer suggestively concludes that 'Nazism was accepted by millions as gospel because it appropriated the language of the gospel'.[28]

In such a context, it's no wonder that superlatives came into their own – with, for instance, 'unique' applied as widely as by our own estate agents. 'Total' too became ubiquitous, as in 'total destruction' and 'total war'; and, again with resonances in current educational jargon, a 'total learning environment' was happily provided in Nazi schools. Likewise, German soldiers, assured that they were the best in the world, and equipped with the best weapons in the world produced by the best workers in the world, could presumably face 'the greatest battle in the history of the world' with confidence – especially with their record of having achieved 'victories the likes of which have never been seen before in the history of the world'. Such use of superlatives is described by Klemperer as part of 'the poison of deliberate mass seduction', and he reminds us also that it is (as in our own time) 'quintessentially advertising mode' (whether for the sale of products or political ideas).[29]

As well as superlatives, euphemisms abounded in the Third Reich, so that victims are just required 'to present themselves' when summoned by the Gestapo, and have simply 'gone away' when they're imprisoned and fail to return home. And (just as Thucydides had so much earlier warned) words take on meanings actually contrary to normal usage: 'fanaticism', for instance, is transformed into a virtue, so becomes 'an inordinately complimentary epithet'; so that, as Klemperer explains, what was previously considered (in normal parlance) 'a confused state of mind, equally close to sickness and criminality, was for twelve years held to be the greatest virtue'.[30]

Altogether, then, Klemperer's lesson reiterates that of Thucydides and Orwell, that we need to heed linguistic usages, especially in times of strife – and what times aren't? Russell Smith has recently described the 'newsspeak' – and the degradation of language – associated with news reports from Iraq, when 'softening up' refers to the exploding of soldiers in their bunkers, and the neologism 'attrited' is coined to describe (or hide) the fact that 'we are slowly killing as many of them as we can'.[31] Language in times of war and crisis has always been most susceptible to such ideologically motivated manipulation, and most likely to be unsettled from any linguistic or moral norm; and it may be wise now to heed the American linguist Noam Chomsky's warning, that 'the terms of political discourse', in our own, no less than Klemperer's time, 'are designed *so as to prevent thought*'.[32]

To recognise that, and to view language as thus changeable and ideologically accommodating, can be highly disconcerting – quite literally un-settling. We may have considered ourselves to be in a world that's 'sorted' – a world that we can describe and predict and control – but of course we're not, and never will be in any such world; and it may be a part of the historian's role to confirm that obvious point. And it's a clarification that brings some compensation, for one very positive outcome is the opening up of new routes through what we call 'reality' – the revelation of possible new 'takes' on it, enabling alternative perceptions, descriptions, and experiences. For by changing our linguistic rules and habits, we're forced to modify our theories and our thoughts – and thereby our actions too.

And that linguistic point is, again, highly relevant for history and for the aspirations we might have for history's functions. Our historical descriptions and representations may no longer be claimed to be 'true', or to be reflecting, describing, or referring directly to, some essence of the past; so that we no longer have the sense of having 'got' the past – grasped it, captured it, made it somehow solid, static. But seen instead as but one proposed stand-point in relation to the past, our histories would no less reveal an attitude – an attitude to the past that can itself either confirm and perpetuate the present, or alternatively open up new ways into a more desirable future. The past would not, in any event, be fixed, but elusive and ambiguous – open to continual modification, in our own interest. It would no longer lack its own potential for trans-formation – not least of us – for the better.

At the end of the war, Victor Klemperer was inspired to complete his book on the language of the Third Reich by a woman who had been imprisoned for insulting Hitler and his political régime – imprisoned, as she put it, "cos of certain expressions' she had used; and he was led to ponder whether it had, 'perhaps been a luxury and egotistical to bury oneself exclusively in academia and avoid worrying about politics'.[33] Linguistic usage and awareness remain core political and educational concerns, to which historians in postmodernity, having renounced the luxury of cultivating exclusive gardens, might aspire to make significant and practical contributions?

5 Transferable qualities

So we're talking here about *qualities* – personal qualities that might be encouraged by historical study. We looked earlier at 'transferable skills', but it might perhaps be more productive, in the context of postmodernity, to give further consideration to transferable *qualities* – or to the sort of human being that we might wish to foster. Following the promptings of Bernard Williams, and in the light of our discussion of our current life and needs, three much needed qualities seem to me to emerge that historians might properly aspire to inculcate (or at least, less prescriptively, to encourage): first, self-reflexivity – a consciousness of ourselves, and of what we're doing and why; second, as we've just considered, linguistic awareness – an alertness to how language is used and abused, adapted and modified in the interests of specific agendas; and third, an ability to live with ambiguity – with sometimes inconsistent and contradictory elements in ourselves and other people, as well as in the past.

These, it will be recalled, are essentially the qualities prescribed by the literary critics – I. A. Richards, F. R. Leavis, and Lionel Trilling – cited in Chapter 1. They constitute characteristics of what I'll now, some generations after them, claim are those of a properly educated person; and I suggest that historical study can (and surely should) make an important contribution towards their development. Let's take them in order.

First, then, historians may sometimes appear in some danger of failing the test of (amongst others) the classical Greek Socrates and the contemporary social theorist Anthony Giddens, concerning what it takes to be a human being – namely, 'to know yourself', 'to know, virtually all of the time, in terms of some description or another, both what one is doing and *why one is doing it*'.[34] Chronologically between those two examples, the poet Coleridge too was concerned to emphasise the importance of what he called a 'philosophic' consciousness, 'which lies beneath or (as it were) behind the spontaneous consciousness natural to all reflecting beings'. For him, it was possible only for 'the true philosopher' to aspire to such heights; and it was 'neither possible or necessary for all men, or for many, to be philosophers'. But in postmodernity, such aspiration, like so much else, has been democratised, and we've earlier seen Zygmunt Bauman's insistence on 'self-monitoring' as being central to the postmodern consciousness *for everyone*.[35]

The problem, then, is to know how that quality, now encompassed by the term 'self-reflexivity', might be encouraged and developed; and it could, I suggest, be one significant outcome of exemplary histories – histories that demonstrate, for instance, the potential evils of succumbing, in an unquestioning, *unreflexive* way, to a perceived 'normality', and that show how alternatives – alternative examples of practical behaviour – *are* actually possible.

This moral message might be derived from Hannah Arendt's treatment of the Nazi war criminal Adolf Eichmann – the bureaucrat responsible for the transportation of Jews in Hitler's 'final solution', brought to trial in Israel in 1961, and subsequently hanged.[36] For one of the points that Arendt emphasises is that Eichmann himself, apart from professional ambition, 'had *no motives at all*' in performing his tasks, and in fact '*never realised what he was doing*'. By that she obviously doesn't mean that he didn't realise that he was making his lists and arranging his transports, but that he never thought to question *why* he was doing it – what all his work was actually *for*. It was, she suggests, not stupidity, nor 'any diabolical or demonic profundity' in him, but 'sheer *thoughtlessness*' that led to his criminal behaviour; and one of the most important lessons to be learnt from his career and trial is that 'such thoughtlessness can wreak more havoc than all the evil instincts taken together'. Bureaucracies tend to dehumanise: they reduce individual human beings to mere cogs in some administrative machine; and it's not until they are brought to court (if they ever are) that such cogs are 'transformed back into perpetrators, that is to say, into human beings'. In other words it's only at that late point that they are forced to take responsibility for their own behaviour – for the way that they themselves have distinguished, or failed to distinguish, between right and wrong.

It's in making such moral distinctions that individuals can (or even must) ultimately be thrown back upon their own resources – their own judgement. For sometimes 'normality' – a seeming consensus all around us – can indicate a course of action that, in our more self-reflexive moments, we ourselves would recognise as wrong. So Arendt describes how 'a ruthless desire for *conformity* at any price' characterised many of the defendants at the 1945 post-war trials in Nuremberg, and notes that it was of a similarly unthinking conformity that Eichmann too was guilty. He 'could see no one, no one at all, who actually was against the Final Solution', so that his actions were in that context 'normal': 'he and the world he lived in ... [were] in perfect harmony'.

The point again, though, is that such harmonious and unthinking conformity with the world we live in needs periodically to be self-consciously questioned; and then, if necessary, it can be contradicted and resisted. And it's just that hope-inspiring possibility of resistance to the norm that can be shown by the historical record. For while it may sometimes seem that the juggernaut, once started, is unstoppable, it has been demonstrated that resistance, once shown, can itself take control. In the case of Nazi policies towards the Jews, it was shown in the case of Denmark, where, in the face of the Danes' maintenance of their own moral standards, 'their [i.e. German] "toughness" ... melted like butter in the sun', and genocide no longer appeared as 'normal' or 'inevitable' at all.

Hannah Arendt's conclusion is, then, that 'under conditions of terror most people will comply but *some people will not* ... [so] the lesson of the countries to which the Final Solution was proposed is that "it could happen" in most places but *it did not happen everywhere*'. And if it did not happen everywhere, it need not happen here – wherever it is that we are; and in showing that, historians perform a vital function. By clarifying that some people could have acted differently (better), and by remembering that other people (as later Hugh Thomson in Vietnam) self-consciously defied the norm and actually did so, historians can give some cause for hope.

Another important by-product of Hannah Arendt's treatment of Eichmann – and another lesson to be learned more generally from history – is my second required quality of linguistic awareness.[37] This is another essential quality to be taught and learnt, not least in our own times of Orwellian-style linguistic distortions. Interestingly in this respect, Arendt claims that Eichmann's 'inability to speak was closely connected with an inability to *think*': he was, as she describes (and as so many of our current political leaders might be described), 'incapable of uttering a single sentence that was not a cliché'; his language expressed, not his own thoughts and feelings, but the euphemisms and platitudes of others. For the SS deliberately adopted new terminology – new 'language rules'; and these 'rules', as Arendt clarifies, were themselves 'what in ordinary language would be called a lie'. But of course they had a function, and in fact 'they proved of enormous help in the maintenance of order and sanity in the various widely diversified services whose co-operation was essential in this matter'.

Thus, 'objectivity' – that quality to which historians so often lay claim, and of which Eichmann remained very proud at his trial – enabled (indeed necessitated) a convenient dissociation from any 'emotional' demands, or any ambiguities or indecisiveness. Mass killings by gas could be (and were quite explicitly at the trial) conveniently subsumed within the seemingly harmless or neutral or even beneficent category of 'medical matters'. Indeed, after Hitler had earlier decreed euthanasia for the mentally sick, gassing was more positively presented as 'the humane way' of killing; and the nasty word 'murder' was replaced with the euphemism 'to grant a mercy death'.

'The net effect of this language system,' as Hannah Arendt explains, 'was not to keep these people ignorant of what they were doing, but to prevent them from equating it with their old, "normal" knowledge of murder and lies.' Linguistic meanings were manipulated, in order to make possible what would previously have been repudiated as beyond the pale of human decency. And within such a distorted normality (or as we sometimes say, 'reality'), people felt justified in shifting any burden of responsibility away from themselves and on to others; so that, when confronted by the horrific results of their own actions, 'instead of saying: What horrible things I did to people!, the murderers would be able to say: What horrible things I had to watch in the pursuance of my duties; how heavily the task weighed upon my shoulders!'

Linked with such ambiguities in language is the inherent ambiguity of experience itself; and the quality of being able to live self-reflexively with the consciousness of ambiguity is the third virtue which I believe historians can aspire to foster. Continuing, then, with our same example, we can see that this might be another thing that history might properly be *for*.[38] For Eichmann was nothing if not of single purpose: once he had his eyes set on a goal, he was not to be distracted or deflected. Seemingly, no doubts or hesitations or ambiguities could enter his consciousness. He enjoyed, or suffered from, a total inability 'to think from the standpoint of somebody else'.

That single-mindedness persisted even in retrospect. His mental harmony appeared to remain intact even throughout his trial, for whatever failed to conform with it was automatically rejected: any alternative and conflicting account of events, as proposed for instance by prosecution witnesses, failed to change his mind. 'It was,' as Hannah Arendt describes, 'as though this story ran along a different tape in his memory, and it was this taped memory that showed itself proof against reason and argument and information and insight of any kind.' And with that sort of rigidity, he believed that he could truthfully record what happened.

It is here that Eichmann's story connects quite explicitly, and chillingly, with history. For, as he claimed: 'One of the few gifts fate bestowed upon me is the *capacity for truth* insofar as it depends upon myself'; so that 'future historians' could use his own account, and should, he asserts, 'be *objective* enough not to stray from the path of this truth recorded here'. 'I shall try to write down the facts ... without any embellishments, in order that future generations will have a true picture.'

Such have been the aspirations of historians through the ages. Supposedly blessed with an extraordinary quality of 'objectivity', they have claimed an ability to record 'the facts' in a simple, clear, and unembellished narrative, and so transmit 'the truth' to future generations. It's doubtful that any aspiring historian of the Nazi 'final solution' would expect to derive 'a true picture' of events from Adolf Eichmann, but his story does have its own lessons to teach – and not least the inadequacy of any single claim to truth. Historians themselves, as they well know, need constantly to juggle with hypothetical alternatives, with other possibilities, with inconsistencies of evidence and ambiguities; and the personal qualities required for that – which include the ability (so lacking in Eichmann) to think from the standpoint of others – are an important part of the heritage to be transmitted through their work.

6   Conclusion

We have to concede that history as currently presented is often *not* concerned with fostering these qualities, and seems unlikely to achieve them. We've looked above at how Ken Burns in the United States aims at a clear historical narrative that can be shared by all, and it's almost inevitable that such popularised history in short doses (such as is seen in documentaries and films – and admittedly in Britain too) should present an authoritative and straightforward (as opposed to an overtly self-reflexive and tentative) account. Uncertainties and ambiguities and open-endedness may sound virtuous to a few academics, but they have less appeal in the real world of an entertainment 'industry'.

Less appeal, too, in an education catering no less for a mass-market. So at a 'special summit' in Berlin (in October 2003), the British were accused of presenting to their students 'a distorted view of German history', with important implications for international relations.[39] The English national history syllabus, it's conceded by the teacher writing the report, is indeed 'unbalanced, to the extent that it focuses almost entirely on the Hitler period'; inspectors have 'warned of a creeping "Hitlerisation"' of history courses; and teachers seem likely 'to keep pandering to their students' enthusiasm for the Third Reich'. 'I was only doing history to study the Nazis,' as one student is reported as explaining. And that may not, of itself, much matter: the young might well be more enthused by Hitler than by Henry VIII, more intrigued by the Third Reich than by the Reformation. But the justification given for the emphasis is what disturbs, and indicates the approach that's taken to the subject. Most importantly, it's claimed, 'This isn't one of those morally ambiguous stories ... it is a tale of right versus wrong'; and needless to add, 'we [British] were absolutely and unequivocally in the right' – so that 'the Germans' {sic} conveniently fulfil our requirement for 'villains'.

With the promulgation of such a simplistic attitude to the infinitely complex events in question, it's hardly surprising that Germans should feel aggrieved; nor surprising that history taught that way leads, however paradoxically, to renewed violence. Which all provokes once more the question of what our history-teaching is and might be *for*, since our ultimate goals will help to determine our approaches. We've just seen how, from some of the events in question, Hannah Arendt drew moral lessons that might well be central to educational aspirations. Seemingly – and sadly – that's not the sort of use to which much history is currently being put. But some is; and to indicate alternative – more positive – approaches, let's turn to specific examples.

Chapter 8

Histories for postmodernity – some examples

It's easy enough to theorise in abstract terms, so let's look here at four specific and practical examples that seem to me to satisfy the criteria I've set for histories in and for postmodernity.

I   Robert A. Rosenstone and Japan

By some happy chance, I had no sooner formulated for myself the personal qualities that seem currently to be particularly needed, and to be such as historical study might well foster (i.e. self-reflexivity, linguistic awareness, and tolerance of ambiguity), than I was introduced to a work that actually exemplifies all three. Robert Rosenstone's *Mirror in the Shrine: American Encounters with Meiji Japan* was published in 1988 but, immersed as I then was in seventeenth-century intellectual history, I missed its then seemingly (to me, as I then was) irrelevant appearance. But it seems to me now to be concerned with just the three qualities about which I've been writing – and to be itself a wonderful vehicle for teaching them.

The book hardly reads like history, but more perhaps like a novel. But history it is, consisting essentially of three historical biographies, and complete with such disciplinary paraphernalia as quotations from archival sources. It recounts the stories of three Americans who went to Japan in the second half of the nineteenth century – a missionary, William Elliott Griffis, a scientist, Edward S. Morse, and a writer, Lafcadio Hearn ('emblematic figures', as the author has more recently explained, 'meant to stand for the larger American experience').[1] Rosenstone's motivation in telling the stories of these three very different men derives from the fact that he himself lived in Japan in 1974–5: he clarifies that his central concern is with 'the American encounter with Japan' – and that encounter clearly has for him personal as well as historical dimensions. His professed aim, then, is to capture 'the meaning that these three lives *still has for us*', with history contributing to the ongoing pursuit of *self-understanding*.[2]

Self-reflexivity is thus at the very core of the work, informing it throughout a history that is deliberately presented as 'conscious of itself as an artifact ... ambiguous and open-ended'. So the historian, *qua* self-reflexive historian, rather than seeking (in the generally approved way) to distance himself from what he writes, periodically and quite deliberately intrudes, and so encourages awareness in the reader of problems encountered and devices adopted. 'How and where to begin?' are the opening words, reminding us that any meaningful narrative – with its tidy beginning and middle and end – is imposed on its subject-matter by the historian, and after the event. Life itself (as we all know from personal experience) can seem shapeless – 'a series of disconnected episodes with no movement toward a climax'; and the author readily confesses that the story of his subjects' lives at times 'becomes difficult to follow'. For it's only in retrospect that our memories contrive to impose a 'smooth narrative' on events, by conveniently forgetting the irritations and problems and conflicts that constitute the rougher edges of real life. Similarly, it's only with 'the safe voice of historical hindsight' that we can talk blandly of it being 'part of a writer's education', as we describe the anxieties experienced by Lafcadio Hearn about where his next meal is coming from; and it's only in retrospect that we can see his journey to New Orleans as being not just a visit to that city, but as a staging-post on his way to the Orient. A biographer, as Robert Rosenstone reminds us, has 'to *make sense* of the messy evidence that is a life' – has to impose on time some 'movement and shape', where none was apparent to the actors at the time.[3]

Conversely, of course, the biographer has to beware of making too much sense – of making both events and people all too orderly and consistent; and here we come to another of my required qualities – that of tolerating ambiguity. Biographical and historical method, as Rosenstone further reminds us, is likely to turn 'a chaotic jumble ... into something systematic and coherent', whereas authenticity requires the writer to 'jam the incompatible elements together and admit the contradictions can never be smoothed away'. The biographer, then, may need to 'settle for quick takes, short sequences, individual scenes, moments of insight' – a less than 'smooth' approach, perhaps, but more indicative of the ambiguities of what went on.[4] In short, the historian here is, again self-reflexively, revealing to the reader his own difficulties in representing the complexities of life as he sees and would wish to convey them: that is no less a part of his job, and of his own objective, than the construction of a finished narrative.

Another problem, as we are further advised, arises particularly in relation to the writer Hearn's own written evidence; for his 'highly literary' journals and letters are 'full of paragraphs so carefully composed, contoured, and balanced that the original experience is at once revealed and hidden'. The imposition of his own crafted narrative makes it impossible to know what he has recorded at the time, and what he has added later, with hindsight, and with wishes of what might have been (rather than what was) the case. So Hearn himself exemplifies a problem explicitly admitted by his later biographer, that often we are ourselves unconscious of how we modify, however slightly, and compress and stretch, however little, what evidence we have; so that we need constantly to remind ourselves of the provisional nature of any conclusions, and remember that our 'task is *not to find the truth, but to create one*'.[5]

The biographer's difficulties are compounded when his subjects' plans and personalities are, as they inevitably must be, thrown into disarray by foreign travel – or at least by travel to somewhere as different from their homeland as was nineteenth-century Japan. Confronting an alien culture, they had to come to terms, to make adjustments; and sometimes they were genuinely torn, wavering, undecided and indecisive, between two value systems that seemed to be at odds. On initially making contact with Japan, Rosenstone's Americans tended to view it as inferior, describing it variously as pagan, heathen, and morally degenerate. But, as their eyes were slowly opened to the virtues of Japanese life, they began to compare it favourably with what they had left behind. Impressed by their aesthetic sense, their refinement and friendship, William Griffis, for instance, came to respect 'the pride and dignity ... diligence, courage, gentlemanly conduct, refinement and affection, truth and honesty, good morals' of samurai, whom he had previously considered 'barbarians'; while Edward Morse wrote of how 'Little by little the realisation of why the Japanese have always called us [Americans] barbarians is dawning upon us'. 'My point of view in many things is repeatedly changed by my experience here'; and it may even be possible, he concludes, 'that *their* way of doing some things is really the best way'.[6]

Caught thus between two 'realities', Morse reminds us of the need to confront existential doubts and ambiguities in the objects of our study (or perhaps ourselves). 'We are not,' as Robert Rosenstone explains, 'trained to see that integrity may lie in contradiction rather than consistency', so that we tend to smooth discrepancies away – 'to deny the splits, to collapse them together, to bridge intellectual and emotional chasms with theories that satisfy a sense of intellectual neatness, completion'. He himself, in undertaking his biographical (and partly autobiographical) work, was forced to rethink conventional disciplinary procedures – to adopt new approaches in his push 'toward fresh visions and new ways of understanding the seamless reality of past and present'.[7]

Rosenstone also describes his need to confront the limitations of language in representing actual experience – and here we reach the third requisite quality, of linguistic awareness. For as perceptions change in the light of admitted ambiguities, there must be linguistic implications: 'words, categories, definitions ... [began] to slip, blend, and overlap in unexpected ways' – not least because direct translation from Japanese to English is impossible, and 'the simplest phrase cannot be translated from one to the other without altering *the form of the thought*'. For the historian, too, linguistic problems recur with the potential hazard of applying anachronistic terminology. Rosenstone quotes from William Griffis's own journal, where he 'rationalises' (as we might say) his projected behaviour in terms of God's will. But 'rationalisation' in that psychological sense was a word unknown in the nineteenth century, so its application here is clearly problematic. It may help us to explain behaviour that we cannot otherwise understand, but Griffis himself, who sincerely believed in obedience to a higher power, would never have interpreted his own behaviour in such terms. So, as Rosenstone insists, we pay a price for any gain in understanding – namely, the loss of some 'immediacy': 'the word can at once obscure and illuminate'; and 'insofar as the concept illuminates [for us] his behaviour, it obscures his [actual] experience'.[8] The anachronistic use of language can prove counter-productive in our attempt to gain real sympathetic understanding.

Altogether, then, Robert Rosenstone's book may not appear to resemble 'history' as it has traditionally been written. But in its often affecting evocation of past places and people, it succeeds in enabling us to come to some understanding of the situation of those, like Hearn, Griffis, Morse, and perhaps Rosenstone himself, who walk their tightrope between and within two different cultures, and though often wracked with indecision become 'able at special moments to live in two worlds'.[9] So in his *Mirror in the Shrine*, Robert Rosenstone reveals just the three qualities that I'm proposing as eminently transferable by historians: self-reflexivity, linguistic awareness, and an ability to live with ambiguity. By displaying all three in his own work – by actually *exemplifying* them in his history – he acts, not only as an advocate but as a practical model; and he thereby indicates an important role for a new-style history in postmodernity.

2   Peter Novick and the Holocaust

My second example might be seen as challenging the sort of history that we saw Ken Burns espousing. Such disciplinary disagreements are nothing new, of course: as we've seen, the past has always been disputed territory, as 'myth' and 'history' conflict and coincide; and the battle for control of personal and national identities is bound to be hard-fought. So let's consider now Peter Novick's provocative analysis of the Holocaust in American 'collective memory'. (Much of what he writes is relevant also for Europe and the wider world.)

The Holocaust seems to provide one example of grounds for what Ken Burns referred to as an 'emotional consensus' on a very widespread scale: it has generally become the indisputable symbol of evil in the twentieth century – indeed constitutes the very paradigm of evil in the whole of history, a moral 'black' with which 'white' may be unambiguously contrasted. Now taken to refer mainly to Hitler's attempted 'final solution of the Jewish problem', and his success in killing some six million Jews, the Holocaust is represented in numberless books and films, is memorialised on special days and in dedicated museums and exhibitions, and is included as an important (and often compulsory) ingredient of school and university syllabuses. In the early twenty-first century, it has taken its place in American and European (and maybe even more widely in our global village times) 'collective memory', providing a focus for 'emotional consensus' and supposedly a moral lesson for the future.

As an historian, Peter Novick is far from relegating that Holocaust to the status of a 'myth', but he has nevertheless felt impelled to examine the *historicity* of the concept – the way that the concept itself emerged and has developed through time. 'Collective memory', after all, is not a substantial entity that flows through the generations, somehow entering consciousness at birth and conveying a simple essence of some people's past: it's what has been decided should be important for us, and what has therefore been transmitted to us through our upbringing, education, and mass media. And an historian's motivation in subjecting that to historical analysis might well derive from a concern about *who* has made the decision concerning its importance, and *why*. History's function then becomes again to raise awareness about the roots of our own norms and presuppositions, and to challenge what might be an over-simplified mono-perspectival consensus, an overly comfortable smoothing out of ambiguities; and it's notable that Novick, while undertaking to do his 'best to make the story understandable', readily admits that he 'can't make it straightforward, or free of contradictions'.[10] That may not sound like much competition for Ken Burns, but it further exemplifies the sort of history that might promote our favoured qualities of self-reflexivity, linguistic awareness, and an ability to live with ambiguity.

What Novick reveals is that 'the Holocaust' is a concept that has grown mightily in strength from the 1970s and 1980s, and that it's only after that time that it has taken its central (even dominating) role in our thinking about the Second World War, and in our defining of Jewish identity. In the earlier 1940s, there was of course much ignorance of what was going on in Germany; and the Nazis' treatment of their 'undesirables' was but one atrocity among many, and so, even when reported, was left largely unexamined. It was only after the liberation of the extermination camps in 1945 that the horrors of the situation became clearer, but even then the particular events uncovered were not immediately subsumed within a general description. So 'the Holocaust' as a proper noun, or label representing a distinct (collective) entity, was 'largely a retrospective construction', conferred only after the event.[11] It is, therefore, another anachronistic, and potentially misleading, usage to apply the word to the time in question – the actual years of the war.

Another linguistic point is made by Novick in relation to the use of the term 'survivor'. He quotes Werner Weinberg writing in 1985 (some forty years after his own liberation) of how he and others had been known first as 'liberated prisoners', then as 'displaced persons', and how only years later he 'noticed that I had been reclassified as a "survivor"' – a reclassification to which he objected, as being 'terminal', or a condition and description from which he could never be freed.[12] And it was a description that originally conferred little honour, implying a self-centred selfishness that enabled survival only at the expense of others: only later did it take on the heroic connotations implicit in the word today.

Survival, at all events, is what seemed appropriate to emphasise at a time, after the war, when an upbeat, optimistic message was required. Through the 1950s and 1960s, then, as Novick writes, 'the Holocaust made scarcely any appearance in American public discourse', but when it did appear, attention was focused, not on atrocities, but on the more inspiring episodes of heroism and resistance. In those years, the status of 'victim' was not, as now, something to be prized, but rather to be treated with a mixture of pity and contempt; so it was a time for stories such as that of Anne Frank, whose diary was published and dramatised in the 1950s, and of the Warsaw Ghetto Uprising, which could be taken to demonstrate (in the words of one writer in 1951) 'the ultimate triumph of humanity despite the temporary victories of barbarism'.[13]

Such examples of resistance may have been rare, and for Novick there is some irony in the fact that the memorialisation of the Warsaw Ghetto Uprising in particular ensured that 'the event most a-typical of the Holocaust was made emblematic of it'. But those were the memories that were deemed salutary in the immediate post-war years by those who were concerned to present Communism as a replacement barbarism that had similarly to be resisted. New political alignments resulted in the re-assimilation of (a rehabilitated, de-Nazified) Germany to the western grouping in the so-called Cold War, and perceptions of the Second World War were re-cycled in that context of new political needs. 'Every generation,' as Novick explains, 'frames the Holocaust, represents the Holocaust, in ways that suit its mood'; and at that time it suited western powers to distance past evils from their present allies.[14]

In the early 1960s, however, the past intruded (as we've seen above) in the person and trial of Adolf Eichmann. Much new material about wartime events then became available and was highly publicised; and it was, Novick claims, as a result of that that 'there emerged in American culture a distinct *thing* called "the Holocaust" [now with a capital 'H']', and that it 'first became firmly attached to the murder of European Jewry' (rather than embracing equally such other victims as gypsies, homosexuals, Communists, and Jehovah's Witnesses).[15]

Lessons to be learnt were now made explicit. What clearly

emerged from Eichmann's trial, and from the freshly delineated Holocaust itself, was the need both to avoid appeasement and to oppose totalitarianism (whether in the form of Nazism or Communism); and the need to insist on those lessons was confirmed by developments in the Middle East. Threats to the very existence of Israel were taken to indicate that another Holocaust might actually be imminent: it was to be seen, not just as a single historical event, but as a continuing possibility; and appeals were made to the memory of past events in order to mobilise opinion against the possibility of future repetitions. Once again, Jews were to be seen as alone and vulnerable, due the support of those who had previously let them down. And that perception of a people as 'persecuted outsiders' has come to be (in the words of the columnist Ellen Willis) 'at the core of what Judaism and Jewishness is all about'.[16] At a time when minorities have become keen to assert their own individualistic identities, the Holocaust has come to constitute the very core of Jewish collective memory.

It's clear that Peter Novick is far from writing history 'for its own sake': as with such other historians as Robert Rosenstone and (as we shall see in the following sections) Sven Lindqvist and Tzvetan Todorov, he defies a number of professional norms, in the service of a self-consciously adopted agenda. Any pretence of 'detachment' is replaced with deliberate personal intrusions – confession of his own status as a Jew, and illustrative anecdotes drawn from his own experience as a teacher or affected museum visitor; and any attempt at definitive, closed narrative is repudiated in favour of the presentation of unanswered (perhaps unanswerable), open-ended questions. In sum, and as he himself readily (and early) concedes, he can't possibly make his story 'straightforward, or free of contradictions'; but what he can do, and does, is to show how historical study might contribute to a positive – a more hopeful – future.

For some lessons do emerge from what he writes – lessons not explicitly or moralistically propounded, but often implicit in analogies drawn between past and present. Thus, for example, the seemingly natural tendency or inclination to go along with everyone else is highlighted, and we are asked 'to consider how readily *we* delegate our moral decision-making to respectable authorities'. That question is posed in the context not only of the historical record of the Nazis, but also of the psychological experiments of Stanley Milgram, who in the 1960s demonstrated our horrifying propensity to obey authority. In the quoted words of the Episcopal Bishop of New York in 1974, 'I think that perhaps any one of us could also have had his or her own My Lai, his or her own Auschwitz';[17] and enhanced awareness of that possibility, and the way that we are presented with (admittedly smaller-scale, but parallel) moral dilemmas in everyday life at least must raise the level of our own self-consciousness at such times.

For, as Novick clarifies, 'all of us are witnesses to injustices, large and small, about which we don't make a fuss', and, in the last decades and even now, we've been witnesses to (complicit with) injustices on a genocidal scale. So we are presented with another question to ponder – as to whether the Holocaust has somehow defined the evil with which we think we ought to be concerned, leaving us free to ignore others (such as world-wide starving children) of which we prefer to remain unaware. The 'indifference', of which by-standers in the 1940s have often been accused, may be something of which we ourselves are guilty now? It's clear that Peter Novick, unlike Nicholas Kinloch, is not an advocate of professional 'neutrality', academic disengagement, or abstention from moral judgement; but he believes that lessons may be learnt from presentation of the past 'in all its messinesss' (back to ambiguities again) – not one 'that's been shaped and shaded' in the service of 'inspiring lessons'.[18]

What we have here, then, is one historian's investigation of one important aspect of collective memory – an investigation undertaken not for its own sake, but very much geared to the future, and to making that future in some way better. For, however unconsciously held, our memories do of course affect us: we act as we do as a result of having certain perceptions of ourselves, and from those perceptions certain expectations. That's why we need to be aware of what memories we hold and why – aware of our reasons for viewing the past as we do. Unless we are aware, memories persist, unquestioned; and for as long as they do that, we too persist unchanged. Constant investigation and adaptation of our memories (both individual and collective) is a precondition of development (and improvement).

As Peter Novick concludes, then, (even in the case of the Holocaust), to be overly mindful and overly focused on past injustices, however terrible, may result in giving a posthumous victory to oppressors, inasmuch as we're allowing our memories (however unconscious) to endorse *their* definitions (not least of ourselves), rather than our own. In individual cases, psycho-therapists would encourage reassessment of the pasts that we unhelpfully retain; but for the public it's clear that historians have the most crucial part to play. It's through their continual reassessments that they are able to loosen the shackles of the past that still confine us, opening routes to a more hopeful future.

3   Sven Lindqvist and bombing

My third example of a history that answers identified needs in post-modernity is Sven Lindqvist's *A History of Bombing*. For not only does it foster the three requisite qualities with which we're here concerned, but it also bears on Richard Rorty's aim to avoid cruelty and engender hope; and it indicates how history might contribute to that programme. As a twenty-first-century history, it is both novel in form and also underpinned by a clear personal and moral agenda. It's an illustration not only of *how* history might be written, but also (and most importantly for us here) of *why*. Despite his carefully modulated tone, it's pretty clear by the end what Lindqvist's history is written *for*.

'This is not a normal book,' writes the author. 'I am trying to give you a new kind of reading experience.'[19] He succeeds: consistently with our remarks above on 'closure', Sven Lindqvist's material is far from being presented in the form of a closed narrative; but, on the contrary, it appears as 399 numbered extracts (mainly single paragraphs, or groups of paragraphs that seldom total more than half a page, itself un-numbered) – a potential quarry of data on his subject, through which (as in the case of the past itself) it's theoretically possible to trace any number of paths. Some paragraphs deal with the history of bombing itself and of related technologies (including especially aviation), others with the effects of bombardments, others with attitudes towards (and legislation concerning) mass destruction and various categories of civilian casualties; and source-material importantly includes novels and the author's personal reminiscences, as well as more conventionally derived evidence from public records, diaries, and eye-witness accounts.

For practical purposes, twenty-two routes through this diverse material are indicated. They deal with such themes as the early history of the subject, questions of 'legality', the bombing of colonials and 'savages' and of Germany and Japan, and the development and effects of 'superweapons'; and subsidiary (or derivative and equally important) themes emerge relating to racism and morality, and the seemingly relentless erosion of human sensibilities. Starting from one numbered section, then, the reader follows arrows to succeeding extracts, and then starts again along another track, until a remarkably rounded picture is achieved, with (at least in my case) considerable impact.

Bombs themselves are identified as early as the eleventh century in China, but their significance was of course hugely increased after the means of delivering them from the air were developed in the early twentieth century. Interestingly, the possibility of aerial bombardment had been envisaged as early as the Montgolfier brothers' first successful balloon flight in 1783: the feasibility of mass-travel has always been linked with that of mass-destruction; and as Lindqvist describes, 'The dream of solving all the problems of the world through mass destruction from the air was already in place before the first bomb was dropped'.[20]

That first drop took place in 1911, in the context of a Eurocentric imperialism that was taken to justify the bombing of 'lesser breeds' in the interest of enlarging the bounds of civilisation. The new technologies were harnessed in aid of Europe's civilising mission – a mission seemingly authorised by Christian and secular sources that justified the violent subjugation of the lawless. Decades before Europeans directed bombs against each other, they had practised their skills – and not least their self-justificatory moral skills – on those who could conveniently be considered as less human than themselves. And with his illuminating juxtaposition of materials, Lindqvist encourages thought about the mindsets of these early perpetrators of mass-destruction from the air, inviting questions about their education and psychology – just as he provokes questioning about the macho posturing of later advocates of military strikes whose outcomes would defy contemplation.

Throughout, too, the author's own personal intrusions add life and point to the unfolding story. He opens with a short description of his own childhood experience of playing at bombs with piss and pine-cones, and periodically links the chronology of his story with his own age and interests at the time in question; he recalls attitudes towards the bombing of Germany that he personally encountered soon after the war on a visit to England; he relates more recent visits to museums and discussions that he has had, with witnesses and survivors for example, in the course of researching his book; and he recalls his own emotional reactions to his father's death and to some external danger to which his own daughter was exposed. Such personal intrusions tend to re-emphasise his own deep involvement with the subject, and establish the ultimately personal and human nature of what he is writing about.

It is, of course, the humanitarian aspect of his subject with which Lindqvist is ultimately concerned, and no reader is likely to feel let off any hook. Allied bombing in the Second World War is shown as paralleling (in some, though not of course all, respects) Nazi attempts at genocide; some blatantly racist overtones of bombing strategy are laid bare, as are the cynical deceptions (concerning, for example, targets and casualties) promulgated, even in nominal democracies, by those in power; and above all the escalating erosion of sensibilities, with revenge following revenge *ad infinitum* and *ad nauseam* until 'People got used even to the unthinkable',[21] is a recurring theme that resonates uncomfortably for those who have seen the 'shock and awe' delivered in their own names since Lindqvist's book was published.

Some main points about this historical study – a study that at first sight might seem a narrowly specialised branch of military history – are, then, that it heightens consciousness about its subject and about the human implications of that subject; that (without any need for explicit sign-posting) it constantly resonates with present concerns; that (without any undue moralising) it raises hugely important moral questions, that make us ponder the future, and the direction into that future that we might wish to take. No reader of Lindqvist's history can escape images of the terrible cruelty that humans inflict on one another (Figure 7); but his message is not without some hope, for, as he says:

> In retrospect, the course of history easily acquires the semblance of inevitability. In retrospect, nothing can be changed, and therefore events are depicted as if they had been unchangeable from the beginning. But while history was unfolding, it *could have been changed*. Other decisions could have been made, which would have turned the course in another direction.[22]

As with our other examples, it's by remembering that things could have been – and can be – changed that we are given cause for hope; and helping to establish that essential point is a hugely important part of what history in postmodernity is *for*.

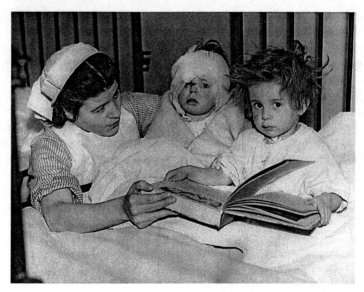

Figure 7 Collateral damage, London 1941. Sally Smith, aged 2, shows a picture
book to her injured sister, Barbara, aged 1, after a bombing raid in
which their mother, father and brother were killed.

4   Tzvetan Todorov and hope

It was only after completing the draft of this book that I came across
my fourth example: Tzvetan Todorov's recently published *Hope and
Memory: Reflections on the Twentieth Century*.[23] Although hardly
written as conventional history, but rather, as indicated in the sub-
title, as 'reflections', it constitutes another good example of what the
subject might now be for; and some discussion of it will enable me
to draw together the threads of my main arguments, while focusing
on matters of crucial importance for the twenty-first century.

Todorov's own reflections on the last century lead him to identify
the rise of totalitarianism – and more specifically of Communist and
Nazi totalitarian ideologies – and its struggle with democracy, as
being the core issue (as it were, the centre of the web) of recent
history. That identification is, as he himself makes clear, the author's
own personal way of making some sense of the past one hundred
years – his own key to enable him to unlock some meaning in them,
or rather perhaps to impose some meaning *on* them. As he reveals
quite explicitly, that choice of key derives from his own background
and experience – from his birth in Bulgaria, his upbringing under a

Communist régime in which his father lost his job for ideological reasons, and, after 1963, his life in France as a cultural and intellectual historian. There are, of course, many possible alternative (and complementary) ways of looking back over the twentieth century, which would obviously lead to quite different conclusions about what is most significant, and about what makes an appropriate organising principle for an infinite amount of data; and indeed a number of attempts have already been made. But what, in the context of this book, is striking about Todorov's account is that his reflections have been driven by a self-consciously adopted and clearly defined *purpose* in relation to the *future*. That purpose derives in brief from the author's own preference for democracy: it is, he believes, only by understanding the challenges by which democracy has been (and may be) confronted that it can hope to survive in the future; and (resonating with another theme of this book) we can, taking inspiration from some specific examples of individual moral excellence, justifiably take *hope* for that future. Todorov in short, has no naive illusions about any possibility of keeping 'use' out of historical study in general, and is, on the contrary, quite clear about what his own particular history is *for*.

Subsidiary or implicit themes in his work seem to me to relate to the three qualities which I have advocated as desirable outcomes of historical study: namely, an ability to live with ambiguity, linguistic awareness, and self-consciousness. It may be, of course, that once one has formulated such themes, one begins to see their presence everywhere, but at all events I'll take them again (in that order) as my own organising principle here for a consideration of *Hope and Memory*.

Totalitarianism, as defined by Todorov, is exemplified first by Communism in Russia, after the revolution of 1917. It started, as was widely perceived, as a utopian project, with its leaders expressing optimism about making the world a better place: the removal of hereditary class privileges and the shackles of hierarchy would, it was believed, pave a way to real equality and human happiness – and that dream spread from Russia itself through eastern Europe and indeed much of the world, persisting, despite some contrary evidence, through much of the twentieth century (at least until European Communism's dissolution in 1989).

As the other form of totalitarianism, Nazism was geographically more confined and had a much shorter life, being essentially German and effectively lasting (despite some other minor outbreaks) only from the 1930s until the defeat and downfall of the Third Reich in 1945. Nazism had much in common with Communism (despite intense mutual hostility): it too promulgated a utopian vision – albeit less universal than that of its competitor – with the prospect for its followers of attaining well-deserved super-eminence, and living happily in a perfected world made free of lesser breeds.

What the two forms of totalitarianism importantly shared, then, was an absolute – an *unambiguous* – conviction of their own rightness. Each fostered the cult of a supreme leader – initially Lenin, followed by Stalin on the one hand, and Adolf Hitler on the other; and each was convinced that their ultimate end or goal justified any actions – any means – by which that end could be achieved. Many may be destined to suffer along the way – and many were: both Stalin and Hitler were responsible for the deaths of millions. But such suffering and sacrifice resulted from (and facilitated) the pursuit of good: it was claimed to be, as we say, all in a good cause. Any massacre of innocents could be 'justified' (at least to its perpetrators) in those terms; for 'Even Herod,' as has been noted, 'did not shed blood in the name of evil; he shed blood in the name of his particular good.'[24]

Any such visions for the future require control of the past, which brings us back to history and its uses; for totalitarian leaders have always taken care to ensure the extension of their power over *memory*. Russian history has been subject to constant revision for political purposes, with participants airbrushed out of photographs, and thence, it's hoped, out of memory, at the whim of current leaders; and, as we have previously seen, similar manipulations were made in Nazi Germany, where, in Primo Levi's words, 'The entire history of the brief "millennial Reich" can be re-read as a war against memory, an Orwellian falsification of memory'[25] – a refusal to admit such memories as failed to cohere with current projects.

Totalitarianism indeed is essentially Manichaean – dividing the world into two mutually exclusive categories: the good and the bad, the right and the wrong, friend and foe, them and us. There's no room there for ambiguity: one of the clearest (and to us most sinister) implications of totalitarianism is the utter self-assurance of its advocates – such assurance of their own goodness and rightness, as justifies annihilation of anything or anyone that begs to differ. For difference in itself implies opposition, and opposition to what is obviously right and good cannot, of course, be brooked. In a world restricted to black and white, there is no room for any shades of grey, no place for (or tolerance of) neutrality or ambiguity. Those who are not *for* are defined as necessarily *against*; there can be no recognition of any equal 'other'.

That decisive categorisation and the attendant repudiation of any doubt, or 'greyness', flies in the face of Todorov's message, as exemplified by some of his chosen individuals. Primo Levi, for instance, with his personal experience of Auschwitz, identified what he referred to as a 'grey zone' in the camps – a zone taken to include all those who seemed to him to fail to fit simplistic categorisations of 'black' and 'white', 'good' and 'evil'. Entering the chaos of a camp, he explains, one tried to make some sense of it, tried to give one's experience of it some meaning; but none of the usual categories gave any purchase on it. Expectations might have included clear differentiation between 'prisoner' and 'guard', 'victim' and 'oppressor'; but the reality proved less than amenable to such terms of what could have constituted a conveniently simple analysis. Instead, there was a whole hierarchy of inmates, with some prisoners promoted to authority in various aspects of camp life; and the boundaries between the different classes were blurred, far from fixed or unambiguous. So Levi, in that abnormal situation – a situation that represented totalitarianism, on a smaller scale, yet even more intensely – came to realise the uselessness of the 'normal' labels by which our lives are ordinarily ordered; and he concluded by admitting to his 'grey zone' both the 'white' and 'black' of convention. 'At that time,' as he recorded, 'we were all grey.'[26]

As another of Todorov's exemplary figures, Romain Gary came to a similar conclusion. Born in Russia in 1914, Gary lived in France from 1928, joined the Free French in London in 1940, and served throughout the war in the air force. What makes him particularly interesting in the present context is his refusal, like Levi, to entertain any Manichaean labelling: on the contrary, as he affirms, 'Black and white, makes me sick. Grey, that's the only thing that's human'. Even the Nazis, he believes (those archetypal enemies against whom he personally fought), demonstrated an aspect of humanity that we in fact all share. Even the Nazis, after all, 'were human. And what was human about them was their inhumanity'. As a character in one of Gary's later novels warns: 'No greater peril lies in ambush for us than the strange difficulty we have in recognising humanity in men.'[27]

Those examples of Primo Levi and Romain Gary, both of whom had personal experience of the moral extremes to which they refer, might well give us pause for thought, as the tendency to reduce to simplistic terms seemingly becomes ever more prevalent in our nominal democracies. The 'foundational rhetorical device' to which Todorov alerts us is 'the excluded middle', whereby those who are not for us are necessarily against, and 'any attempt to introduce nuances into the argument is seen as treason'. By such means we are encouraged to dehumanise our enemies – whether as a Jewish plague of rats or as the tentacled monster of Al Qaeda – and that makes their elimination all the more urgent as well as all the more acceptable (and even desirable). It's worth quoting Todorov's own conclusion, which has itself taken on additional urgency with additional resonances since he wrote it (before the invasion of Iraq), and which bears a clear message for the future in relation to the toleration of ambiguities:

> If we want to be free of the Manichaean world view dividing humanity into mutually exclusive categories of good and bad – a view akin to totalitarian doctrines – then a good way to start would be to avoid becoming Manichaean ourselves. A maxim for the twenty-first century might well be to start not by fighting evil in the name of good, but by attacking the certainties of people who claim always to know where good and evil are to be found. We should struggle not against the devil himself but against what allows the devil to live – Manichaean thinking itself.[28]

If Todorov there provides an example of a tolerant and humane advocacy of life sustained without dogmatic certainties – of life embracing the necessity of ambiguity – he also conveniently (for me) links it with another desired quality, that of linguistic awareness. And as a man who bears personal witness to life in a totalitarian country in the 1950s, his own interest in that subject is hardly surprising; for recalling that time, he writes of how 'My friends and I felt we were living in a world of lies, where words designating ideals – peace, freedom, equality, prosperity – had come to mean their opposites.' Totalitarian leaders need to control not only memory, but also language – to make words fit their own requirements, promoting what supports them and expunging (first from language, then from experience itself, and memory) anything that might oppose. Words are manipulated, so that they hide as much as they reveal. Thus, for example, in early Communist Russia, Lenin can, without any recogni-

tion of irony, proclaim that 'The enemies of liberty must be extermi-
nated without mercy' – an assertion that not only illustrates his utter
conviction of the rightness of his own cause, and his utter ruthlessness
in seeking his own ends, but also demonstrates his appropriation of
the word 'liberty' for his own party. Henceforth anyone opposing him
opposes 'liberty', so clearly warrants extermination without mercy –
with the help, perhaps, of the Russian General, who proclaimed at
the head of his invading army that he was bringing 'peace and happiness' on the 'tips of our bayonets'. 'War is Peace', as the Party slogan
went in Orwell's *Nineteen Eighty-Four*, and words do indeed 'come to
mean their opposites'.[29]

Such linguistic manipulations – particularly rife during times of
war, when popular opinion needs to be mobilised in required patriotic or ideological directions – are not confined to totalitarian
régimes alone: Vaclav Havel, the famously anti-totalitarian president of the Czech Republic, has much more recently referred, with
no apparent recognition of paradox, to the 'humanitarian bombs'
that were dropped on Kosovo in the name of democracy; and
Todorov reminds us of similar contortions that permit description
of 'what the other side calls "crimes against humanity" (civilian
deaths) as "collateral damage"'. These linguistic contortions (like
those we've considered in the context of the Third Reich) are, as he
suggests, marks of 'a particularly docile public, or one that is keen
to preserve its good conscience'; and they are marks too, as we
might add, of a people insufficiently aware of the uses (abuses) to
which their language is constantly subject.[30]

For it suits self-congratulatory democratic leaders to consolidate
their own positions by distancing themselves from their assumed
opposites. Totalitarian leaders such as Stalin and Hitler, or others
(chronologically nearer home) such as Saddam Hussein and Osama
bin Laden, are to be described as 'irrational', 'mad', and 'paranoid'.
For in that way they can be viewed as aberrations, deserving expul-
sion from the ranks of 'normal' human beings. But as Todorov
reminds us, those men were (or are) in fact and in their own ways
perfectly rational, in the sense that, starting from the aims they set
themselves, they acted (and act) quite rationally (methodically and
ruthlessly) in order to achieve them. It is their 'end' – their conception of 'good' – that needs to be questioned; and it's just possible
that such questioning (which is again at least in part a matter of
language: what is 'good'?) may be provoked by historical study. For
it is, after all, that study which reveals (or can be used to reveal)

other and earlier examples of those who thought they had the answer – of those who were so certain of their own rightness that they set out to impose it on the rest of the world.

The attempts by Europeans, for instance, to impose the good of their own Christian religion on others have been well rehearsed. The Crusades of the eleventh to thirteenth centuries, the conquest of America in the fifteenth and sixteenth centuries, and far-flung European colonisation in the nineteenth and twentieth centuries, have all been justified in conveniently altruistic terms. But in the light of history, such attempts to impose a good – whether religious or social or political – on other people can often be revealed as problematic; for with the benefit of hindsight, we can sometimes see that means have not invariably been justified by (increasingly questionable and debatable) ends. The aspiration finally to eradicate evil and injustice (as defined by us) harks back to 'those totalitarian utopias that dreamed of improving the human race and creating paradise on earth'; and we might do well, as Todorov concludes, to beware of taking on again the task of curing humanity of all its ills. 'The dream of universal goodness is itself evil, for it puts abstract aim in the place of real people ... [and] If we have to become totalitarian in order to crush totalitarianism, then totalitarianism has won.'[31]

If Todorov's reflections serve to re-emphasise this book's two themes concerning ambiguity and language, the third – relating to self-consciousness – also appears, most obviously in his introduction of exemplary figures. For it is by reading about men and women who have exemplified the best qualities of human beings (as we would wish them to be) that we are (or may be) alerted to the (possibly less than adequate) nature of our own selves. That sort of revelation has, as we have seen, long been considered one of the main moral points of historical study, and the examples given illustrate what Todorov himself approvingly refers to as 'critical humanism'. Those examples may be few in number, but they are important in demonstrating human qualities maintained against great odds; for in whatever awful circumstances these people found themselves, they 'never stopped believing, in spite of everything, that actual human beings provide the only legitimate ideal for human aspiration'. Importantly, then, they 'help us to avoid despair' – or even, as we might say more positively, they give us cause for hope.[32]

Thus, Primo Levi is well known as a self-conscious witness of Auschwitz, where he was himself imprisoned as an Italian Jew. In writing books about his experiences, he might have been expected to sound cynical, bitter, accusatory, and to have induced despair about the level to which supposedly civilised human beings can sink. But in fact the reverse is the case: through his own qualities, Levi somehow transcends the beastliness of his descriptions, and as Todorov maintains, the reader actually 'emerges strengthened'. It's not his historical subject-matter that gives us hope – how could it? – but the attitude that he's adopted in relation to it. 'The light doesn't come from the world that Levi describes, but from Levi himself.' For he has refused to accept what might have been considered the 'real' or 'natural' (or even 'only') way of looking at what happened – has somehow refused to accept any negative implications of his past experience. And it is precisely that 'unwillingness to be content with the bitter conclusions that he could not avoid reaching', that 'makes him particularly precious to us today'.[33]

Another witness introduced by Todorov is Margarete Buber-Neumann, who similarly retained her own humane values despite experiencing the inhumanity of both Russian and German totalitarianism. As a prisoner in concentration camps, she too, like Levi, managed to avoid falling into the sort of despair that we might be tempted to think would have been all too 'natural' or 'normal'; and she did that by focusing, not on the generality of evil all around her, but on any particular 'signs of human goodness', however rare these might have been. Her particular importance for Todorov lies in her refusal to discriminate between the evils of the two totalitarian régimes, so that after the war she bravely spoke out against the still existing Russian camps, even after it had become politically inexpedient to do so. 'My hatred for German concentration camps,' she insisted, 'is no greater and no smaller than my hatred of the camps of Stalin the dictator'; and she 'used her remaining strength to fight the still unvanquished evil of the Communist totalitarian régime'.[34]

A central lesson derived from his reflective narratives by Todorov himself is that 'Each of us can find the means to stand up to the trend of our times; as Rousseau said, we are free to "acquiesce or resist"'.[35] The records of his exemplary people – their histories (and there are others whom I've not included here) – provoke our reconsideration of what qualities human beings can show even in extreme situations; they encourage us to re-define our concept of 'humanity'; and they compel us not least to be self-conscious – aware of how we might measure up to (or fall short of) their exacting standards.

Todorov thus shows the vital importance of certain sorts of history in relation to the future. It's because the past is so important for that future that we need to be aware of what we're doing with it. Control of the past was (and remains) essential to totalitarianism: both Nazi and Communist leaders carefully retained (or purloined) that power for themselves – deciding which parts of the past would 'disappear' and which be publicly available, deciding how their own selections from the past would be interpreted, and where they would be seen to lead. That is the power that historians possess – that is the power (whether consciously or not) they wield.

So in our privileged democracies we'd do well to remain alert to those insistent demands (so frequently heard of late) to 'draw lines' beneath what's inconvenient, and 'move on' – and so by implication simply forget what's past. 'Nobody else,' as Todorov insists, 'has a right to tell us what image to have of our own past, *even if many try to do so.*' For 'Free access to the past unfettered by centralised control is one of the fundamental, inalienable freedoms of democratic countries'. That may sound so obvious as not to need re-stating. But such reminders are far from out of place in societies where longer-term aspiration is replaced by immediate gratification, and where 'the vain pleasures of the instant' are not always unrelated to 'the crime of forgetting'.[36]

Todorov's 'reflections' lead him to a position of which Richard Rorty surely would approve – a position where 'memory' has to do with 'hope'. So a democracy, he insists, 'does not have to resign itself to accepting the world as it is'; it 'also seeks to replace what *is* with what *should be*'. And it is, of course, in the prospective journey from one to the other, that we can see again what history might be for. 'In judging a work of history,' Todorov suggests, 'we use "truth" to signify the power to unveil the underlying meaning of an event.'[37] 'Unveil' may be a problematic concept here, inasmuch as meaning is not to be found inherent in the past, but rather constructed or imposed by the historian. But if personal and public histories are (as I too believe) about the attribution of some meaning to the past, then one could do worse than choose to reflect upon that past in such a way as to indicate, as Todorov does, a hopeful future – warning against prospective dangers, proposing more positive alternatives, and offering exemplifications of humanity defined in such ways as we approve. With that message of hope, we find another indication here of what history can be *for*.

Afterword

It is a naïve illusion to believe that use can be kept out of history.

(Tzvetan Todorov)[1]

Maybe we write to change the world in some way.

(Greg Dening)[2]

I hope that in the course of this book I've shown that the old ideal of 'history for its own sake' has been finally discredited, and that, as Tzvetan Todorov indicates in the quotation above, it's at best naïve to retain any belief in the illusion that a history can ever be 'useless'. As Claude Lévi-Strauss (cited in the Preface) long since indicated, history just can't help being *for* something. Which is far from being any cause to lament: on the contrary, it serves once again to re-emphasise how extraordinarily powerful and important history *necessarily* is.

Historians, then, can't any longer pretend to be engaged in a self-indulgent, solipsistic cultivation of their own gardens. Rather, they are bound to be aware that the manner of their digging in the past, of their pruning and preserving, uprooting and discarding, the nature of the interpretative seeds they sow, the designs and plans they work to, their intellectual harvesting – all will impact profoundly upon the wider social, political, and moral environment. That may be either in ways to confirm some *status quo*, or, as Greg Dening indicates above, in ways that might actually effect some *change*.

To take the former first – their stabilising function – it is historians whose role it has been to supply remembrance and identify traditions by which lives are to be ordered; it is they who have assumed responsibility for the construction of personal and national identities, providing requisite narratives for their underpinning; it is they who have served to encourage acceptance and assimilation of such conventions as have glued both individual people and societies together. In such ways, historians have often been a force for comforting conservatism, and it's not for nothing that history has traditionally been prescribed as an essential part of education.

But historically derived cohesion tends to come at a price – the price of inertia and un-receptiveness towards alternatives. And when, like Pyrrho in the fourth century BC, we're confronted now by cultural diversity, we are forced to realise that change and possible alternatives do need to be considered. For nothing – and least of all the past – is essentially one thing rather than another: what matters is our response to it. As Pyrrho put it, 'no single thing [and here we must include the past] is *in itself* any more this than that'; so, unless we take remedial action, it remains unconsciously adopted habits – 'custom and convention' – that determine our responses, and so 'govern human action'.[3]

And that's where we come to the possibility of history effecting change. For as a remedy for such un-self-aware enslavement, what's required is historical study of the sort that (in the last chapter) we've just been looking at – histories that encourage self-consciousness about both the existence and the foundations of our customs and conventions; for it's that self-consciousness that enables questioning and change. 'The requirement,' then, as Foucault has described, 'is for critical analyses of prevailing "régimes of truth", analyses which explore the connections, encounters, supports, blockages, plays of forces, strategies and so on which at a given moment establish what subsequently counts as being self-evident, universal, and necessary.'[4] So, reverting to the discussion in Chapter 1, it becomes once more the task of the humanities – and not least of history in particular – to adopt a 'therapeutic' role, by provoking doubts and questioning the status and validity of what's otherwise too easily accepted unthinkingly as self-evident, natural, and inevitable.

As the force of existing conventions, inscribed in and confirmed by former histories, is challenged and dissipates, new possibilities emerge; for with a changed orientation to (perception of) our past, a whole new future opens up. That may, as Anthony Giddens and others have warned, induce some anxiety; for as earlier signposts, previously established and confirmed by historical or mythical traditions, are rendered blank once more, we are inevitably faced with uncertainties about which path – which future – to take. But there's a positive dimension to that predicament: we're left with real choice, endowed with 'the capability to disturb the fixity of things, [and] open up new pathways'; and those pathways may, if we so determine, lead to hope for human betterment, as we contemplate our ability to 'colonise a segment of a *novel* future'.[5]

In the early twentieth century, the Vice-Chancellor of Birmingham University, Charles Grant Robertson, envisaged a future when 'Not philosophers but the philosophical historians will be kings in a progressive society, and The Institute of Historical Research will be subsidised by a grateful nation in priority even to the Committee for Scientific and Industrial Research'. That amazing (and, as it now appears, unlikely) situation would come about through widespread realisation that, because the future is indeed a blend of the present with the inherited past, it's important that we take cognisance of that past, assessing it in relation not only to the gains we've made, but also to the losses we've sustained along the way – gaining awareness of 'what we have lost and why we have lost it'.[6]

Two years later, in his Inaugural Lecture as Regius Professor at Oxford, F. M. Powicke insisted that 'the study of history cannot be dissociated from concern with political and wider ethical problems'. History should, he believed, have a constructive purpose: it might in particular engage in 'the search for the forces which have confirmed in mankind the sense of fair dealing and mutual under-standing ... a search for equity'. 'The dominant conception' with which we need to be concerned 'is the need of mutual under-standing and equitable behaviour between man and man, nation and nation, race and race'; so that we might arrive at a future where 'wanton cruelty and destructiveness ... will be condemned'.[7]

That returns us to the prospect offered by Greg Dening with his unashamed ambition actually to change the world, with histories that might disturb 'the moral lethargy of the living to change in their present the consequences of their past';[8] which returns us in turn and again to our preliminary discussion of 'therapeutic' educa-tion. For we sometimes do need to be disturbed from our lethargy and reminded that, yes, we do have a choice about how to view our pasts – about how to respond to them, and thence about what consequences to derive from them. 'Historical fact and falsehood,' as Clive Bell noted long ago in relation to history of art, 'are of no consequence to people who try to deal with realities. They need not ask, "Did this happen?"; they need ask only, "Do I feel this?"'[9] It's not so much what we (intellectually) 'know' about our past, as how we (more emotionally) feel about it that will affect (if not determine) its consequences for us, and so the way we face and encounter the future. So some moral disturbance to provoke an openness to reassessment seems highly desirable, especially when, to generalise hugely, we can see that world events in the early twenty-first century have done little to boost confidence in the future, but have rather served to emphasise the apparent impotence of people, even in nominal democracies, to influence the direction that 'history' is to take.

Those events have also rendered even more unlikely our ability to construct any plausible narrative of progress, which makes it even more important that such a narrative in fact be constructed – not by looking back at what has happened and, by extrapolation from the past, making (no doubt rationally) dire predictions for the future, but rather by articulating first some moral goals to which we may aspire and then providing such underpinning as they may require for their fulfilment. That implies the rejection of any aspiration to tell a final or 'definitive' story that inhibits flexibility; it implies the rejection of any dogmatic exclusiveness (in the name of patriotism or 'professionalism' or anything else); and it implies the rejection of any quest for the certainty of final 'truth'.

That may in turn itself sound negative or nihilistic, but is surely the reverse. For as is well known, but sometimes forgotten, it was recognition of his own ignorance that qualified Socrates to be the wisest man in the world; and in similar (at first sight seemingly paradoxical) vein the German poet Schiller reaffirmed a belief that 'In error only is there life, and knowledge must be death'.[10] It's the assumed fixity of knowledge that militates against life, and it's the continued (always unsuccessful) striving to achieve a better future – that travelling hopefully which is better than premature arrival – which overcomes death. It's the process of inquiry (*historia* in Greek) that is important; for by ongoing adjustments and the acceptance of apparent opposites and incompatibilities (rather than by denials and exclusions), growth and development are facilitated, both individual and (thence) socio-political. In a continuing evolution, there are no final 'winners' and 'losers' – no exclusions from any exclusive, absolute, or finally arrived at truth. And an encouragement towards such inclusiveness, with its implication of acceptance, tolerance, and even love, may provide another answer to our question of what history is *for*?

Further reading

This book comes as the culmination of my thinking on the nature(s) and purpose(s) of history, as shown in *History: What and Why? Ancient, Modern, and Postmodern Perspectives* [1996], 2nd edn, London, Routledge, 2001; *Why Bother with History? Ancient, Modern, and Postmodern Motivations*, Harlow, Longman, 2000; and *Postmodernism in History: Fear or Freedom?* London, Routledge, 2003. Each of these earlier studies is designed to put our own situation into some historical context, and each has a bibliography and suggestions for further reading. With regard more specifically to the question of what history has been, is, and might be *for*, the following is a listing of some of the books and articles that I have found interesting, provocative and/or intellectually stimulating.

On the general issue of the humanities and what I have called 'therapeutic' education, I have obviously been inspired by works of Richard Rorty, including especially *Contingency, Irony, and Solidarity*, Cambridge, Cambridge University Press, 1989, and the collection of essays significantly entitled *Philosophy and Social Hope*, Harmondsworth, Penguin, 1999. These last provide a particularly accessible entrée to Rorty's thought on the potentially *practical* effects of pragmatic philosophy. As models of much earlier therapeutically inclined thinkers, see Cicero, *The Nature of the Gods*, transl. Horace C. P. McGregor, Harmondsworth, Penguin, 1972; Lucretius, *On the Nature of the Universe*, transl. R. E. Latham, Harmondsworth, Penguin, 1951; and Seneca, *Letters from a Stoic*, transl. Robin Campbell, Harmondsworth, Penguin, 1969; and for up-to-date commentary on these and other important ancient (but still relevant) philosophies, see Martha C. Nussbaum, *The Therapy of Desire: Theory and Practice in Hellenistic Ethics*, Princeton, Princeton University Press, 1994. For literature, key works are (for Britain)

F. R. Leavis, *The Great Tradition*, Harmondsworth, Penguin, 1972, and (for the USA) Lionel Trilling, *The Liberal Imagination: Essays on Literature and Society*, London, Secker & Warburg, 1951; and for a rather less accessible, more linguistically orientated approach, try I. A. Richards, *Mencius on Mind: Experiments in Multiple Definition*, London, Kegan Paul, 1932.

The long-lived tradition of knowledge for its own sake goes back at least to Plato: for the quest for Truth in the guise of beauty and love, his *Symposium* makes a good start, transl. Walter Hamilton, Harmondsworth, Penguin, 1951; and then try Socrates' 'Apology' (or self-defence) in *The Last Days of Socrates*, transl. Hugh Tredennick, London, Penguin, 1959. For the development of this tradition in the nineteenth century, see, for a classic contemporary source, John Henry Newman, *On the Scope and Nature of University Education* [1852], London, J. M. Dent & Sons, 1916; and for an excellent recent historical commentary George Levine, *Dying to Know: Scientific Epistemology and Narrative in Victorian England*, London, Chicago University Press, 2002. On history more specifically, the own-sakist tradition in the twentieth century is well represented by Geoffrey Elton, *The Practice of History*, London, Fontana, 1969, and *Return to Essentials*, Cambridge, Cambridge University Press, 1991; and see also J. H. Plumb, *The Death of the Past*, Harmondsworth, Penguin, 1973. For continuing subscribers in the twenty-first century, try Arthur Marwick, *The New Nature of History: Knowledge, Evidence, Language*, Basingstoke, Palgrave, 2001 (which incorporates a revealingly intemperate attack on 'postmodernists'); and M. C. Lemon, *Philosophy of History: A Guide for Students*, London, Routledge, 2003. Of related interest, a study of the Holy Grail itself was published too late for me to use, but has been well reviewed: Richard Barber, *The Holy Grail: Imagination and Belief*, London, Allen Lane, 2004.

On the professed purposes (as well as natures) of history, some useful edited collections include Donald R. Kelley (ed.), *Versions of History from Antiquity to the Enlightenment*, New Haven and London, Yale University Press, 1991, which includes much of relevance from antiquity, the Middle Ages and Renaissance; and, with convenient chronological complementarity, Robert M. Burns and Hugh Rayment-Pickard (eds), *Philosophies of History from Enlightenment to Postmodernity*, Oxford, Blackwell, 2000, which brings the story up to date. On the latter period, Fritz Stern (ed.), *Varieties of History from Voltaire to the Present*, 2nd edn, London, Macmillan, 1970, remains useful, although 'the present' reaches only as far as the 1960s. Back in the nineteenth century, William Stubbs writes on the purposes, as well as methods, of historical study in *Seventeen Lectures on the Study of Mediaeval and Modern History and Kindred Subjects*, 3rd edn, Oxford, Clarendon Press 1900; and, with its revealing title, see also W. E. H. Lecky, *The Political Value of History*, London, Edward Arnold, 1892. Most theoretical writing on history in the twentieth century has focused on its nature, but J. H. Plumb writes on 'the *role* of history' in *The Death of the Past* (as above); and Elton has a few pages on 'Purpose' in *The Practice of History*. As we reach the new millennium, historians' increased awareness of such matters is indicated by Eric Foner in e.g. *Freedom's Lawmakers: A Directory of Black Officeholders during Reconstruction*, revised edn, Baton Rouge and London, Louisiana State University Press, 1996, and *Who Owns History? Rethinking the Past in a Changing World*, New York, Hill & Wang, 2002; and, for all his apparent misunderstanding of 'postmodernism', J. C. D. Clark has interesting things to say in *Our Shadowed Present: Modernism, Postmodernism and History*, London, Atlantic Books, 2003.

The hidden agendas to which historians have (often unconsciously) worked are brilliantly revealed in my two main case-studies: Reba N. Soffer, *Discipline and Power: The University, History, and the Making of an English Élite, 1870–1930*, Stanford, Stanford University Press, 1994; and Bonnie G. Smith, *The Gender of History: Men, Women, and Historical Practice*, London, Harvard University Press, 1998. There are interesting papers in the nicely entitled collection of Keith Wilson (ed.), *Forging the Collective Memory*, Oxford, Berghahn, 1996; and on the case of Germany, there is chilling material in Gilmer W. Blackburn, *Education in the Third Reich: A Study of Race and History in Nazi Textbooks*, Albany, State University of New York Press, 1985. Further revealing accounts of post-war German historiography are to be found in Mary Fulbrook, *German National Identity after the Holocaust*, Cambridge, Polity, 1999; Mary Fulbrook and Martin Swales (eds), *Representing the German Nation: History and Identity in Twentieth-Century Germany*, Manchester, Manchester University Press, 2000; and Peter Baldwin (ed.), *Reworking the Past: Hitler, the Holocaust, and the Historians' Debate*, Boston, Beacon, 1990. Another illuminating book on the (often obscured) relationship between history/historiography and practical politics came to my attention after concluding my own: Oliver J. Daddow, *Britain and Europe since 1945: Historiographical*

Perspectives on Integration, Manchester, Manchester University Press, 2004. While focusing on Britain's relationship with Europe, issues raised are of more general application and practical relevance.

On life and needs in postmodernity, the works of the social theorist Zygmunt Bauman are indispensable – illuminating about our present condition and eminently accessible to the lay person: try e.g. *Modernity and Ambivalence*, Cambridge, Polity, 1991, and *Postmodernity and its Discontents*, Cambridge, Polity, 1997. The work of Anthony Giddens too is central and readable (and influential): see e.g. *The Consequences of Modernity*, Cambridge, Polity, 1990, and *Modernity and Self-Identity: Self and Society in the Late Modern Age*, Cambridge, Polity, 1991. Another of my own favourites is David Harvey, *The Condition of Postmodernity: An Enquiry into the Origins of Cultural Change*, Oxford, Blackwell, 1989; for a succinct introduction, try Barry Smart, *Postmodernity*, London, Routledge, 1993; and for a prescient analysis of prospective problems, see Alvin Toffler, *Future Shock*, London, Bodley Head, 1970. Particularly important in relation to issues of identity are writings by Nikolas Rose: see *Governing the Soul: The Shaping of the Private Self* [1989], 2nd edn, London, Free Association Books, 1999; 'Assembling the Modern Self', in Roy Porter (ed.), *Rewriting the Self: Histories from the Renaissance to the Present*, London, Routledge, 1997, pp. 224–48; and *Inventing Our Selves: Psychology, Power, and Personhood*, Cambridge, Cambridge University Press, 1998.

On some prospects and aspirations for history in postmodernity, an obvious starting-point is Keith Jenkins (ed.), *The Postmodern History Reader*, London, Routledge, 1997, which includes numerous key texts, together with commentary and bibliography; and for a philosophically challenging follow-up try Frank Ankersmit, *Historical Representation*, Stanford, Stanford University Press, 2001. On story-telling and narrativisation, Richard Kearney is particularly interesting and eminently readable in *On Stories*, London, Routledge, 2002; and Hilary Lawson writes clearly and suggestively on 'closure' in *Closure: A Story of Everything*, London, Routledge, 2001. For contemporary historians who have a clear idea of *why* they are writing, and profess to idealistic motivations, see Eric Foner and J. C. D. Clark, as listed above; and for a theorist who continues to break new historiographical ground, with a wealth of cultural cross-reference, try Frank Ankersmit, whose draft of *Sublime Historical Experience*, Princeton, Princeton University Press, forthcoming, I have been privileged to read. Greg Dening's article, 'Performing on the Beaches of the Mind: An Essay', in *History and Theory* 41, 2002, pp. 1–24, indicates a way forward by reintroducing a 'moral' dimension into historical study that I believe is crucial; and in relation to both moral and therapeutic roles for history, see the important and suggestive work of Dominick LaCapra – e.g. *History and Memory after Auschwitz*, Ithaca and London, Cornell University Press, 1998. Further indications of a renewed interest in the relationship of historians and ethics is the issue of *History and Theory* 43, 2004, devoted to that theme and published after this book was concluded.

For histories that might qualify as actually 'postmodern', and which certainly seem to me to indicate future directions for history in postmodernity, I have introduced my four examples, all of which would repay further more detailed study: Robert A. Rosenstone, *Mirror in the Shrine: American Encounters with Meiji Japan*, Cambridge, Mass. and London, Harvard University Press, 1988; Peter Novick, *The Holocaust and Collective Memory: The American Experience*, London, Bloomsbury, 2000; Sven Lindqvist, *A History of Bombing*, London, Granta, 2001; and Tzvetan Todorov, *Hope and Memory: Reflections on the Twentieth Century*, London, Atlantic Books, 2003. Of particular relevance to some of the important issues raised, especially in the last three of my examples, is a book that came to my attention only after completion of my own: W. G. Sebald, *On the Natural History of Destruction*, London, Penguin, 2004. Additionally, as its name implies, up-to-the-minute examples of 'postmodern' practice, as well as theory, can be found in *Rethinking History: The Journal of Theory and Practice*.

Notes

Preface

1 Claude Lévi-Strauss, *The Savage Mind*, London, Weidenfeld & Nicolson, 1966, p. 257 (my emphasis).
2 Richard Rorty, *Philosophy and Social Hope*, Harmondsworth, Penguin, 1999, p. 69 (my emphases).
3 Frank Ankersmit, 'Invitation to Historians', *Rethinking History: The Journal of Theory and Practice* 7, 2003, p. 416.
4 John Dewey, *Reconstruction in Philosophy*, London, University of London Press, 1921, p. 27 (my emphases).

1 Humanities and therapeutic education

1 Richard Rorty, *Philosophy and Social Hope*, Harmondsworth, Penguin, 1999, Preface, p. xiii.
2 The (momentarily) most recent demand in Britain for 'clear usefulness', coupled with the relegation of mediaevalists to 'ornamental purposes', comes from Charles Clarke, Education Secretary, in May 2003: see e.g. *Times Higher Education Supplement*, 9 May 2003.
3 Fundamental question attributed to the intellectual historian Arthur O. Lovejoy by Donald R. Kelley, 'Reflections on a Canon', in Donald R. Kelley (ed.), *The History of Ideas: Canon and Variations*, Rochester, Rochester University Press, 1990, p. ix.
4 R. G. Collingwood, quoted by Bonnie G. Smith, *The Gender of History: Men, Women, and Historical Practice*, London, Harvard University Press, 1998, p. 86.
5 Rorty, *Social Hope*, p. 69 (my emphasis).
6 Lucretius, *On the Nature of the Universe*, transl. R. E. Latham, Harmondsworth, Penguin, 1951, pp. 128–9. On Hellenistic philosophy as therapeutically orientated, see Martha C. Nussbaum, *The Therapy of Desire: Theory and Practice in Hellenistic Ethics*, Princeton, Princeton University Press, 1994, whose opening quotation (p. 13) is from Epicurus: 'Empty is that philosopher's argument by which no human suffering is therapeutically treated.'
7 Seneca, *Letters from a Stoic*, transl. Robin Campbell, Harmondsworth, Penguin, 1969, p. 64.

8 Thomas White, *An Exclusion of Scepticks from All Title to Dispute*, London, John Williams, 1665, Preface.

9 Diogenes Laertius, *Lives of Eminent Philosophers*, transl. R. D. Hicks, 2 vols; London, William Heinemann, 1925, vol. 2, p. 481.

10 Ludwig Wittgenstein, *Philosophical Investigations*, 2nd edn, transl. G. E. M. Anscombe, Oxford, Blackwell, 1958, Part 1, paras 133 (my emphases), 255, 309, 129; and cf. 415.

11 Basil Willey, *Nineteenth Century Studies*, London, Chatto & Windus, 1964, p. 252.

12 Matthew Arnold, *Literature and Dogma: An Essay towards a Better Apprehension of the Bible*, London, Smith, Elder, 1873, p. 108.

13 Matthew Arnold, 'The Scholar-Gipsy', in Arthur Quiller-Couch (ed.), *The Oxford Book of English Verse, 1250–1900*, Oxford, Clarendon Press, 1926, pp. 899, 898, 900 (my emphases).

14 Willey, *Nineteenth Century*, p. 255 (my emphasis).

15 Graham Swift, *Waterland*, London, Picador, 1992, pp. 62–3.

16 Isak Dinesen, quoted by Raimond Gaita, *A Common Humanity*, London, Routledge, 2002, p. 98.

17 For material on I. A. Richards, I am indebted to Terry Eagleton's review of his *Selected Works 1919–38*, in *London Review of Books*, 25 April 2002, pp. 13–15. See also Richards' own *Mencius on the Mind: Experiments in Multiple Definition*, London, Kegan Paul, 1932.

18 F. R. Leavis, *The Great Tradition*, Harmondsworth, Penguin, 1972, p. 10 (my emphasis).

19 Leavis, *Great Tradition*, pp. 16, 18, 22, 27–8, 33, 38 (word order changed).

20 Lionel Trilling, 'Manners, Morals, and the Novel' (1947), in *The Liberal Imagination: Essays on Literature and Society*, London, Secker & Warburg, 1951, p. 222.

21 See Carolyn Steedman, *Dust*, Manchester, Manchester University Press, 2001.

22 For Petrarch, see Donald R. Kelley (ed.), *Versions of History from Antiquity to the Enlightenment*, London, Yale University Press, 1991, pp. 221–6; W. E. H. Lecky, *The Political Value of History*, London, Edward Arnold, 1892, p. 19; Geoffrey Elton, *The Practice of History*, London, Fontana, 1969, p. 11; Hampton Court advertisements seen May 2003.

23 Diane Ravitch, 'The Controversy over National History Standards', in Elizabeth Fox-Genovese and Elisabeth Lasch-Quinn (eds), *Reconstructing History*, London, Routledge, 1999, p. 242.

24 Elizabeth Fox-Genovese, 'History in a Postmodern World', in Fox-Genovese and Lasch-Quinn (eds), *Reconstructing*, p. 53.

25 Anthony Giddens, *Modernity and Self-Identity*, Cambridge, Polity, 1991, pp. 71–2, 180.

26 Rorty, *Social Hope*, p. 52 (my emphasis).

2 History for its own sake

1 Richard Cobb quoted in John Tosh (ed.), *Historians on History*, Harlow, Pearson, 2000, p. 45.

2 H. H. Milman (1847), quoted by Peter Mandler in Stefan Collini, Richard Whitmore and Brian Young (eds), *History, Religion and Culture: British*

Intellectual History 1750–1950, Cambridge, Cambridge University Press, 2000, p. 228.

3 Thucydides, *History of the Peloponnesian War*, I.22, transl. R. Crawley, London, J. M. Dent & Sons, 1910, p. 11.

4 This response was attributed to Jowett in Max Beerbohm's cartoon, 'The Sole Remark Likely to Have Been Made by Benjamin Jowett about the Mural Paintings at the Oxford Union'. See Richard Barber, *The Holy Grail: Imagination and Belief*, London, Allen Lane, 2004, p. 270.

5 Johan Huizinga, 'The Task of Cultural History' (1926), in *Men and Ideas: History, the Middle Ages, the Renaissance*, Princeton, Princeton University Press, 1959, p. 43.

6 Leopold von Ranke, 'On the Character of Historical Science' (manuscript of 1830s), in Leopold von Ranke, *The Theory and Practice of History*, ed. Georg G. Iggers and Konrad von Moltke, New York, Bobbs-Merrill, 1973, p. 39; Johann Droysen, quoted by Frederick Jackson Turner, 1891, in Fritz Stern (ed.), *The Varieties of History from Voltaire to the Present*, New York, Meridian Books, 1956, p. 208 (my emphasis); Friedrich Meinecke, in Stern (ed.), *Varieties*, p. 274 (my emphasis).

7 Plato, *Phaedo* §64, in B. Jowett (ed.), *The Dialogues of Plato*, 5 vols; Oxford, Clarendon Press, 1875, vol. 1, p. 436.

8 See the fascinating study by George Levine, *Dying to Know: Scientific Epistemology and Narrative in Victorian England*, London, Chicago University Press, 2002, to which I am indebted for this section.

9 Samuel Smiles, *Character* (1871), London, John Murray, 1910, pp. 184–6; *Life and Labour* (1887), London, John Murray, 1907, p. 48.

10 John Tyndall, *Fragments of Science* (1899), quoted by Levine, *Dying*, p. 4.

11 Karl Pearson, *The Grammar of Science*, London, Walter Scott, 1892, pp. 7–9 (my emphases).

12 Charles Darwin, *Autobiography*, quoted by Levine, *Dying*, p. 93.

13 John Henry Newman, *On the Scope and Nature of University Education* (1852), London, J. M. Dent & Sons, 1915, p. 94; further quotations from pp. 238, 36–7. Coleridge had earlier (1817) cited with approval Leibniz's 'criterion of a true philosophy; namely that it would at once explain and collect the fragments of truth scattered through systems apparently the most incongruous'. *Biographia Literaria*, ed. George Watson, London, J. M. Dent, 1965, pp. 140–1.

14 Houston Stewart Chamberlain, *The Foundations of the Nineteenth Century* (1899), transl. John Lees, 2 vols; London, John Lane, 1911, vol. 1, p. lxi. Chamberlain's reputation was later much tainted by his enthusiasm for Nazism.

15 William Stubbs, Inaugural lecture, 1867, in *Seventeen Lectures on the Study of Mediaeval and Modern History and Kindred Subjects*, 3rd edn, Oxford, Clarendon Press, 1900, p. 15.

16 Quoted by Julien Benda, *The Great Betrayal* (*La Trahison des Clercs*), transl. Richard Aldington, London, Routledge, 1928, p. 38. Following quotations are from pp. 31, 56, 84, 145, 74, 162.

17 G. R. Elton, *The Practice of History*, London, Fontana, 1969, pp. 69, 68, 65, 86; cf. J. H. Plumb, *The Death of the Past*, Harmondsworth, Penguin, 1973, pp. 12–15.

18 Cicero, *The Offices* I.vi, I.xliv, transl. Thomas Cockman (1699), London, J. M. Dent, 1909, pp. 9, 69.

19 Michael Howard, 'The Lessons of History: An Inaugural Lecture given in the University of Oxford, March 1981', in *The Lessons of History*, Oxford, Clarendon Press, 1991, pp. 13, 16, 18, 20.

20 Raymond Gaita, *A Common Humanity*, London, Routledge, 2000, p. 85.

21 Gerda Lerner, *Why History Matters: Life and Thought*, Oxford, Oxford University Press, 1998, p. 128 (my emphasis).

22 Alan Kors, in Elizabeth Fox-Genovese and Elisabeth Lasch-Quinn (eds), *Reconstructing History*, London, Routledge, 1999, pp. xxi, 13–14 (my emphases); the following quotation is from p. 17.

23 Hugh Trevor-Roper, *History: Professional and Lay* (Inaugural Lecture), Oxford, Clarendon Press, 1957, p. 14.

24 M. C. Lemon, *Philosophy of History: A Guide for Students*, London, Routledge, 2003, pp. 303, 331–2, 344.

25 A. J. P. Taylor, of himself in the 1920s, *A Personal History*, London, Hamish Hamilton, 1983, pp. 83–4 (my emphasis); Geoffrey Barraclough, 'The Historian in a Changing World', in *History in a Changing World*, Oxford, Blackwell, 1955, p. 8; Charles C. Gillispie, 'A Professional Life in the History of Science', *Historically Speaking* 5, January 2004, p. 3.

26 John Simpson, *Sunday Telegraph*, 10 November 2002, p. 17 (my emphasis).

27 As reported in the *Daily Telegraph*, 5 November 2002, p. 3.

28 As reported in the *Daily Telegraph*, 7 October 2002; *The Times*, 21 July 2003. Professor Starkey did start his own undergraduate work with an advantage shared by few: by the time he went to Cambridge, 'I'd read everything of importance published about the sixteenth century'.

29 Blurb for John Lukacs, *The Hitler of History*, London, Weidenfeld and Nicolson, 1997 (my emphasis).

30 Paul Begg, *Jack the Ripper: The Definitive History*, Harlow, Longman, 2002. Other presumptuous examples include D. J. Taylor, *Orwell: The* [sic] *Life*, London, Chatto & Windus, 2003, and Leycester Coltman, *The Real* [sic] *Fidel Castro*, New York and London, Yale University Press, 2003. Compare Miranda Carter's more persuasive title for her biography of Britain's art historian–spy: *Anthony Blunt: His Lives* [in the plural], London, Macmillan, 2001.

31 Mary Fulbrook, *Historical Theory*, London, Routledge, 2002, pp. 74, 152, 192, 154, 71 (my emphases).

32 Timothy Garton Ash, *History of the Present: Essays, Sketches and Dispatches from Europe in the 1990s*, London, Allen Lane, 1999, p. xvi (my emphasis).

33 Steven Weinberg, quoted by Richard Rorty, *Philosophy and Social Hope*, Harmondsworth, Penguin, 1999, pp. 183, 186.

34 Stephen Hawking, *A Brief History of Time from the Big Bang to Black Holes*, London, Bantam, 1988, p. 175.

35 Gaita, *Humanity*, pp. 248, 252.

36 J. R. Seeley, Lecture to Cambridge undergraduates, 1881–2, in *The Expansion of England*, ed. with introduction by John Gross, Chicago, University of Chicago Press, 1971, p. 8.

37 Seeley, *Expansion*, p. 243.

fessed purposes

1 Leopold von Ranke, 'On the Character of Historical Science' (manuscript of 1830s), in *The Theory and Practice of History*, ed. Georg G. Iggers and Konrad von Moltke, New York, Bobbs-Merrill, 1973, p. 35.

2 Thomas Carlyle, 'On History Again' (1833), in *English and Other Critical Essays*, London, J. M. Dent & Sons, 1915, p. 91 (my emphasis).

3 Geoffrey Elton, *The Practice of History*, London, Fontana, 1969, p. 17.

4 William Stubbs, 'Of the Purpose and Methods of Historical Study' (1877), in *Seventeen Lectures on the Study of Mediaeval and Modern History and Kindred Subjects*, 3rd edn, Oxford, Clarendon Press, 1900, p. 83.

5 South Bank University, London, advertisement, April 2003.

6 W. E. H. Lecky, *The Political Value of History* (Presidential Address, Birmingham, 1892), London, Edward Arnold, 1892, pp. 47–8.

7 E. H. Carr, *What is History?*, Harmondsworth, Penguin, 1964, pp. 26, 117; cf. pp. 55, 86.

8 J. H. Plumb, *The Death of the Past*, Harmondsworth, Penguin, 1973, pp. 16, 85.

9 Peter Laslett, *The World We Have Lost*, London, Methuen, 1971, pp. 242, 244.

10 Lord Acton, 'Beginning of the Modern State', in *Lectures on Modern History*, ed. J. N. Figgis and R. V. Laurence, London, Macmillan, 1906, p. 33.

11 Elizabeth Fox-Genovese and Elisabeth Lasch-Quinn (eds), *Reconstructing History*, London, Routledge, 1999, p 5.

12 History Subject Benchmarking Group, Initial Statement, London, Quality Assurance Agency, January 1999, pp. 2, 3.

13 Polybius, quoted by Donald R. Kelley (ed.), *Versions of History from Antiquity to the Enlightenment*, London, Yale University Press, 1991, pp. 36, 39.

14 Maiolino Bisaccioni, *History of the Recent Civil Wars* (2nd edn, 1653), quoted by Peter Burke, *The Renaissance Sense of the Past*, London, Edward Arnold, 1969, pp. 98–9.

15 Pier Paolo Vergerio, in Kelley, *Versions*, p. 255.

16 Leonardo Bruni (1370–1444), in Kelley, *Versions*, pp. 245–6.

17 Stubbs, Address, 1889, in *Seventeen Lectures*, pp. 465–6.

18 Matthew Arnold, quoted by Peter A. Dale, *The Victorian Critic and the Idea of History*, London, Harvard University Press, 1977, p. 5.

19 Carlyle, quoted by Dale, *Victorian Critic*, pp. 6, 49.

20 G. R. Elton, *Return to Essentials*, Cambridge, Cambridge University Press, 1991, p. 8.

21 See Keith Jenkins, *On 'What is History?'*, London, Routledge, 1995, p. 71.

22 Scott Fitzgerald quoted by Thomas J. Peters and Robert H. Waterman Jr, *In Search of Excellence: Lessons from America's Best-Run Companies*, New York, Harper & Row, 1982, p. 89.

23 Denis Diderot, *Conversation between D'Alembert and Diderot*, transl. Leonard Tancock, Harmondsworth, Penguin, 1966, p. 163.

24 Bernard Williams, *Truth and Truthfulness: An Essay in Genealogy*, Princeton, Princeton University Press, 2002, p. 260.

25 Leonardo Bruni, in Kelley, *Versions*, p. 245.

26 Henry St John, Lord Bolingbroke, *Reflections upon Exile*, London, A. Millar, 1752, pp. 444–5.

27 Bolingbroke, *Letters on the Study and Use of History*, London, A. Millar, 1752, pp. 25–7; and cf. Macaulay: 'The effect of historical reading is analogous, in many respects, to that produced by foreign travel'; Fritz Stern (ed.), *The Varieties of History from Voltaire to the Present*, New York, Meridian Books, 1956, p. 85. The past, after all, is another country.

28 Lecky, *Political Value*, pp. 53, 49.

29 Elton, *Essentials*, p. 8.

30 Jinty Nelson, 'Letter from the President', *Royal Historical Society Newsletter*, Spring 2003.

31 Williams, *Truth*, pp. 162–3.

32 So Antonio Filarete, *Treatise on Architecture*, Bk. XXIV, quoted by Burke, *Renaissance Sense*, p. 27.

33 Gabriel Naudé, *Additions to the History of Louis XI* (1630), p. 25, quoted by Burke, *Renaissance Sense*, p. 74.

34 Roland Barthes, *Mythologies* (1957), transl. Annette Lavers, London, Vintage, 1993, pp. 142–5.

35 Lorenzo Valla, in Kelley, *Versions*, pp. 250–1.

36 Geoffrey of Monmouth, *The History of the Kings of Britain*, transl. Lewis Thorpe, Harmondsworth, Penguin, 1966, p. 72.

37 Polydore Vergil, in Kelley, *Versions*, p. 256; and see John Kenyon, *The History Men: The Historical Profession in England since the Renaissance*, 2nd edn, London, Weidenfeld & Nicolson, 1993, p. 3.

38 Dialogue of the Exchequer, quoted by R. H. C. Davis, *The Normans and their Myth*, London, Thames & Hudson, 1976, pp. 124, 131.

39 Jonathan Clark, *Our Shadowed Present: Modernism, Postmodernism and History*, London, Atlantic Books, 2003, esp. ch. 5. I am indebted to this work for the following paragraphs.

40 Clark, *Shadowed Present*, p. 246.

41 Clark, *Shadowed Present*, p. 183 (my emphasis).

42 Pieter Geyl, *Napoleon: For and Against* (1949), Harmondsworth, Penguin, 1965, pp. 25–6, 400.

43 Ian Kershaw, *The 'Hitler Myth': Image and Reality in the Third Reich*, Oxford, Clarendon Press, 1987, p. 2

44 Kershaw, *'Hitler Myth'*, pp. 5, 48, 151.

45 Kershaw, *'Hitler Myth'*, pp. 253, 269.

46 Vespasiano da Bisticci, in Kelley, *Versions*, p. 252.

47 Thomas Carlyle, *Past and Present*, London, Ward Lock, n.d., Book 2, ch. XVII, p. 90.

48 Arrian, *The Campaigns of Alexander*, transl. Aubrey de Selincourt, Harmondsworth, Penguin, 1971, pp. 67–8.

49 The Aztec figure with three faces (*Cabeza con tres rostros, c. 250–700 Teotihuacan?*, from Col. Museo Universitario de Ciencias y Arte, Universidad Nacional, Autonoma de Mexico, Ciudad de Mexico, 08–741814) was exhibited at the Royal Academy, London, in April 2003.

50 See e.g. Michael Shermer and Alex Grobman, *Denying History*, London, University of California Press, 2000, pp. 17, v.

51 Tony Judt, 'Anti-Americans Abroad', in *The New York Review of Books*, 1 May 2003, p. 25, referring to Thierry Meyssan.

52 Luke 24.44.

53 Charles Rollin, *The Ancient History of the Egyptians, Carthaginians, Assyrians, Babylonians, Medes and Persians, Grecians and Macedonians*, 18th edn, London, Ward Lock, 1881, Preface, p. iii.

54 Houston Stewart Chamberlain, *The Foundations of the Nineteenth Century* (1899), transl. John Lees, 2 vols; London, John Lane, 1911, vol. 1, pp. 5, 8.

55 Field-Marshall Alanbrooke, *Diaries*, quoted in *London Review of Books*, 21 March 2002.

56 Chamberlain, *Foundations*, vol. 2, p. 564.

57 On Chamberlain, see Geoffrey G. Field, *Evangelist of Race: The Germanic Vision of Houston Stewart Chamberlain*, New York, Columbia University Press, 1981.

58 C. V. Wedgwood, 'The Historian and the World' (1942), in *Velvet Studies*, London, Jonathan Cape, 1946, pp. 157–8.

59 Herodotus, *The History*, transl. G. Rawlinson, 2 vols; London, J. M. Dent & Sons, 1910, vol. 1, p. 1; for the quotation from Sima Qian, I am indebted to Zhang Longxi, 'History and Fictionality: Insights and Limitations of a Literary Perspective', *Rethinking History: The Journal of Theory and Practice*, 8, 2004, p. 389.

60 Vespasiano da Bisticci, in Kelley, *Versions*, pp. 252–4.

61 Jules Michelet, quoted by Carolyn Steedman, *Dust*, Manchester, Manchester University Press, 2001, p. 39.

62 Peter Mandler, *History and National Life*, London, Profile Books, 2000, p. 2.

63 I am indebted for this paragraph to Richard J. Golsan, 'History and the "Duty to Memory" in Postwar France: The Pitfalls of an Ethics of Remembrance', in Howard Marchitello (ed.), *What Happens to History: The Renewal of Ethics in Contemporary Thought*, New York, Routledge, 2001, pp. 23–39.

64 Eric Foner, *Who Owns History? Rethinking the Past in a Changing World*, New York, Hill & Wang, 2002, pp. 19–20; *Freedom's Lawmakers: A Directory of Black Officeholders during Reconstruction*, revised edn, Baton Rouge and London, Louisiana State University Press, 1996, pp. xii–xiii.

65 Foner, *Who Owns?* pp. 19, 41, 22, 74, 69–70.

66 Tzvetan Todorov, *Hope and Memory: Reflections on the Twentieth Century*, London, Atlantic Books, 2003, p. 175, citing *Le Monde*, 15 June 2000.

67 Lyotard in Geoffrey Bennington, *Lyotard: Writing the Event*, Manchester, Manchester University Press, 1988, p. 112.

4 Hidden agendas

1 See press reports, 18 July 2003.

2 I am indebted for this quotation to a letter in the *Guardian*, 21 July 2003.

3 Ernest Renan, 'What is a Nation?' (lecture at the Sorbonne, 1882), reprinted in Homi K. Bhabha (ed.), *Nation and Narration*, London, Routledge, 1990, pp. 8–22.

4 On Cotton, see John Kenyon, *The History Men: The Historical Profession in England since the Renaissance*, 2nd edn, London, Weidenfeld & Nicolson, 1993, p. 23; Giolitti in relation to Cavour, quoted by Keith Wilson, in Keith

Wilson (ed.), *Forging the Collective Memory*, Oxford, Berghahn, 1996, p. 4; the quotation in the following paragraph is from p. 14. See also Wilson's revealing paper (ch. 8) on 'The Imbalance in *British Documents on the Origins of the War, 1898–1914*' – a case-study in the tensions between historians and politicians.

5 Noble Frankland, *History at War: The Campaigns of an Historian*, London, Giles de la Mare, 1998, p. vii, and cover.

6 Leopold von Ranke, *The Theory and Practice of History*, ed. Georg G. Iggers and Konrad von Moltke, New York, Bobbs-Merrill, 1973, p. 59.

7 See e.g. *Daily Telegraph*, 21 November 2003, p. 18. One might take heart from the quoted comment of one aspiring history teacher: 'If the Americans write our history, they will put in only good things about themselves. If that's the case, I won't follow the book.'

8 Napoleon's note is quoted in Julien Benda, *The Great Betrayal*, transl. Richard Aldington, London, Routledge, 1928, p. 176.

9 Johan Huizinga, 'Historical Ideals of Life', Inaugural Lecture as Professor of History at the University of Leiden, 27 January 1915, in *Men and Ideas*, transl. James S. Holmes and Hans van Marle, Princeton, Princeton University Press, 1959, p. 94.

10 Baron de Courcel, quoted in Wilson (ed.), *Collective Memory*, p. 29.

11 Holger H. Herwig, 'Self-Censorship in Germany after the Great War', in Wilson (ed.), *Collective Memory*, p. 93.

12 See Ellen L. Evans and Joseph O. Baylen, 'History as Propaganda: The German Foreign Ministry and the "Enlightenment" of American Historians on the War-Guilt Question, 1930–1933', in Wilson (ed.), *Collective Memory*, ch. 5.

13 Adolf Hitler, *Mein Kampf*, quoted by Gilmer W. Blackburn, *Education in the Third Reich: A Study of Race and History in Nazi Textbooks*, Albany, State University of New York Press, 1985, p. 36.

14 Virgil, *Aeneid* , Bk 1, line 33.

15 Quoted by Blackburn, *Education*, p. 57.

16 Blackburn, *Education*, pp. 76, 83, 40.

17 Textbooks (1945, 1943), quoted by Blackburn, *Education*, pp. 46–7.

18 Josef Goebbels, quoted by Blackburn, *Education*, p. 103.

19 Quoted by Blackburn, *Education*, p. 167.

20 See Mary Fulbrook, *German National Identity after the Holocaust*, Cambridge, Polity, 1999; 'Re-presenting the Nation: History and Identity in East and West Germany', in Mary Fulbrook and Martin Swales (eds), *Representing the German Nation: History and Identity in Twentieth-Century Germany*, Manchester, Manchester University Press, 2000, pp. 172–92; and for further reading, see Stefan Berger, *The Search for Normality: National Identity and Historical Consciousness in Germany since 1800*, Oxford, Berghahn, 1997.

21 Fulbrook, 'Re-presenting', p. 176.

22 Fulbrook, 'Re-presenting', p. 175.

23 Friedrich Meinecke, quoted by Fulbrook, *National Identity*, p. 114.

24 Fulbrook, *National Identity*, p. 125. See also Peter Novick, *The Holocaust and Collective Memory: The American Experience*, London, Bloomsbury, 2000, discussed in Ch. 8, §2 of this volume.

25 See Peter Baldwin (ed.), *Reworking the Past: Hitler, the Holocaust, and the Historians' Debate*, Boston, Beacon, 1990.

26 See Jonathan Clark, *Our Shadowed Present*, London, Atlantic Books, 2003, ch. 7.

27 Norman Davies, *Europe: A History*, London, Pimlico, 1997, p. 41 (my emphasis).

28 Davies, *Europe*, p. 45.

29 Richard J. Evans, *In Defence of History*, London, Granta, 1997, p. 206.

30 Herbert Butterfield, *The Englishman and His History* (1944), Hamden, Conn., Archon, 1970, p. 1.

31 See J. H. Plumb, *The Death of the Past*, Harmondsworth, Penguin, 1973, ch. 1.

32 Nikolas Rose, *Inventing Our Selves: Psychology, Power, and Personhood*, Cambridge, Cambridge University Press, 1998, p. 27.

33 Rose, *Inventing*, p. 106.

34 This section is largely derived from Reba N. Soffer, *Discipline and Power: The University, History, and the Making of an English Élite, 1870–1930*, Stanford, Stanford University Press, 1994.

35 Soffer, *Discipline*, p. 83.

36 H. W. C. Davis, quoted by Soffer, *Discipline*, p. 142.

37 H. W. C. Davis, *The Study of History*, Oxford, Clarendon Press, 1925, pp. 18–19.

38 William Stubbs, *Seventeen Lectures on the Study of Mediaeval and Modern History and Kindred Subjects*, 3rd edn, Oxford, Clarendon Press, 1900, pp. 10, 465 (from, respectively, Inaugural Lecture of 1867 and Address of 1889).

39 J. R. Seeley, *Lectures and Essays*, London, Macmillan, 1870, pp. 296–8.

40 Seeley, *Lectures*, p. 298; A. L. Smith, 'The Teaching of Modern History', in Christopher Cookson (ed.), *Essays on Secondary Education*, Oxford, Clarendon Press, 1898, p. 180; Stubbs, 'Of the Purpose and Methods of Historical Study' (1877), in *Seventeen Lectures*, pp. 86, 95.

41 E. Barker *et al.*, *Why We are at War: Great Britain's Case*, By Members of the Oxford Faculty of Modern History, Oxford, Clarendon Press, 1914, pp. 5, 122.

42 Soffer, *Discipline*, p. 206.

43 This section is largely derived from Bonnie G. Smith, *The Gender of History: Men, Women, and Historical Practice*, London, Harvard University Press, 1998.

44 Susan Bordo's important piece on 'The Cartesian Masculinisation of Thought' (1987) is conveniently reprinted in Lawrence Cahoone (ed.), *From Modernism to Postmodernism: An Anthology*, Oxford, Blackwell, 1996, pp. 638–64.

45 For examples, see e.g. Brian Easlea, *Witch Hunting, Magic and the New Philosophy: An Introduction to Debates of the Scientific Revolution, 1450–1750*, Brighton, Harvester Press, 1980.

46 Fustel de Coulanges, quoted by Fritz Stern (ed.), *The Varieties of History*, New York, Meridian Books, 1956, p. 25.

47 For the 'manner of discourse' of early modern scientists and modern historians, see, respectively, Thomas Sprat, *The History of the Royal Society*, London, J. Martyn, 1667, pp. 111–15; *English Historical Review* I, 1886, 'Prefatory Note', p. 5.

48 Smith, *Gender*, pp. 49, 62 (my emphasis).

49 Smith, *Gender*, pp. 161, 205, 67.

50 Geoffrey Elton, *The Practice of History*, London, Fontana, 1969, p. 33; Arthur Marwick, *The New Nature of History: Knowledge, Evidence, Language*, Basingstoke, Palgrave, 2001, p. 35. Elton writes elsewhere of 'amateurism, knowing nothing with the certainty, sufficiency and clear understanding of the

professional': 'Second Thoughts on History at the Universities', *History* 54, 1969, p. 66. Cf. Macaulay, who in the nineteenth century distinguished between, on the one hand, historical novelists such as Walter Scott, who worked with the 'eye of a sculptor' and produced *imaginative* landscapes, and, on the other hand, proper historians such as Henry Hallam, who more closely resembled 'an anatomist' and supplied maps with *exact information*. Thomas Babington Macaulay, *Critical and Historical Essays*, ed. A. J. Grieve, London, J. M. Dent & Sons, 1933, pp. 1–2.

51 Smith, *Gender*, pp. 103f.
52 Rose, *Inventing*, p. 55; cf. Michel Foucault: 'Truth ... is produced only by virtue of multiple forms of constraint'; *Power/Knowledge: Selected Interviews and Other Writings 1972–1977*, ed. Colin Gordon, New York, Harvester, 1980, p. 131.
53 Rose, *Inventing*, pp. 42–3.
54 Rose, *Inventing*, p. 43.

5 Life and needs in postmodernity

1 Zygmunt Bauman, *Modernity and Ambivalence*, Cambridge, Polity, 1991, p. 272; cf. p. 4.
2 Barry Smart, *Postmodernity*, London, Routledge, 1993, p. 62.
3 John Henry Newman, *On the Scope and Nature of University Education*, London, J. M. Dent, 1915, pp. 258–9.
4 Smart, *Postmodernity*, pp. 51, 81, 83 (my emphases).
5 Antony Giddens, *Modernity and Self-Identity: Self and Society in the Late Modern Age*, Cambridge, Polity, 1991, p.185.
6 Giddens, *Modernity*, pp. 3, (my emphases), 21, 9, 201.
7 David Burns, Chief Executive of the Football League, as reported in the *Daily Telegraph*, 16 April 2002. The quotation from Camus is taken from an advertisement for philosophyfootball.com in *London Review of Books*, 14 November 2002, p. 1. Analysis of contemporary Englishness is from Paul Laity's review of Richard Weight's *Patriots*, *London Review of Books*, 28 November 2002, p. 25.
8 Bauman, quoted by Smart, *Postmodernity*, pp. 62–3.
9 Alexander Pope, *The Dunciad* (1728) Bk IV, lines 629–32, in *The Poetical Works of Alexander Pope*, ed. Adolphus W. Ward, London, Macmillan, 1908, p. 423.
10 Smart, *Postmodernity*, p. 41.
11 Pope, *Dunciad*, Bk IV, line 647.
12 Matthew Arnold, *Culture and Anarchy: An Essay in Political and Social Criticism* (1869), London, Thomas Nelson, n.d., pp. 239, 81.
13 Newman, *University Education*, pp. 104, 129 (my emphases); cf. p. 90.
14 Newman, *University Education*, pp. 130–1 (my emphases).
15 Pope, *Dunciad*, Bk IV, lines 653–6.
16 Adolf Eichmann, quoted by Hannah Arendt, *Eichmann in Jerusalem: A Report on the Banality of Evil* (1963), London, Penguin, 1994, p. 32 (my emphasis).
17 Diogenes Laertius, *Lives of Eminent Philosophers*, transl. R. D. Hicks, 2 vols; London, William Heinemann, 1925, vol. 2, p. 483.
18 Keith Jenkins, for example, characterises postmodernity as 'the era of the raising to consciousness of the "aporia"': 'On Disobedient Histories', *Rethinking History: The Journal of Theory and Practice* 7, 2003, p. 371.

19 Anthony Giddens, *The Consequences of Modernity*, Cambridge, Polity, 1990, p. 49 (my emphasis).

20 Friedrich Nietzsche, *The Gay Science*, transl. Walter Kaufmann, New York, Vintage, 1974, p. 336 (original emphasis).

21 Alvin Toffler, *Future Shock* (1970), quoted in Donald S. Gochberg (ed.), *Classics of Western Thought*, 4 vols; New York, Harcourt Brace Jovanovich, 1980, vol. IV, pp. 641–60.

22 Alphonse Daudet, quoted by William James, *The Varieties of Religious Experience*, London, Longmans Green, 1902, p. 164.

23 For St Paul, see Romans 7.19; St Augustine, *Confessions*, transl. R. S. Pine-Coffin, Harmondsworth, Penguin, 1961, p. 164.

24 James, *Varieties*, pp. 166–7.

25 Michael Drayton, 'To my noble friend Mister William Browne, of the evil time', quoted by Christopher Hill, *Intellectual Origins of the English Revolution*, Oxford, Clarendon Press, 1965, p. 8. Cf. the poet of the Great War, Edward Thomas: 'This is no case of petty right or wrong/ That politicians or philosophers/ Can judge' (Imperial War Museum, London, Anthem for Doomed Youth exhibition, December 2002).

26 Samuel Taylor Coleridge, *Biographia Literaria* (1817), ed. George Watson, London, J. M. Dent, 1965, p. 142.

27 See esp. Linda Colley, *Britons: Forging the Nation, 1707–1837*, London, Yale University Press, 1992. This point holds, perhaps yet more strongly, if we accept J. C. D. Davis's critique of Colley, which implies a much longer period through which English national identity has developed.

28 See e.g. Richard Weight, *Patriots: National Identity in Britain, 1940–2000*, London, Macmillan, 2002; Tom Nairn, *Pariah: Misfortunes of the British Kingdom*, London, Verso, 2002; Robert Colls, *Identity of England*, Oxford, Oxford University Press, 2002 – all reviewed by Paul Laity in *London Review of Books*, 28 November 2002, pp. 24–8, to whom I am also indebted for the following quotation from Churchill.

29 Coleridge, quoted by Basil Willey, *Nineteenth Century Studies*, London, Chatto & Windus, 1964, p. 29; D. H. Lawrence, *À Propos of Lady Chatterley's Lover*, London, Mandrake Press, 1930, p. 55.

30 I am indebted for this analysis to Andrew Graham-Dixon, *Sunday Telegraph Magazine*, 3 November 2002, p. 89, from whom quotations are taken.

6 History in postmodernity: future prospects

1 George Orwell, quoted by Raymond Gaita, *A Common Humanity*, London, Routledge, 2002, p. 188.

2 Christopher Hill, *Intellectual Origins of the English Revolution*, Oxford, Clarendon Press, 1965, p. 299 (my emphasis).

3 Richard J. Evans, *In Defence of History*, London, Granta, 1997, p. 75.

4 Richard Rorty, *Philosophy and Social Hope*, Harmondsworth, Penguin, 1999, p. 119.

5 William James, quoted by Rorty, *Social Hope*, p. 149; John Dewey (1920), quoted by S. J. Curtis and M. E. A. Boultwood, *A Short History of Educational Ideas*, London, University Tutorial Press, 1961, p. 475.

6 John Dewey, *Reconstruction in Philosophy*, London, University of London Press, 1921, p. 177.

7 Zygmunt Bauman, *Modernity and Ambivalence*, Cambridge, Polity, 1991, p. 272 (cf. Ch. 5, §2 above).

8 Hilary Lawson, *Closure: A Story of Everything*, London, Routledge, 2001, p. 138. My brief discussion of Lawson here is indebted in par-ticular to pages 5f., 137f., 205f.

9 G. R. Elton, *The Practice of History*, London, Fontana, 1969, pp. 19, 68; Arthur Marwick, *The New Nature of History*, Basingstoke, Palgrave 2001, pp. 217, 251 (my emphases).

10 Lawson, *Closure*, p. 209.

11 Cézanne, quoted by Lawson, *Closure*, p. 352, n. 2.

12 Andrew Graham-Dixon, 'In the Picture', *Sunday Telegraph Magazine*, 31 August 2003, p. 73. Lyotard writes interestingly of Cézanne's search for 'elementary sensations ... hidden in ordinary perception, which remains under the hege-mony of habitual or classical ways of looking', and the aim 'to make seen what makes one see, and not what is visible'; Jean-François Lyotard, *The Inhuman: Reflections on Time*, transl. Geoffrey Bennington and Rachel Bowlby, Cambridge, Polity, 1991, p. 102.

13 Salman Rushdie, quoted by Brenda K. Marshall, *Teaching the Postmodern: Fiction and Theory*, London, Routledge, 1992, pp. 173–4. See ch. 5 of Brenda Marshall's work for a discussion of Rushdie, together with other examples of historiographic metafiction. On this see also Linda Hutcheon, *A Poetics of Postmodernism: History, Theory, Fiction*, London, Routledge, 1988.

14 Marshall, *Teaching*, p. 178.

15 Carlos Fuentes, *Terra Nostra*, transl. Margaret Sayers Peden, Harmondsworth, Penguin, 1978, p. 644 (my emphases). My attention was drawn to this work by the discussion in Brian McHale, *Postmodernist Fiction*, London, Routledge, 1987 – a reference for which I am grateful to John Ibbett.

16 Fuentes, *Terra Nostra*, pp. 643–6 (my emphases).

17 Johann Droysen, quoted by Frederick Jackson Turner in Fritz Stern (ed.), *The Varieties of History*, New York, Meridian Books, 1956, p. 201.

18 Anthony Giddens, *Modernity and Self-Identity: Self and Society in the Late Modern Age*, Cambridge, Polity, 1991, p. 169.

19 James Hamilton-Paterson, *Loving Monsters*, London, Granta, 2002, p. 38.

20 Jules Michelet, quoted by Carolyn Steedman, *Dust*, Manchester, Manchester University Press, 2001, p. 39 (my emphasis); cf. Ch. 3, §6 above.

21 Arthur Mitzman, quoted by Steedman, *Dust*, p. 71.

22 Report quoted by Gaita, *Humanity*, p. 116. This is now the subject of a film, *Rabbit-Proof Fence*, released in England in November 2002.

23 Gaita, *Humanity*, p. 97.

24 Barry Smart, *Postmodernity*, London, Routledge, 1993, p. 125, citing Paul Hirst.

25 Steedman, *Dust*, p. 77.

26 Giddens, *Modernity*, p. 52.

27 Cf. J. Raichman, 1985, quoted by Smart, *Postmodernity*, p. 84: 'We are ... "really" free because we can identify and change those procedures or forms through which our stories become true.'

28 Michel Foucault in Lawrence Cahoone (ed.), *From Modernism to Postmodernism: An Anthology*, Oxford, Blackwell, 1996, pp. 372–6.

29 Kelly Oliver, 'Witnessing Otherness in History', in Howard Marchitello (ed.), *What Happens to History: The Renewal of Ethics in Contemporary Thought*, London, Routledge, 2001, pp. 40–66; quotations are from p. 47.

30 Nikolas Rose, 'Assembling the Modern Self', in Roy Porter (ed.), *Rewriting the Self: Histories from the Renaissance to the Present*, London, Routledge, 1997, p. 234 (my emphasis).

31 Elizabeth Fox-Genovese, 'History in a Postmodern World', in Elizabeth Fox-Genovese and Elisabeth Lasch-Quinn (eds), *Reconstructing History*, London, Routledge, 1999, p. 50.

32 G. R. Elton, *Return to Essentials*, Cambridge, Cambridge University Press, 1991, p. 24.

33 John Dewey quoted by Rorty, *Social Hope*, p. 29.

34 Oscar Wilde, quoted by Peter A. Dale, *The Victorian Critic and the Idea of History*, London, Harvard University Press, 1977, p. 224.

35 Nikolas Rose, *Inventing Our Selves: Psychology, Power, and Personhood*, Cambridge, Cambridge University Press, 1998, pp. 17–18 (my emphases).

36 For an account of Hugh Thomson, see Seymour M. Hersh, *My Lai 4: A Report on the Massacre and its Aftermath*, New York, Random House, 1970.

37 Samuel Taylor Coleridge, *Biographia Literaria*, ed. George Watson, London, J. M. Dent, 1956, ch. xiv, p. 169.

38 Walter Pater, *The Renaissance: Studies in Art and Poetry* (1873), ed. Donald L. Hill, Berkeley and Los Angeles, University of California Press, 1980, pp. 188–9.

39 Giddens, *Modernity*, pp. 41, 114, 129.

40 Hugh Rayment-Pickard, in R. M. Burns and Hugh Rayment-Pickard (eds), *Philosophies of History*, Oxford, Blackwell, 2000, p. 132 (emphases in original).

41 Evans, *Defence*, p. 134.

42 Matthew Arnold, *Culture and Anarchy* (1869), London, Thomas Nelson, n.d., p. 79.

43 Arnold, *Culture*, pp. 132, 139 (cf. 263), 364, 261–2.

44 Arnold, *Culture*, pp. 11, 56 (and passim), 80, 11–12.

45 Arnold, *Culture*, pp. 378–9, 11–12, 15 (my emphasis).

46 Arnold, *Culture*, pp. 17, 274, 16 (my emphasis).

47 Jonathan Swift, *The Battle of the Books*, ed. A. Guthkelch, London, Chatto & Windus, 1908, p. 21.

48 Arnold, *Culture*, pp. 129, 50, 162 (my emphasis).

49 Zygmunt Bauman, *Intimations of Postmodernity*, London, Routledge, 1992, p. xi; Rorty, *Social Hope*, pp. 234, 231.

50 Smart, *Postmodernity*, p. 103.

51 Steedman, *Dust*, p. 148.

52 John Wilkins, *Mathematical Magick: or The Wonders that may be Performed by Mechanical Geometry* (1648), 4th edn, London, Ric. Baldwin, 1691, p. 3.

53 Trevor-Roper, quoted in John Tosh (ed.), *Historians on History*, Harlow, Pearson, 2000, pp. 199–200; and Hugh Trevor-Roper, 'A Case of Co-existence: Christendom and the Turks', in *Historical Essays*, London, Macmillan, 1957, pp. 177–8 (my emphasis).

54 J. C. D. Clark, *Our Shadowed Present: Modernism, Postmodernism and History*, London, Atlantic Books, 2003, p. 29 (my emphasis).

55 Clark, *Shadowed Present*, p. 54.
56 A. L. Smith, 'The Teaching of Modern History', in Christopher Cookson (ed.), *Essays on Secondary Education*, Oxford, Clarendon Press, 1898, p. 179.
57 H. W. C. Davis, Inaugural Lecture as Regius Professor of Modern History at Oxford, in *The Study of History*, Oxford, Clarendon Press, 1925, p. 20.
58 Ralph Waldo Emerson, *The Complete Prose Works*, London, Ward Lock, 1890, p. 614.

7 Histories for postmodernity – some aspirations

1 F. M. Powicke, 'After Fifty Years', Address to Historical Association meeting, 1944, in *Modern Historians and the Study of History: Essays and Papers*, London, Odhams, 1955, p. 237.
2 Herbert Spencer, *Education*, London, Williams & Norgate, 1910, p. 14; cf. pp. 4, 39–44.
3 Henry Thomas Buckle (1861), in Robert M. Burns and Hugh Rayment-Pickard (eds), *Philosophies of History*, Oxford, Blackwell, 2000, p. 128 (my emphasis).
4 Nicholas Kinloch, 'Learning about the Holocaust: Moral or Historical Question?' *Teaching History* 93, 1998 (my emphasis).
5 Kinloch, *Teaching History* 93 (my emphasis); 'Parallel Catastrophes? Uniqueness, Redemption and the Shoah', *Teaching History* 104, 2001, p. 13.
6 'James Mill's Article on Education', in F. A. Cavenagh (ed.), *James and John Stuart Mill on Education*, Cambridge, Cambridge University Press, 1931, p. 21.
7 Thomas Carlyle, 'On History Again', in *English and Other Critical Essays*, London, J. M. Dent & Sons, 1915, pp. 95–6.
8 Barry Smart, *Postmodernity*, London, Routledge, 1993, pp. 70f., 78.
9 Bernard Williams, *Truth and Truthfulness: An Essay in Genealogy*, Princeton, Princeton University Press, 2002, pp. 244, 248.
10 Williams, *Truth*, p. 267.
11 Peter Gay, *Style in History*, London, Jonathan Cape, 1975, p. 199.
12 Williams, *Truth*, pp. 261, 257, 241, 266.
13 Janette Rainwater, *Self-Therapy: A Guide to Becoming Your Own Therapist*, Wellingborough, Turnstone Press, 1989, pp. 99–100.
14 Williams, *Truth*, pp. 262–3.
15 David Harlan, 'Ken Burns and the Coming Crisis of Academic History', in *Rethinking History: The Journal of Theory and Practice*, 7, 2003, pp. 169–92. I am obviously indebted to this interesting and important article for what follows, from which quotations are taken unless otherwise noted. Harlan is concerned with an American phenomenon, but there are no doubt (existing or impending) parallels elsewhere, awaiting analysis.
16 Ken Burns, as reported in Thomas Cripps, 'Historical Truth: An Interview with Ken Burns', *The American Historical Review* 100, 1995, p. 745.
17 Burns, quoted by Cripps, 'Interview', p. 741.
18 Burns in Cripps, 'Interview', pp. 746, 748.
19 For an enlightening criticism, see Eric Foner, *Who Owns History? Rethinking the Past in a Changing World*, New York, Hill & Wang, 2002, pp. 189–204.

20 Ludwig Wittgenstein, *Philosophical Investigations*, 2nd edn, transl. G. E. M. Anscombe, Oxford, Blackwell, 1958, p. 82e.
21 Raimond Gaita, *A Common Humanity*, London, Routledge, 2002, pp. 15–16 (my emphasis).
22 Sextus Empiricus, *Outlines of Pyrrhonism*, transl. R. G. Bury, London, Heinemann, 1933, p. 291.
23 Wittgenstein, *Philosophical Investigations*, p. 51e.
24 Stuart Hampshire, *Thought and Action*, London, Chatto & Windus, 1965, p. 25.
25 W. G. Sebald, *Austerlitz*, London, Penguin, 2002, p. 175.
26 Victor Klemperer, *The Language of the Third Reich*, transl. Martin Brady, London, Athlone Press, 2000, p. 15.
27 Klemperer, *Language*, p. 23.
28 Klemperer, *Language*, pp. 111, 114, 117.
29 Klemperer, *Language*, pp. 219–20, 215, 222.
30 Klemperer, *Language*, pp. 185, 60–1.
31 Russell Smith, 'The New Newsspeak', *The New York Review of Books*, 29 May 2003, p. 19.
32 Noam Chomsky, *Understanding Power: The Indispensable Chomsky*, ed. Peter R. Mitchell and John Schoeffel, London, Vintage, 2003, p. 41 (my emphasis).
33 Klemperer, *Language*, pp. 286, 284.
34 Anthony Giddens, *Modernity and Self-Identity*, Cambridge, Polity, 1991, p. 35 (my emphasis).
35 See Samuel Taylor Coleridge, *Biographia Literaria*, London, J. M. Dent & Sons, 1965, pp. 136–9; for Zygmunt Bauman, see Chapter 5, §2 in this volume.
36 Hannah Arendt, *Eichmann in Jerusalem: A Report on the Banality of Evil* (1963), Harmondsworth, Penguin, 1994. The following quotations are from pp. 287–9, 116, 175, 52, 233 (my emphasis pp. 287 and 175, otherwise emphasis as in original).
37 Quotations in this section are taken from Arendt, *Eichmann*, pp. 48–9, 85, 69, 108, 86, 106 (emphasis in original).
38 Quotations in this section are taken from Arendt, *Eichmann*, pp. 78, 54 (my emphases), 241.
39 My material here is taken mainly from Andrew Cunningham's article 'Why We are So Obsessed with Hitler', in the *Daily Express*, 14 October 2003, supplemented by Jemima Lewis, 'Don't Mention Hitler', *Sunday Telegraph*, 12 October 2003.

8 Histories for postmodernity – some examples

1 Robert A. Rosenstone, 'Confessions of a Postmodern (?) Historian', *Rethinking History: The Journal of Theory and Practice* 8, 2004, p. 158.
2 Robert A. Rosenstone, *Mirror in the Shrine: American Encounters with Meiji Japan*, Cambridge, Mass. and London, Harvard University Press, 1988, pp. ix, xi (my emphasis). This section owes everything to Robert Rosenstone's fascinating and deeply affecting work.
3 Rosenstone, *Mirror*, pp. xiii, 1, 187, 96, 16, 74, 77, 114 (my emphasis), 122.
4 Rosenstone, *Mirror*, pp. 173, 189.

5 Rosenstone, *Mirror*, pp. 151–2 (my emphasis).
6 Rosenstone, *Mirror*, pp. 117, 27, 137, 127 (my emphasis).
7 Rosenstone, *Mirror*, pp. 103–4, 275.
8 Rosenstone, *Mirror*, pp. 103, 159, 68, 53.
9 Rosenstone, *Mirror*, p. 222.
10 Peter Novick, *The Holocaust and Collective Memory: The American Experience*, London, Bloomsbury, 2000, p. 6.
11 Novick, *Holocaust*, p. 20.
12 Novick, *Holocaust*, p. 67.
13 Novick, *Holocaust*, pp. 103, 121, 115.
14 Novick, *Holocaust*, pp. 138, 120.
15 Novick, *Holocaust*, pp. 144, 133.
16 Ellen Willis, quoted by Novick, *Holocaust*, p. 191.
17 Novick, *Holocaust*, pp. 245 (my emphasis), 236.
18 Novick, *Holocaust*, pp. 247, 257, 261.
19 Sven Lindqvist, *A History of Bombing*, London, Granta, 2001, §22.
20 Lindqvist, *Bombing*, §73.
21 Lindqvist, *Bombing*, §208.
22 Lindqvist, *Bombing*, §272 (my emphasis).
23 Tzvetan Todorov, *Hope and Memory: Reflections on the Twentieth Century*, London, Atlantic Books, 2003.
24 Vasily Grossman, *Life and Fate*, London, Harvill Press, 1995, p. 405.
25 Primo Levi, *The Drowned and the Saved*, transl. Raymond Rosenthal, London, Abacus, 1989, p. 18.
26 Primo Levi, quoted by Todorov, *Hope*, p. 180.
27 Romain Gary, quoted by Todorov, *Hope*, pp. 214, 221, 223.
28 Todorov, *Hope*, pp. 192, 195.
29 Todorov, *Hope*, pp. 44, 33, 276; George Orwell, *Nineteen Eighty-Four*, Harmondsworth, Penguin, 1954, p. 7.
30 Todorov, *Hope*, pp. 258–60.
31 Todorov, *Hope*, pp. 283, 289, 142.
32 Todorov, *Hope*, p. 4.
33 Todorov, *Hope*, p. 186.
34 Todorov, *Hope*, pp. 111, 104, 107.
35 Todorov, *Hope*, p. 197.
36 Todorov, *Hope*, pp. 129 (my emphasis), 118–19.
37 Todorov, *Hope*, pp. 31 (my emphasis), 122.

Afterword

1 Tzvetan Todorov, *Hope and Memory: Reflections on the Twentieth Century*, London, Atlantic Books, 2003, p. 128.
2 Greg Dening, 'Performing on the Beaches of the Mind: An Essay', *History and Theory* 41, 2002, p. 6.
3 Diogenes Laertius, *Lives of Eminent Philosophers*, 2 vols, London, William Heinemann, 1925, vol. 2, p. 475.
4 Michel Foucault, *Power/Knowledge: Selected Interviews and Other Writings 1972–1977*, ed. Colin Gordon, New York, Harvester, 1980, p. 131.

5 Anthony Giddens, *Modernity and Self-Identity: Self and Society in the Late Modern Age*, Cambridge, Polity, 1991, pp. 82, 133 (my emphasis).
6 Charles Grant Robertson, *History and Citizenship* (Creighton Lecture, 1927), Oxford, Clarendon Press, 1928, p. 15.
7 F. M. Powicke, 'Historical Study in Oxford', Inaugural Lecture as Regius Professor at Oxford, 1929, in *Modern Historians and the Study of History: Essays and Papers*, London, Odhams, 1955, pp. 172, 177.
8 Dening, 'Performing', p. 14.
9 Clive Bell, *Art* (1914), ed. J. B. Bullen, Oxford, Oxford University Press, 1987, p. 100.
10 Schiller, quoted by Hans Vaihinger, *The Philosophy of 'As If'*, transl. C. K. Ogden, London, Kegan Paul, Trench, Trubner, 1924, p. xxv.

Bibliography

Acton, Lord, 'Beginning of the Modern State', in *Lectures on Modern History*, ed. J. N. Figgis and R. V. Laurence, London, Macmillan, 1906.

Ankersmit, Frank, 'Invitation to Historians', *Rethinking History: The Journal of Theory and Practice* 7, 2003, 413–37.

Arendt, Hannah, *Eichmann in Jerusalem: A Report on the Banality of Evil* [1963], London, Penguin, 1994.

Arnold, Matthew, *Culture and Anarchy: An Essay in Political and Social Criticism* [1869], London, Thomas Nelson, n.d.

—— *Literature and Dogma: An Essay towards a Better Apprehension of the Bible*, London, Smith, Elder, 1873.

—— 'The Scholar-Gipsy', in Arthur Quiller-Couch (ed.), *The Oxford Book of English Verse, 1250–1900*, Oxford, Clarendon Press, 1926.

Arrian, *The Campaigns of Alexander*, transl. Aubrey de Selincourt, Harmondsworth, Penguin, 1971.

Augustine, St, *Confessions*, transl. R. S. Pine-Coffin, Harmondsworth, Penguin, 1961.

Baldwin, Peter (ed.), *Reworking the Past: Hitler, the Holocaust, and the Historians' Debate*, Boston, Beacon, 1990.

Barber, Richard, *The Holy Grail: Imagination and Belief*, London, Allen Lane, 2004.

Barker, E. *et al.*, *Why We are at War: Great Britain's Case*, by Members of the Oxford Faculty of Modern History, Oxford, Clarendon Press, 1914.

Barraclough, Geoffrey, *History in a Changing World*, Oxford, Blackwell, 1955.

Barthes, Roland, *Mythologies* [1957], transl. Annette Lavers, London, Vintage, 1993.

Bauman, Zygmunt, *Modernity and Ambivalence*, Cambridge, Polity, 1991.

—— *Intimations of Postmodernity*, London, Routledge, 1992.

Bell, Clive, *Art* [1914], ed. J. B. Bullen, Oxford, Oxford University Press, 1987.

Benda, Julien, *The Great Betrayal* (*La Trahison des Clercs*), transl. Richard Aldington, London, Routledge, 1928.

Bennington, Geoffrey, *Lyotard: Writing the Event*, Manchester, Manchester University Press, 1988.

Blackburn, Gilmer W., *Education in the Third Reich: A Study of Race and History in Nazi Textbooks*, Albany, State University of New York Press, 1985.

Bolingbroke, Lord Henry St John, *Letters on the Study and Use of History*, London, A. Millar, 1752.

—— *Reflections upon Exile*, London, A. Millar, 1752.

Bordo, Susan, 'The Cartesian Masculinisation of Thought' (1987), in Lawrence Cahoone (ed.), *From Modernism to Postmodernism: An Anthology*, Oxford, Blackwell, 1996, pp. 638–64.

Burke, Peter, *The Renaissance Sense of the Past*, London, Edward Arnold, 1969.

Burns, Robert M. and Rayment-Pickard, Hugh (eds), *Philosophies of History*, Oxford, Blackwell, 2000.

Butterfield, Herbert, *The Englishman and His History* [1944], Hamden, Conn., Archon, 1970.

Cahoone, Lawrence (ed.), *From Modernism to Postmodernism: An Anthology*, Oxford, Blackwell, 1996.

Carlyle, Thomas, *Past and Present*, London, Ward, Lock, n.d.

—— *English and Other Critical Essays*, London, J. M. Dent & Sons, 1915.

Carr, E. H., *What is History?*, Harmondsworth, Penguin, 1964.

Cavenagh F. A. (ed.), *James and John Stuart Mill on Education*, Cambridge, Cambridge University Press, 1931.

Chamberlain, Houston Stewart, *The Foundations of the Nineteenth Century* [1899], transl. John Lees, 2 vols; London, John Lane, 1911.

Chomsky, Noam, *Understanding Power: The Indispensable Chomsky*, ed. Peter R. Mitchell and John Schoeffel, London, Vintage, 2003.

Cicero, *The Offices*, transl. Thomas Cockman [1699], London, J. M. Dent, 1909.

Clark, Jonathan, *Our Shadowed Present: Modernism, Postmodernism and History*, London, Atlantic Books, 2003.

Coleridge, Samuel Taylor, *Biographia Literaria* [1817], ed. George Watson, London, J. M. Dent, 1965.

Colley, Linda, *Britons: Forging the Nation, 1707–1837*, London, Yale University Press, 1992.

Cripps, Thomas, 'Historical Truth: An Interview with Ken Burns', *The American Historical Review* 100, 1995, 741–64.

Curtis, S. J., and Boultwood, M. E. A., *A Short History of Educational Ideas*, London, University Tutorial Press, 1961.

Dale, Peter A. *The Victorian Critic and the Idea of History*, London, Harvard University Press, 1977.

Davies, Norman, *Europe: A History*, London, Pimlico, 1997.

Davis, H. W. C., *The Study of History*, Oxford, Clarendon Press, 1925.

Davis, R. H. C., *The Normans and their Myth*, London, Thames & Hudson, 1976.

Dening, Greg, 'Performing on the Beaches of the Mind: An Essay', *History and Theory* 41, 2002, 1–24.

Dewey, John, *Reconstruction in Philosophy*, London, University of London Press, 1921.

Diderot, Denis, *Conversation between D'Alembert and Diderot*, transl. Leonard Tancock, Harmondsworth, Penguin, 1966.

Diogenes Laertius, *Lives of Eminent Philosophers*, transl. R. D. Hicks, 2 vols; London, William Heinemann, 1925.

Easlea, Brian, *Witch Hunting, Magic and the New Philosophy: An Introduction to Debates of the Scientific Revolution, 1450–1750*, Brighton, Harvester Press, 1980.

Elton, G. R., *The Practice of History*, London, Fontana, 1969.

—— 'Second Thoughts on History at the Universities', *History* 54, 1969, 60–7.

—— *Return to Essentials*, Cambridge, Cambridge University Press, 1991.

Emerson, Ralph Waldo, *The Complete Prose Works*, London, Ward Lock, 1890.

Evans, Richard J., *In Defence of History*, London, Granta, 1997.

Fisher, H. A. L., *A History of Europe*, London, Edward Arnold, 1936.

Foner, Eric, *Freedom's Lawmakers: A Directory of Black Officeholders during Reconstruction*, revised edn, Baton Rouge and London, Louisiana State University Press, 1996.

—— *Who Owns History? Rethinking the Past in a Changing World*, New York, Hill & Wang, 2002.

Foucault, Michel, *Power/Knowledge: Selected Interviews and Other Writings 1972–1977*, ed. Colin Gordon, New York, Harvester, 1980.

Fox-Genovese, Elizabeth and Lasch-Quinn, Elisabeth (eds), *Reconstructing History*, London, Routledge, 1999.

Frankland, Noble, *History at War: The Campaigns of an Historian*, London, Giles de la Mare, 1998.

Fuentes, Carlos, *Terra Nostra*, transl. Margaret Sayers Peden, Harmondsworth, Penguin, 1978.

Fulbrook, Mary, *German National Identity after the Holocaust*, Cambridge, Polity, 1999.

—— 'Re-presenting the Nation: History and Identity in East and West Germany', in Mary Fulbrook and Martin Swales (eds), *Representing the German Nation: History and Identity in Twentieth-Century Germany*, Manchester, Manchester University Press, 2000, pp. 172–92.

—— *Historical Theory*, London, Routledge, 2002.

Gaita, Raymond, *A Common Humanity*, London, Routledge, 2000.

Garton Ash, Timothy, *History of the Present: Essays, Sketches and Dispatches from Europe in the 1990s*, London, Allen Lane, 1999.

Gay, Peter, *Style in History*, London, Jonathan Cape, 1975.

Geoffrey of Monmouth, *The History of the Kings of Britain*, transl. Lewis Thorpe, Harmondsworth, Penguin, 1966.

Geyl, Pieter, *Napoleon: For and Against* [1949], Harmondsworth, Penguin, 1965.

Giddens, Anthony, *The Consequences of Modernity*, Cambridge, Polity, 1990.

—— *Modernity and Self-Identity: Self and Society in the Late Modern Age*, Cambridge, Polity, 1991.

Gillispie, Charles C., 'A Professional Life in the History of Science', *Historically Speaking* 5, January 2004.

Gochberg, Donald S. (ed.), *Classics of Western Thought*, 4 vols; New York, Harcourt Brace Jovanovich, 1980.

Golsan, Richard J., 'History and the "Duty to Memory" in Postwar France: The Pitfalls of an Ethics of Remembrance', in Howard Marchitello (ed.), *What Happens to History: The Renewal of Ethics in Contemporary Thought*, New York, Routledge, 2001, pp. 23–39.

Grossman, Vasily, *Life and Fate*, London, Harvill Press, 1995.

Hamilton-Paterson, James, *Loving Monsters*, London, Granta, 2002.

Hampshire, Stuart, *Thought and Action*, London, Chatto & Windus, 1965.

Harlan, David, 'Ken Burns and the Coming Crisis of Academic History', in *Rethinking History: The Journal of Theory and Practice*, 7, 2003, 169–92.

Hawking, Stephen, *A Brief History of Time from the Big Bang to Black Holes*, London, Bantam, 1988.

Herodotus, *The History*, transl. G. Rawlinson, 2 vols; London, J. M. Dent & Sons, 1910.

Hersh, Seymour M., *My Lai 4: A Report on the Massacre and its Aftermath*, New York, Random House, 1970.

Hill, Christopher, *Intellectual Origins of the English Revolution*, Oxford, Clarendon Press, 1965.

Howard, Michael, *The Lessons of History*, Oxford, Clarendon Press, 1991.

Huizinga, Johan, *Men and Ideas: History, the Middle Ages, the Renaissance*, Princeton, Princeton University Press, 1959.

Hutcheon, Linda, *A Poetics of Postmodernism: History, Theory, Fiction*, London, Routledge, 1988.

James, William, *The Varieties of Religious Experience*, London, Longmans Green, 1902.

Jenkins, Keith, *On 'What is History?'*, London, Routledge, 1995.

—— 'On Disobedient Histories', *Rethinking History: The Journal of Theory and Practice* 7, 2003, 367–85.

Kelley, Donald R. (ed.), *The History of Ideas: Canon and Variations*, Rochester, Rochester University Press, 1990.

—— (ed.), *Versions of History from Antiquity to the Enlightenment*, London, Yale University Press, 1991.

Kenyon, John, *The History Men: The Historical Profession in England since the Renaissance*, 2nd edn, London, Weidenfeld & Nicolson, 1993.

Kershaw, Ian, *The 'Hitler Myth': Image and Reality in the Third Reich*, Oxford, Clarendon Press, 1987.

Kinloch, Nicholas, 'Learning about the Holocaust: Moral or Historical Question?', *Teaching History* 93, 1998, 44–6.

—— 'Parallel Catastrophes? Uniqueness, Redemption and the Shoah', *Teaching History* 104, 2001, 8–14.

Klemperer, Victor, *The Language of the Third Reich*, transl. Martin Brady, London, Athlone Press, 2000.

Laslett, Peter, *The World We Have Lost*, London, Methuen, 1971.

Lawrence, D. H., *À Propos of Lady Chatterley's Lover*, London, Mandrake Press, 1930.

Lawson, Hilary, *Closure: A Story of Everything*, London, Routledge, 2001.

Leavis, F. R., *The Great Tradition*, Harmondsworth, Penguin, 1972.

Lecky, W. E. H., *The Political Value of History*, London, Edward Arnold, 1892.

Lemon, M. C., *Philosophy of History: A Guide for Students*, London, Routledge, 2003.

Lerner, Gerda, *Why History Matters: Life and Thought*, Oxford, Oxford University Press, 1998.

Levi, Primo, *The Drowned and the Saved*, transl. Raymond Rosenthal, London, Abacus, 1989.

Levine, George, *Dying to Know: Scientific Epistemology and Narrative in Victorian England*, London, Chicago University Press, 2002.

Lévi-Strauss, Claude, *The Savage Mind*, London, Weidenfeld & Nicolson, 1966.

Lindqvist, Sven, *A History of Bombing*, London, Granta, 2001.

Longxi, Zhang, 'History and Fictionality: Insights and Limitations of a Literary Perspective', *Rethinking History: The Journal of Theory and Practice*, 8, 2004, 387–402.

Lucretius, *On the Nature of the Universe*, transl. R. E. Latham, Harmondsworth, Penguin, 1951.

Lyotard, Jean-François, *The Inhuman: Reflections on Time*, transl. Geoffrey Bennington and Rachel Bowlby, Cambridge, Polity, 1991.

McHale, Brian, *Postmodernist Fiction*, London, Routledge, 1987.

Macaulay, Thomas Babington, *Critical and Historical Essays*, ed. A. J. Grieve, London, J. M. Dent & Sons, 1933.

Mandler, Peter, *History and National Life*, London, Profile Books, 2000.

—— '"Race" and "nation" in mid-Victorian thought', in Stefan Collini, Richard Whitmore and Brian Young (eds), *History, Religion and Culture: British Intellectual History 1750–1950*, Cambridge, Cambridge University Press, 2000, pp. 224–44.

Marshall, Brenda K., *Teaching the Postmodern: Fiction and Theory*, London, Routledge, 1992.

Marwick, Arthur, *The New Nature of History: Knowledge, Evidence, Language*, Basingstoke, Palgrave, 2001.

Nelson, Jinty, 'Letter from the President', *Royal Historical Society Newsletter*, Spring 2003.

Newman, John Henry, *On the Scope and Nature of University Education* [1852], London, J. M. Dent & Sons, 1915.

Nietzsche, Friedrich, *The Gay Science*, transl. Walter Kaufmann, New York, Vintage, 1974.

Novick, Peter, *The Holocaust and Collective Memory: The American Experience*, London, Bloomsbury, 2000.

Nussbaum, Martha C., *The Therapy of Desire: Theory and Practice in Hellenistic Ethics*, Princeton, Princeton University Press, 1994.

Oliver, Kelly, 'Witnessing Otherness in History', in Howard Marchitello (ed.), *What Happens to History: The Renewal of Ethics in Contemporary Thought*, London, Routledge, 2001, pp. 41–66.

Orwell, George, *Nineteen Eighty-Four*, Harmondsworth, Penguin, 1954.

Pater, Walter, *The Renaissance: Studies in Art and Poetry* [1873], ed. Donald L. Hill, Berkeley and Los Angeles, University of California Press, 1980.

Pearson, Karl, *The Grammar of Science*, London, Walter Scott, 1892.

Peters, Thomas J. and Waterman, Robert H. Jr, *In Search of Excellence: Lessons from America's Best-Run Companies*, New York, Harper & Row, 1982.

Plato, *The Dialogues*, ed. Benjamin Jowett, 5 vols; Oxford, Clarendon Press, 1875.

Plumb, J. H., *The Death of the Past*, Harmondsworth, Penguin, 1973.

Pope, Alexander, *The Poetical Works*, ed. Adolphus W. Ward, London, Macmillan, 1908.

Porter, Roy (ed.), *Rewriting the Self: Histories from the Renaissance to the Present*, London, Routledge, 1997.

Powicke, F. M., *Modern Historians and the Study of History: Essays and Papers*, London, Odhams, 1955.

Rainwater, Janette, *Self-Therapy: A Guide to Becoming Your Own Therapist*, Wellingborough, Turnstone Press, 1989.

Ranke, Leopold von, *The Theory and Practice of History*, ed. Georg G. Iggers and Konrad von Moltke, New York, Bobbs-Merrill, 1973.

Renan, Ernest 'What is a Nation?', in Homi K. Bhabha (ed.), *Nation and Narration*, London, Routledge, 1990, pp. 8–22.

Robertson, Charles Grant, *History and Citizenship*, Oxford, Clarendon Press, 1928.

Rollin, Charles, *The Ancient History of the Egyptians, Carthaginians, Assyrians, Babylonians, Medes and Persians, Grecians and Macedonians*, 18th edition, London, Ward Lock, 1881.

Rorty, Richard, *Philosophy and Social Hope*, Harmondsworth, Penguin, 1999.

Rose, Nikolas, 'Assembling the Modern Self', in Roy Porter (ed.), *Rewriting the Self: Histories from the Renaissance to the Present*, London, Routledge, 1997, pp.224–48.

—— *Inventing Our Selves: Psychology, Power, and Personhood*, Cambridge, Cambridge University Press, 1998.

Rosenstone, Robert A. *Mirror in the Shrine: American Encounters with Meiji Japan*, Cambridge, Mass. and London, Harvard University Press, 1988.

—— 'Confessions of a Postmodern (?) Historian', *Rethinking History: The Journal of Theory and Practice* 8, 2004, 149–66.

Sebald, W. G., *Austerlitz*, London, Penguin, 2002.

Seeley, J. R., *Lectures and Essays*, London, Macmillan, 1870.

—— *The Expansion of England*, ed. with introduction by John Gross, Chicago, University of Chicago Press, 1971.

Seneca, *Letters from a Stoic*, transl. Robin Campbell, Harmondsworth, Penguin, 1969.

Sextus Empiricus, *Outlines of Pyrrhonism*, transl. R. G. Bury, London, Heinemann, 1933.

Shermer, Michael and Grobman, Alex, *Denying History*, London, University of California Press, 2000.

Smart, Barry, *Postmodernity*, London, Routledge, 1993.

Smiles, Samuel, *Character* [1871], London, John Murray, 1910.

—— *Life and Labour* [1887], London, John Murray, 1907.

Smith, A. L., 'The Teaching of Modern History', in Christopher Cookson (ed.), *Essays on Secondary Education*, Oxford, Clarendon Press, 1898, pp. 177–95.

Smith, Bonnie G., *The Gender of History: Men, Women, and Historical Practice*, London, Harvard University Press, 1998.

Smith, Russell, 'The New Newsspeak', *The New York Review of Books*, 50 (9), 29 May 2003.

Soffer, Reba N., *Discipline and Power: The University, History, and the Making of an English Élite, 1870–1930*, Stanford, Stanford University Press, 1994.

Spencer, Herbert, *Education*, London, Williams & Norgate, 1910.

Sprat, Thomas, *The History of the Royal Society*, London, J. Martyn, 1667.

Steedman, Carolyn, *Dust*, Manchester, Manchester University Press, 2001.

Stern, Fritz (ed.), *The Varieties of History from Voltaire to the Present*, New York, Meridian Books, 1956.

Stubbs, William, *Seventeen Lectures on the Study of Mediaeval and Modern History and Kindred Subjects*, 3rd edn, Oxford, Clarendon Press, 1900.

Swift, Graham, *Waterland*, London, Picador, 1992.

Swift, Jonathan, *The Battle of the Books*, ed. A. Guthkelch, London, Chatto & Windus, 1908.

Taylor, A. J. P., *A Personal History*, London, Hamish Hamilton, 1983.

Thucydides, *History of the Peloponnesian War*, transl. R. Crawley, J. M. Dent & Sons, 1910.

Todorov, Tzvetan, *Hope and Memory: Reflections on the Twentieth Century*, London, Atlantic Books, 2003.

Tosh, John (ed.), *Historians on History*, Harlow, Pearson, 2000.

Trevor-Roper, Hugh, *Historical Essays*, London, Macmillan, 1957.

—— *History: Professional and Lay*, Oxford, Clarendon Press, 1957.

Trilling, Lionel, *The Liberal Imagination: Essays on Literature and Society*, London, Secker & Warburg, 1951.

Vaihinger, Hans, *The Philosophy of 'As If': A System of the Theoretical, Practical and Religious Fictions of Mankind*, transl. C. K. Ogden, London, Kegan Paul, Trench, Trubner, 1924.

Virgil, *The Aeneid* , transl. David West, London, Penguin, 2003.

Wedgwood, C. V., *Velvet Studies*, London, Jonathan Cape, 1946.

White, Thomas, *An Exclusion of Scepticks from All Title to Dispute*, London, John Williams, 1665.

Wilkins, John, *Mathematical Magick: or The Wonders that may be Performed by Mechanical Geometry* [1648], 4th edn, London, Ric. Baldwin, 1691.

Willey, Basil, *Nineteenth Century Studies*, London, Chatto & Windus, 1964.

Williams, Bernard, *Truth and Truthfulness: An Essay in Genealogy,* Princeton, Princeton University Press, 2002.

Wilson, Keith (ed.), *Forging the Collective Memory*, Oxford, Berghahn, 1996.

Wittgenstein, Ludwig, *Philosophical Investigations*, 2nd edn, transl. G. E. M. Anscombe, Oxford, Blackwell, 1958.

Index